AF698777

Post-Crisis Risk Management

Bracing for the Next Perfect Storm

Post-Crisis Risk Management

Bracing for the Next Perfect Storm

TSUYOSHI OYAMA

WILEY

John Wiley & Sons (Asia) Pte. Ltd.

POST-CRISIS RISK MANAGEMENT
Copyright © 2010 by Tsuyoshi Oyama
English translation rights arranged with Kinzai Institute for Financial Affairs, Inc. through Japan UNI Agency, Inc., Tokyo

Published in 2010 by John Wiley & Sons (Asia) Pte. Ltd.
2 Clementi Loop, #02-01, Singapore 129809

All rights reserved.

No part of this publication may be reproduced, stored in a retrieval system, or transmitted in any form or by any means, electronic, mechanical, photocopying, recording, scanning, or otherwise, except as expressly permitted by law, without either the prior written permission of the Publisher, or authorization through payment of the appropriate photocopy fee to the Copyright Clearance Center. Requests for permission should be addressed to the Publisher, John Wiley & Sons (Asia) Pte. Ltd., 2 Clementi Loop, #02-01, Singapore 129809, tel: 65-6463-2400, fax: 65-6463-4605, e-mail: enquiry@wiley.com.

This publication is designed to provide accurate and authoritative information in regard to the subject matter covered. It is sold with the understanding that the publisher is not engaged in rendering professional services. If professional advice or other expert assistance is required, the services of a competent professional person should be sought.

Neither the authors nor the publisher are liable for any actions prompted or caused by the information presented in this book. Any views expressed herein are those of the authors and do not represent the views of the organizations they work for.

Other Wiley Editorial Offices

John Wiley & Sons, 111 River Street, Hoboken, NJ07030, USA
John Wiley & Sons, The Atrium, Southern Gate, Chichester, West Sussex, P019 8SQ, United Kingdom
John Wiley & Sons (Canada) Ltd., 5353 Dundas Street West, Suite 400, Toronto, Ontario, M9B 6HB, Canada
John Wiley & Sons Australia Ltd, 42 McDougall Street, Milton, Queensland 4064, Australia
Wiley-VCH, Boschstrasse 12, D-69469 Weinheim, Germany

Library of Congress Cataloging-in-Publication Data
ISBN 978-0-470-82537-2

Typeset in 10/12pt Sabon by Macmillan Publishing Solutions
Printed in Singapore by Toppan Security Printing Pte. Ltd.

10 9 8 7 6 5 4 3 2 1

Contents

Foreword

After having been triggered by the subprime loan problem, the financial turmoil turned out to be a fully fledged credit crisis and has not yet seen its conclusion. Still, we have surely managed to withstand the worst of the fire that needed to be put out and have gradually moved to the next phase—designing and building a new house (financial system) to replace the one that was burned down.

This book tries to tackle the central issues of this phase of designing the new financial system. For example, the issues include "how should individual financial institutions reestablish their risk management so as to avoid the recurrence of the financial crisis?," "how should the authorities conduct macroprudential policy to preempt the future crisis?" and "how should we establish an appropriate relationship between banks and regulators to manage the crisis smoothly?"

The author, Mr. Oyama, worked for a long time for the Bank of Japan and was engaged there in the issues of risk management of financial institutions. He decided to write this book on the occasion of moving to the private sector, being less constrained in expressing his own views than before. In this sense, he is indeed the best person to discuss the issues dealt with here.

This book provides us with many insights that contribute to deepening discussions about important financial stability issues. Among them, particularly innovative and constructive, is the proposal of having an agreement to share extreme stresses between regulators and banks. This idea is to specify the scope of extreme risks to be faced and thus managed by individual financial institutions in advance and thus indicate the risks beyond this scope left for the authorities to be shared. This is worth seriously considering to keep the stability of the financial system while avoiding the moral hazard of financial institutions.

This book also makes many other important policy suggestions that should be listened to by financial institutions and regulators. Therefore I hope many who take an interest in the stability of the financial system read this book.

Kazuhito Ikeo

Kazuhito Ikeo, who resides in Tokyo, has been a professor of economics at Keio University since 1995. He was the president of the Nippon Financial Association (2002–2004), and is the chairman of the committees of the Japanese government's Financial Council and of the Industrial Structure Council.

Acknowledgments

There are many people I have to thank for finishing this book, first in Japanese and later in English. Particularly, I would like to show my appreciation for the very helpful comments on the Japanese version from Kenji Nishiguchi, Toshinori Kurihara, Masaaki Misawa, Shun Kobayashi, Yasuhiro Harada, Yuka Oku, Tomoyuki Shimoda, and Tetsuji Miyaji. Besides, I must thank Prof. Kazuhito Ikeo (Keio University), who kindly provided me with a foreword, and Toshishiko Fukui (former governor of the Bank of Japan), who gave me helpful advice on this book's publication. I also would like to give thanks for the many useful comments given on my presentations in the international meetings after the publication of the Japanese version, from Krirk Vanikkul, Charles Littrell, Takashi Kozu, Shinichiro Nakano, Luo Ping, Mohd Zabidi Md. Nor, Ian Woolford, and Tam Ming Soong. Of course, I could not forget Nick Wallwork and the many other staff at John Wiley & Sons for their kind and incredibly speedy assistance, and also Peter Hoflich, who kindly introduced me to this excellent company. Finally, I have to thank my wife, Mariko, for her patience in allowing me to be away in my room over every weekend for as long as six months.

Introduction

Almost one-and-a-half years have passed since the eruption of the financial crisis. This turmoil was originally supposed to be limited to the local market of non-banks' and their special products known as "subprime loans." However, it rapidly extended to other countries, other markets, and the core of the financial system, that is, the banking system. Some called it the worst event to have occurred since the end of the Second World War, and soon they were calling it the worst in the past 100 years.

In the midst of the crisis, many major countries' regulatory agencies and international organizations have made recommendations and actually introduced various measures. Despite all their efforts, the crisis has not yet ended (as of this writing in December 2008).

This crisis has offered us various policy challenges to overcome. The challenges are not limited to the area of macroprudential policy, or how to deal with financial bubbles. They also include risk management issues for individual banks. Also, the crisis has forced us to ponder the issue of how to design the regulatory system so that all financial institutions, including non-banks, are properly supervised. In the area of social policy, the crisis provides a challenge in how to formulate housing policy for poor families.

Among them, this book focuses on the challenges facing individual financial institutions in their risk management, and also the challenges facing regulatory agencies in how to design the financial system and implement macroprudential policy. The author has this focus because he has long been involved in these areas.

The Basel Committee of Bank Supervision (hereafter, the Basel Committee), or the group of regulatory agencies of major countries, and many subgroups under this committee have made substantial efforts to implement the Basel II accord smoothly for the past few years. The capital requirement under Basel II was designed to be more sensitive to the risks taken by financial institutions than that in Basel I. Moreover, the Basel II framework allows the advanced risk management systems developed by financial institutions to be incorporated into the regulation. For all these reasons, many naturally expected that Basel II implementation would bring a more robust financial system than before.

Some countries, including Japan, Hong Kong, and major European countries, had already started to implement Basel II in 2007, and have begun to bring in all the available approaches, including advanced ones, in 2008. Among major countries, the US was expected to start Basel II only in 2009. Consequently, whether Basel II, having consumed the bulk of regulators' energy until recently, and the current financial crisis are related may be a good question to be considered. Some doubt the effectiveness of Basel II in the current crisis, while others suggest that we would have seen very different developments had Basel II been implemented much earlier.

This issue will be discussed in detail later in this book. One thing, however, that I would like to note here is that up to early 2007, in other words not more than two years ago, all the major financial institutions in the US and Europe, and also their managers, had retained strong confidence in the stability of the global financial system. For example, the Financial Stability Report (FSR) published by the Bank of England (BOE) in April 2007 noted the continuing robustness of the financial system as a whole, despite some increase in risk factors. Likewise, the Global Financial Stability Report (GFSR) published by the International Monetary Fund (IMF) in 2006 noted increases in some risk factors, but concluded that at base the chances of financial market stability were rosy.

These views were strongly backed by their belief in advanced financial technology and risk management techniques, which have been established over past years, and also the refined institutional setting that oversees risk-taking and risk management of financial institutions in a sophisticated way. Owing to this strong belief, no one suspected that risk factors that were surely observed even in 2006 could turn into a global crisis.

What in the world went wrong with financial institutions' risk management and regulatory framework, which had supported their (mainly the US and European) strong belief in the entrenched stability of the financial system up to just two years ago? What do we need to fix these problems? Are the various recommendations and countermeasures recently published by many parties enough to fix them? If not, what should we do to tackle them? Finally, how should financial institutions and regulators in the Asian region establish their global strategies for increasing their presence in the world, capitalizing on the lessons learned from the financial crisis? These are the main topics of this book.

The following is the concrete organization of the book. Chapter 1 reviews the development of the current financial crisis, that is how a local, non-bank market event developed into a global financial crisis. This chapter also notes a commonality between the current financial crisis and the Japanese banking crisis in the 1990s, founded in both representing a malfunctioning of a macroeconomic system that had long worked as the main engine behind high economic growth.

Chapter 2 presents an overall picture of the current financial crisis, by identifying 1) the causes of generating the financial bubble and of triggering its burst; 2) why the bubble was allowed to expand for a long period; and 3) how the repercussions of the bubble bursting were amplified.

The chapter first points out that the generation of a financial bubble itself is nothing new to us, and that bubbles occur cyclically with a mechanism deeply rooted in the incentive structure of financial institutions. Concerning the triggering factors, referring to other studies, the chapter cites a widespread understanding of risk undervaluation, represented by loosened loan origination discipline in the US subprime market (the micro-perspective), and tightening monetary policy after a long easing in the US (macro-perspective).

Then the chapter notes two factors that allowed for an expansion of the bubble for a long period, which are an excessive expansion of information asymmetry due to the boom of the originate and distribute model among banks and their overconfidence in risk management techniques to manage this information asymmetry. The chapter also discusses several factors that amplified the repercussions, which are the failures of functions of various market and social infrastructures that were supposed to support the marketization and socialization of financial risks. They were the accounting system, disclosure practices, market liquidity management, silo-type risk management of individual banks, and the macroprudential policy framework.

Chapter 3 introduces recommendations and policy reactions made by international organizations, regulators, and banks in the aftermath of the financial crisis. This chapter, however, points out that many recommendations seem to bring a feeling of déjà vu.

Chapter 4 discusses why the same recommendations have been repeated in past crises, but to no avail. The chapter identifies four causes, of which the first three concern the difficulties in forming consensus on risk to be assumed by financial institutions, and the last concerns the issue of incentive compatibility, that is the condition in which financial institutions are not sufficiently motivated to prepare for these risks. These four causes are as follows:

1) The core part of a financial institution's risk management is something of an "art," which is very hard to express in a precise way. There are surely limits to it and an inappropriate use of risk-expressing techniques such as value at risk (VaR) and stress testing, which led major stakeholders of banks to a failure to capture an important part of the risks faced by financial institutions.

2) Regulatory and supervisory authorities have not clearly conveyed their messages of the degree of stresses to be assumed in the capital adequacy assessment by financial institutions. Lack of consensus on how to share the losses under extreme stresses between banks and regulators have aggravated the problem.

3) In the crisis, financial institutions and also regulatory authorities tended to lack in their efforts to make a deeper analysis of the causes of the financial crisis. The countermeasures they introduced tended to target the avoidance of the "same" event recurring, but stopped short of studying the common mechanism behind the various crises so that they could avoid the next one.

4) The current financial system has been ill equipped with the incentive mechanism to discourage the generation of a financial bubble, so long as some

financial institutions have huge externalities, thus cause systemic risk. So we need massive changes in the design of the financial system to stem the causes of generating the financial bubble and subsequent financial crisis. This discussion leads to the design of a new financial system, with recommendations later in the book.

Based on the findings in chapter 4, chapter 5 makes some policy recommendations, which consist of macroprudential policies that try to end the current vicious circle, in which regulatory improvement has always been followed by regulatory arbitrage, and of microregulatory policies that improve risk identification and measurement under variable external environments. These micro policies actually constitute the required foundations for banks and regulators to agree on the macro policies.

The macroprudential policies consist of 1) clarifying the burden sharing of extreme stresses between banks and regulators using objective criteria for the degree of stresses, thereby minimizing the room for moral hazard not only for banks but also for regulators; and 2) introducing a proactive macroprudential policy to smooth cyclical effects.

Meanwhile, the microregulatory policies consist of 1) establishing a stress evaluation technique that can support the implementation of macroregulatory policies, such as the introduction of a new yardstick to measure the degree of stresses and of measures to increase the robustness of stress scenarios, and also of their inducing technique of risk quantification; and 2) introducing a compensation scheme for senior managers of banks that encourages them to establish a long-term strategy, rather than a short-term one.

Furthermore, the chapter compares the idea of system design explained in this book with that of Kashyap, Rajan, and Stein (2008).

Chapter 6 discusses how regulators and banks in the Asian region should react proactively to the lessons learned from the current financial crisis and increase their presence in the world. The chapter first discusses the reasons behind Asian parties' minor role in dealing with the current financial crisis, which was mainly triggered by the US and European financial institutions due to their lack of well-planned strategies. Then the chapter recommends policy coordination among the regional regulators, so that they can take the initiative in establishing a new global standard in banking regulation.

Chapter 7 concludes by summarizing all the discussions developed in the previous chapters and by indicating a common thread in my arguments for the new risk management framework to be established by the regulatory/supervisory agencies as well as financial institutions, such as the need for a public element into stress pricing as is the case of carbon dioxide (CO_2) pricing.

Finally, the Epilogue overviews the developments of events since the end of December 2008 when I finished drafting the Japanese version of my book, and concludes that many international policy initiatives observed during this period actually reinforce my concerns mentioned in chapter 4.

CHAPTER 1

Developments of the Current Financial Crisis

THE ENVIRONMENT BEFORE THE SUMMER OF 2007

Around the summer of 2008, many journals carried articles featuring the "one-year anniversary" of the current crisis and reviewing its developments. While there might be no strict definition, many cited the so-called "Paribas shock," which occurred in July 2007, as the start of the crisis. This was the shock caused by the big French bank, BNP Paribas, which stopped calculating prices and redemption of some financial products sold by affiliated funds over its counter because some fund products included securitized products related to subprime loans.

Even before the summer of 2007, however, there were some reports that something was wrong in the market for so-called subprime loans in the US. For example, US regulators jointly announced a somewhat unusual caution against declining discipline in subprime loan origination in March 2007. Moreover, there was a report that the US subsidiary of HSBC made a huge provision for subprime loans, and decided on the closure of its US business in February 2007.

Around the same time came the news that many US non-banks specializing in subprime loan origination faced solvency problems. News indicating ominous changes in the US subprime loan market gradually increased from late 2006 to the beginning of 2007.

Still, many experts in this area actually regarded this issue as local to the US, and a very specific market problem until about June 2007. The US subprime loan market had been growing very rapidly over recent years, and consequently reached a relatively huge size. Still, it was small in size compared with the prime mortgage market (about a little more than 10 percent at the end of 2006, as shown in figure 1.1). Besides, the subprime loan market is very special, dealing with households that are usually not

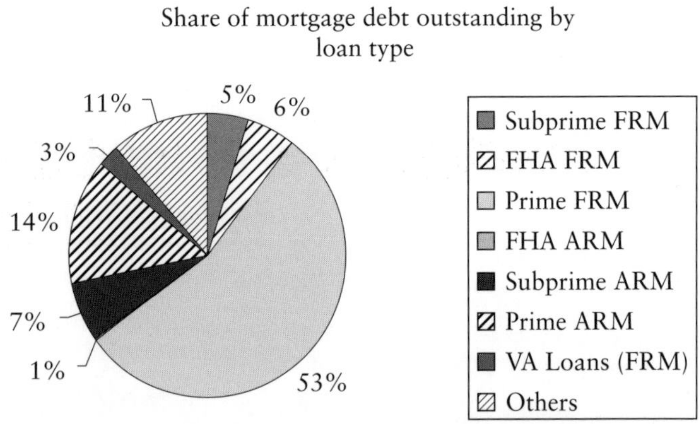

Figure 1.1 Subprime loan share of the US mortgage market
Source: Duncan and Verg (2007) based on material from the MBA 2006Q3 National Delinquency Survey

accepted by ordinary banks. Moreover, only a few non-banks that had aggressively originated reckless loans faced serious solvency problems at that time.

So the US perception of this crisis in the beginning stage up to the middle of 2007 was that it was surely a big problem particularly from the social justice point of view, but not so serious for the whole financial system, or from a macroeconomic point of view.

THE SUMMER OF 2007: PRELUDE

This type of observation changed dramatically around July 2007. First came the "Paribas shock." In addition, major global rating agencies announced a series of downgrades of securitized products around the same time. It was indeed a shock because all the major rating agencies at once started to downgrade products that were previously rated "AAA" or "AA," or "ultra safe."

These events gradually changed the characteristics of the crisis from a problem in the US subprime loan market to a problem of subprime loan-related "securitization," or a global problem for investors who invested in these products.

Another notable event was the report of a problem for a small German financial institution, IKB, on July 30. According to the report, this bank suffered huge losses because of its investments in securitized products related to subprime loans. Even though it is a small institution, this news was shocking enough to many financial experts (particularly bank regulators) because the subprime loan problem had long been believed to be a problem for non-banks, and now had for the first time clearly been recognized in the banking system, which was supposed to be supervised by regulators.

Clearly, the problem was no longer just a problem of the US market. In Germany, another bank called Sachsen LB also became substantially bankrupt due to its own structured investment vehicle (SIV), which was heavily exposed to subprime loan markets.

In the midst of a series of these unbelievable failures, financial institutions had started to doubt even the credit of their counterparties in the money market. The consequence of this was the emergence of gridlock, or the evaporation of liquidity in short-term money markets, where banks provide funds to other banks. This problem first became serious in Europe and then in the US, particularly after August 2007. A symbolic event of this liquidity crisis was the failure of a British bank called Northern Rock.

Northern Rock is a middle-sized British bank with assets of £17 billion ($34 billion), mainly engaged in mortgage loans. This bank's special business model of originating mortgage loans with wholesale funding, however, came under the spotlight partly because of its rapid growth. Northern Rock fell into a liquidity trap not because of its direct exposure to subprime loans, but because of its business model itself.

So, after the summer of 2007, the subprime loan problem turned from a local non-bank problem into a global banking problem through global financial institutions' investments in subprime-related securitized products, and then into a liquidity problem for banks, which were plagued by a distrust of each other in the market without any certain asset impairment information.

AFTER THE SUMMER: CONTINUOUS SURPRISES

These issues, particularly the liquidity turmoil, was temporarily contained, mainly thanks to the joint liquidity provision by major countries' central banks (see figure 1.2). At that time, banks and regulators expected that the announcement of banks' P/L during the second and third quarters could bring further turmoil up to the end of the year, but at the same time they hoped that this would be followed by the return of stability at the beginning of 2008.

Around that time, all financial experts expected that the delinquency and default rates of subprime loan markets were likely to rise during the

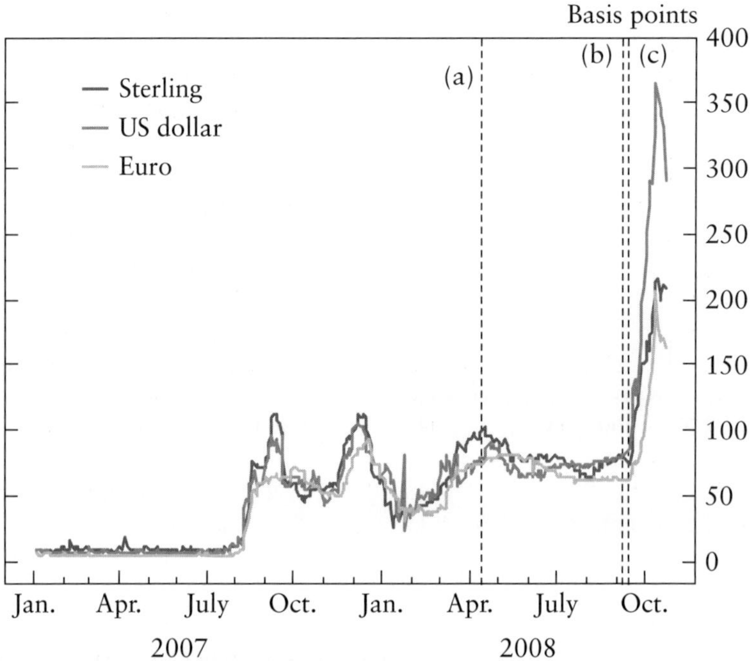

Spread of three-month Libor to three-month overnight indexed swap rates. Data to close of business on October 20, 2008.

(a) April 2008 Report.

(b) Fannie Mae and Freddie Mac taken into conservatorship.

(c) Lehman Brothers Holdings files for Chapter 11 bankruptcy protection.

Figure 1.2 Three-month interbank rate and policy rate
Source: BOE (2008b)

course of 2008. Provided that the problem was limited to the US subprime loan market, however, many agreed that financial institutions in general had enough capital to overcome it.

One optimistic idea after another fell victim to events after the summer of 2007. Actually, market participants' distrust expanded from subprime loan-related products to others that were only indirectly related to subprime loans. Moreover, they started to distrust products that were likely to be affected by the financial system, whose problems were revealed by the crisis. For example, problems arose from the loss of confidence in rating agencies, and from the imperfect model behind the design of securitized products.

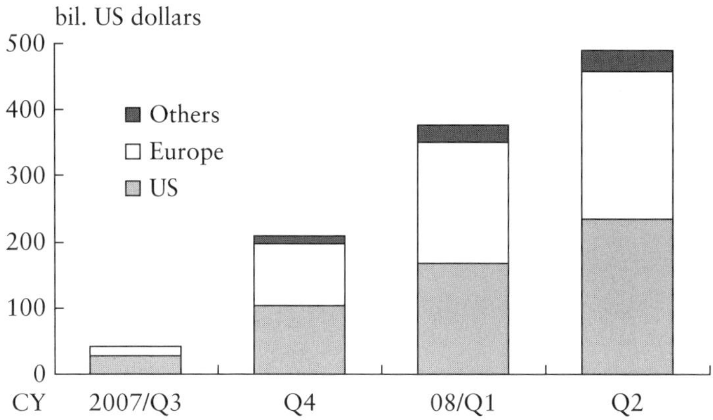

Figure 1.3 Subprime-related losses of major financial institutions
Source: Bloomberg, L.P.

By some measures, we can view these as a result of speculative transactions by some market participants, which tried to capitalize on the others' misfortune. Such volatile market movements should surely offer precious chances for some market participants to gain huge profits. While even aggressive agitation by market participants cannot easily cause such a quasi-panic situation in the ordinary environment, they could easily do so in an environment in which all the participants had lost their confidence in its long-established conventions. In other words, the shock was too big to be reacted to normally.

This "confidence debacle" included the buy-back of certain assets once believed to be detached from the balance sheet for reputational reasons. Moreover, this included frequent changes in accounting methods, which led to the expansion of financial institutions' losses. In this environment, against prior expectation, the losses of globally active financial institutions became bigger quarter by quarter (see figure 1.3). In this process, the US's fifth-biggest investment bank, Bear Sterns, faced a liquidity squeeze and was finally bailed out by the New York Federal Reserve.

The objects of the market's attack were then further expanded to other securitized products, including CDOs (securitized products backed by other securitized products backed by subprime loans) and monoline insurance companies (US insurance companies that specialize in financial guarantees). These were previously mainly engaged in the insurance of municipal bonds, but in recent years had expanded rapidly into the insurance of structured products (including CDOs), leveraged loans, and government-sponsored enterprises (GSEs) such as Fanny Mae and Freddie Mac.

They were not necessarily affected by the performance of subprime loans. Some were just inspired by the association with subprime loans or securitization (e.g. ordinary mortgage loans including prime loans or highly leveraged transactions). Or some were businesses that were inherently defective but had not long been noticed thanks to the financial bubble (e.g., monoline insurers and GSEs).

This expansion of attack objectives was actually encouraged by the general worsening of the US macroeconomy. With hindsight, the financial experts' optimism seen in the summer of 2007 was conditional on very naïve assumptions that the market turmoil would be limited mainly to the US subprime and highly leveraged loan markets, and that subsequent shocks to profits of major financial institutions would be limited to declines from historic record levels. There was surely a serious problem for the stability of the financial system, but it would not necessarily wreck the macroeconomy itself.

This type of logic was also observed in Japan just after the debacle of the financial bubble in the 1990s. The events that followed again rebutted this somewhat optimistic logic observed in the US, however. The problems in the mortgage loan markets spread from subprime to prime loans. Moreover, the economic slump also went beyond the financial and real estate sectors to the whole macro-level, as private consumption became sluggish and the service and durable goods manufacturing industries felt the pinch.

THE SUMMER OF 2008 AND AFTER: FULLY FLEDGED CRISIS

The series of events after the summer of 2008 were dramatic enough for many still to remember them vividly. The US Congress finally approved then Treasury Secretary Paulson's proposal to inject public funds into the GSEs on July 26, and then the Treasury effectively nationalized them on September 7. The total budget to buy their preferred stocks was set at $200 billion, which suddenly more than doubled the size of the government's liability (the total outstanding debt issued by the two GSEs was more than the outstanding amount of the government bonds.).

Given that a large part of the GSEs' issued securities was owned by foreign financial institutions and central banks (see table 1.1), this reaction of the US government was very understandable. From the foreign investors' point of view, GSEs have long been equal to the US government. This means that defaults of the GSEs could trigger fear of default of the US government itself. This would surely be a disaster to be avoided by any means.

Table 1.1 Outstanding GSE-issued securities (at end of June 2007)

GSE-related securities		$5.3 trillion
	Agency bonds	$1.6 trillion
	RMBS	$3.7 trillion
Owned by foreign investors		$1.3 trillion
	Chinese	$370 billion
	Japanese	$228 billion
Owned by the three Japanese megabanking groups		¥4.7 trillion
Owned by top four Japanese insurance companies		more than ¥4 trillion

Source: Reuters reports 2008

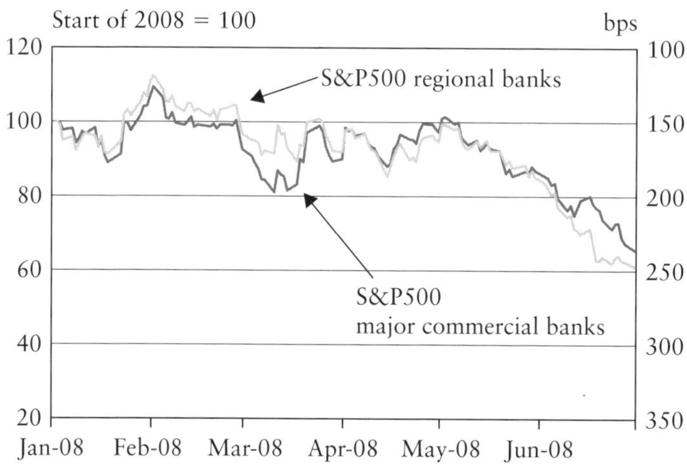

Figure 1.4 Share prices of the US financial sector
Source: Bloomberg, L.P.

Even this historical bailout could not stop the progress of the crisis though. The failure of a US representative investment bank, Leman Brothers in raising funds in the market in the same week had further amplified the mutual distrust in the US and European markets (as shown in figure 1.2), and escalated the attacks against their share prices (see figure 1.4). The result is a long unforgettable event of massive restructuring of the US financial system that took only a week.

After the fifth-biggest US investment bank, Bear Stearns, disappeared in March 2008, the third- (Merrill Lynch) and fourth- (Lehman Brothers) biggest also went under during the weekend of September 13 and 14 (Merrill Lynch was bought by Bank of America and Leman Brothers went bust). The remaining two (Goldman Sachs and Morgan Stanley) were also forced to set up bank holding companies, which would be supervised by the Federal Reserve Bank (FRB). Also, Morgan Stanley raised capital from Tokyo Mitsubishi UFJ, indicating a stronger alliance between banks.

Some similarities can be seen with the Japanese banking crisis, in which Sanyo and Yamaichi Securities went bankrupt, Nikko Securities fell under the umbrella of foreign bank's capital, Daiwa Securities established a strong alliance with a Japanese megabank, and only Nomura Securities remained distinct from the banks. Indeed, events in the US reminded us of the vulnerability of their business models, that is, high leverage and wholesale funding.

The shock did not only hit investment banks. In the same week that two investment banks had disappeared, the US government announced a bailout package for the US's biggest insurance company, AIG, which faced the risk of downgrading by rating agencies. The then-decided total amount of the FRB's bridge loan reached a maximum $85 billion, which accounted for about 10 percent of the FRB's total assets at that time. (The FRB's outstanding assets was about $900 billion in September 2008, but increased rapidly to reach more than $2 trillion in December 2008). This amount was also more than double the FRB's capital of the time ($41 billion).

For those who knew the developments after the summer of 2008, all these figures were no longer any surprise (a sign of surprise fatigue, maybe). Still, these events indicated an historic first turnaround in the FRB's policy to maintain the soundness of the central bank's balance sheet.

In 1985, FRB of New York once provided liquidity of $24 billion for the Bank of New York (BONY), which suffered from computer system troubles and a subsequent cash drain of $32 billion. It is said that the FRB of New York worked through the night to assess the values of all the assets held by BONY, including its real estate, to ensure that the collateral was big enough to cover the FRB's exposures. Meanwhile, the FRB provided a few times more than this to AIG, a company that is not directly supervised by the FRB. Naturally, it is difficult to assess the value of collateral covering such a huge risk taken by the FRB.

Indeed, this FRB lending to AIG was a straight loan without any collateral based on Article 13(3) of the Federal Reserve Act. This lending is normally understood to be used only for emergency purposes, and even in such a case, the government usually guarantees the lending. This time, however, the government announced only the "plan" to purchase AIG preferred securities corresponding to 80 percent of its capital. In other words, the FRB was forced to make its decision even before ensuring that there was security provided to the government for its lending.

After the failures of investment banks and insurance companies, the market again targeted banks. In this process, the US's biggest savings and loan bank, Washington Mutual, failed, and was taken over by JP Morgan Chase. Also, the sixth-biggest US bank, Wachovia, which bought a Californian mortgage company in 2006, suffered from the accompanying nonperforming loans, and was finally taken over by Wells Fargo.

All these events forcefully pushed the US government to take more draconian steps, including mobilization of all available measures to stabilize the financial system. The Emergency Economic Stabilization Act, which includes the measures of purchasing nonperforming loans and of injecting capital into financial institutions, was first voted down by Congress and scorned by the world, but later, on October 3, 2008, finally approved.

With this new act, the government first planned to buy nonperforming assets up to a maximum $700 billion from financial institutions, but then also decided to inject capital into financial institutions, which finally crowded the original buying plan out of the budget. As a result, some roles of buying up risk assets of the private sector had shifted from the government to the central bank, FRB, which announced that it would embark on purchasing various mortgage-related assets. The government also provided guarantees for further losses arising from nonperforming loan assets detached from the balance sheets of financial institutions, thereby saving the use of its budget while accepting the risks.

The repercussions of this financial turmoil naturally spread after the summer of 2008 from the US to European countries, and also to Asian countries including Japan. First, liquidity evaporated in the short-term financial markets in many countries, and interbank rates rose sharply. This was particularly true of dollar markets against the background of the huge dollar funding needs of some European banks (see figure 1.5).

To calm this turmoil, the central banks of major countries, including the Bank of Japan, jointly took some stabilization measures. In addition to the increase in liquidity provision to the markets, some central banks, including the Bank of Japan, kickstarted their domestic currency lending with dollar asset collateral or dollar lending.

It was not only the short-term money markets that were at the mercy of the turmoil. Indeed, many financial institutions in Europe defaulted or were rescued by the public authorities because of their liquidity problems. For example, after the tenth-biggest bank in Denmark, Roskilde Bank, defaulted in August 2008; a large British bank, HBOS, was forced to be sold to Lloyds TSB; and another British bank, Bradford & Bingley, was partially nationalized. Moreover, Belgium and its neighboring countries' authorities injected

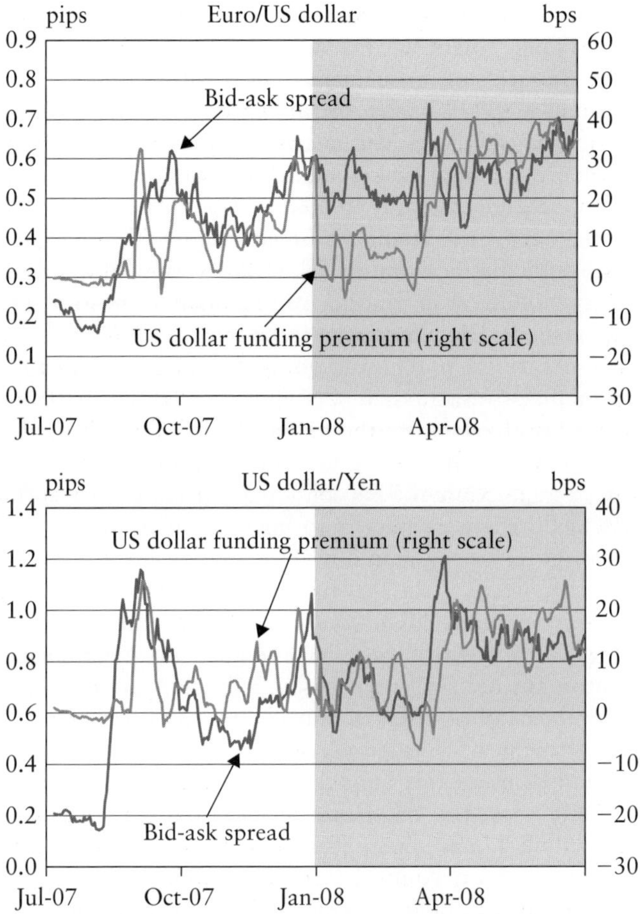

Note: 5-day moving average. US dollar funding premium indicates the spread between the FX swap implied US dollar rate and US dollar LIBOR.

Figure 1.5 Dollar funding premium
Source: Bloomberg, L.P. Meitan tradition

capital into Belgium's biggest bank, Fortis, and another major bank, Dexia. Likewise, some major banks in Iceland and Ireland received relief from their authorities.

Injection of public funds into financial institutions' capital gathered momentum once the UK government announced the bold step on October 7 of injecting £50 billion into major banks' capital by the end of the year.

Announcements of similar measures by other European countries, including Germany and France, followed. Furthermore, as stated, the US also joined in this European effort to inject capital into major financial institutions. According to media reports (*Nihon Keizai-Shimbun*, dated October 15, 2008), the total outstanding of the capital injection reached €270 billion in Europe, of which Germany accounts for €80 billion, France for €40 billion, Spain for €30–50 billion, and Italy €20–30 billion.

Around the same time, many European countries raised their levels of maximum deposit insurance guarantees. For example, the UK raised it from £350,000 to £500,000 on October 3, and Germany, Ireland, and Denmark went as far as announcing blanket protection.

According to the GFSR published by the IMF in April 2008, financial institutions' total losses that could occur in the coming two years, including not only direct losses related to the financial crisis, but also indirect losses such as those related to the economic slump, were $945 billion. The previously reported figure (October 2007) included only subprime loan-related losses at $240 billion. Even using the same definition, however, this figure increased to $525 billion in April 2008.

Against these estimates, for example, the report published by the OECD economists (Blundell-Wignell 2008) insisted that the substantive loss amounts of financial institutions should be about $422 billion if based on their fundamental values. This report assumed a recovery ratio for subprime loan assets of about 40 percent, indicating that the figure estimated by the IMF, using only market prices, was likely to be an overestimate. The latest GFSR published by the IMF in October 2008, however, showed that total losses, $945 billion in April 2008, had further expanded to $1.4 trillion.

Developments up to the end of 2008 were an unprecedented sharp fall in major economies in a remarkably synchronized way, the subsequent reactions of central banks through a series of drastic monetary easings (the US Fed finally introduced a zero interest rate policy on December 16), an almost compulsory public capital infusion into major financial institutions, and the further expansion of the safety net to cover non-banks and some core industries such as automobiles (the US Fed started to purchase commercial paper [CP] issued by corporates and RMBS and so on).

Even in Japan, where the impact could have been minimal, business conditions worsened significantly because of the rapid appreciation of the yen against other major currencies and a sharp drop in foreign demand, and credit conditions tightened, particularly for small and midsized enterprises. In this environment, the Bank of Japan (BoJ) again reduced its policy rate close to zero on December 19, and also announced that it would purchase CP and other risk assets through financial institutions. Moreover, the Japanese government expanded its budget significantly for possible public capital injection into financial institutions, and decided to purchase shares held by financial institutions and CP issued by business corporates, using the Development Bank of Japan.

This way, the local, special market problem dramatically changed into a global financial crisis at a certain point, and then further evolved into a once-in-100-years global financial crisis. Recently, we have experienced various financial crises or shocks, such as "Black Monday" (1987), "the LTCM shock" (1998), "9/11" (2001), and "the Asian Crisis" (1997) or "Russian Crisis" (1998). None of those crises, however, could even rival the size and spread of the impact of the current crisis. What in the world could cause the differences between the past and the current crisis?

SOME SIMILARITIES BETWEEN THE CURRENT CRISIS AND THE JAPANESE BANKING CRISIS

As the crisis in the US deepened, more arguments were seen to focus on the similarities between the current crisis and the Japanese banking crisis of the 1990s. I would like to touch on this issue here because it could give us a hint of the reasons the current financial crisis deviated from other past crises to become a far more serious crisis than ever before.

Because the current financial crisis is still going on, it is a little hard to draw a crystal clear conclusion on this issue at this point. The most important commonality between the current crisis and the Japanese banking crisis, however, seems to be that many factors behind the turmoil led to the loss in confidence of the mechanisms that had long supported high economic growth.

In the case of the current crisis, these mechanisms are "securitization," "ratings given by rating agencies," "fair value accounting," "VaR," or "Basel II." In the case of the US, it is also social policy, which effectively provides a guarantee for mortgage financing despite its strong emphasis on the mechanism of market economy in other areas. In other words, many implicit assumptions behind the "new financial system," which had long supported the robust economic growth of the US and some European countries, were simply put in doubt.

These elements are not necessarily found in other past crises. The central issues of the past crises, for example, hedge funds or emerging markets, tended to be peripheral; in other words, the crisis never entered into the core of major countries' financial systems.

In this sense, the current financial crisis can be seen as quite similar to the Japanese banking crisis during the 1990s. In the Japanese banking crisis, no one expected that the bubble bursting could evolve into such a tremendously serious crisis. In the early 1990s, many financial experts and economists were rather optimistic in saying that the Japanese economy would be on track once it adjusted excess capital formation, although it would takc some years. Needless to say, the reality was different.

Asset prices in Japan fell significantly, particularly real estate prices, which continued to fall until 2004 (see figure 1.6). The real economy had also been sluggish, recording three years of negative growth (FY1993, FY1998, and FY2001), with an average growth rate of only a little more than 1 percent over the past 15 years (during FY1992 to FY2006). During this period, the share of Japanese GDP in the world economy fell from 14.1 percent in 1997 to just 8.1 percent in 2007 (see figure 1.7). The Japanese economy was actually overshadowed by other rapidly growing economies such as those of Brazil, Russia, India, and China (BRIC) and even the US and European economies.

Concerning the banking system, many financial institutions, including large ones, went bankrupt, and the government injected huge amounts of public capital into some of them to sustain financial system stability. Moreover, the central bank went so far as to introduce very abnormal measures for purchasing the shares held by financial institutions. During this period, bank lending continued to fall to 2004 (see figure 1.8). Japanese banks' position in the world also dropped sharply in terms of asset size or capitalization value. For example, *American Banker* reported in 1986 that among the top 10 banks in the world in terms of deposits outstanding, seven banks, including the number one, were Japanese. In 2006, however, among the top 10 banks in terms of asset size, there was only one Japanese bank, ranked eighth.

The seriousness of the problems of the Japanese banking system thus also stemmed from collapsing confidence in the financial system, which had long supported the miraculous economic growth after the Second World War. This system was represented by the loans with real estate collateral based on the myth of ever-increasing prices, relationship banking and cross-share holding between banks and corporations, assuming ever-continuing high economic growth, and finally banking regulation and supervision in this environment. Once the confidence in them collapsed, it should naturally take a long time and huge costs to establish a new system that could regain the confidence.

Many systems that lost users' confidence in the current crisis were related to the banks' relatively new business model, called originate and distribute (O&D). This business model will be detailed later but, putting it simply, unlike the traditional model, in which the bank originates loans and keeps them on its balance sheet, in this model, the bank originates loans to be securitized and sold to investors in the market. Consequently, banks can earn commissions from the process of origination and sale of loans while

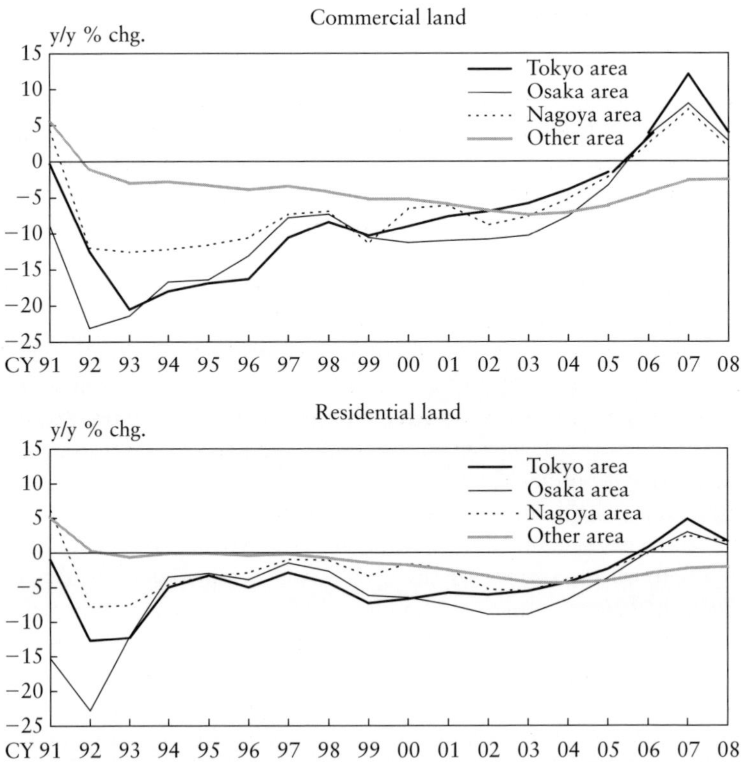

Note: Prefectural Land Price Survey, surveyed by prefecture officials, shows the land prices as of July 1.

Figure 1.6 Development of Japanese real estate prices
Source: Bank of Japan 2008c; material from Ministry of Land, Infrastructure, Transport and Tourism, "Survey of Land Prices"

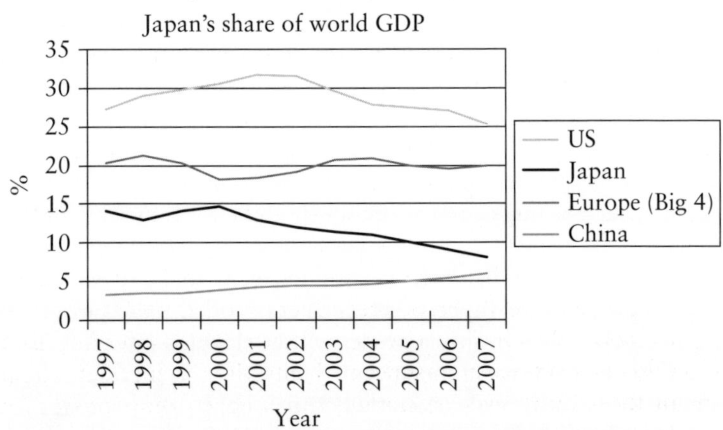

Figure 1.7 Japanese GDP's share of the world economy
Source: Economic and Social Research Institute 2008

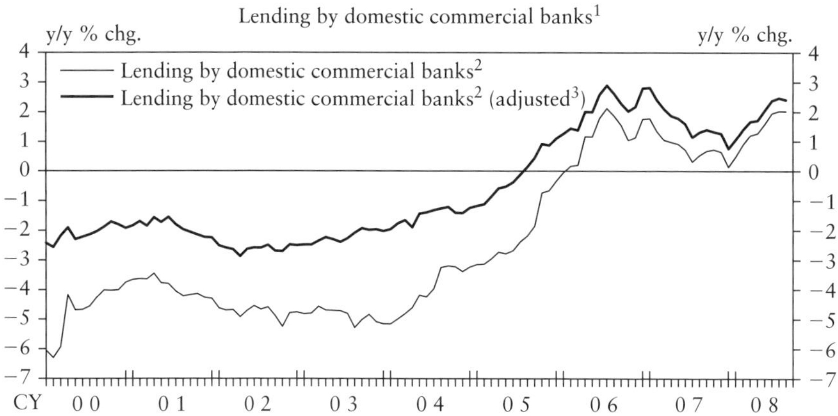

Notes: [1]Percent changes in average amounts outstanding from a year earlier.
[2]"Domestic commercial banks" refers to city banks, regional banks, and regional banks II.
[3]Adjusted to exclude
(1) Fluctuations due to the liquidation of loans.
(2) Fluctuations in the yen value of foreign currency-denominated loans due to changes in exchange rates.
(3) Fluctuations due to loan write-offs.
(4) The transfer of loans to the former Japan National Railways Settlement Corporation to the General Account.
(5) The transfer of loans to the former Housing Loan Administration Corporation to the Resolution and Collection Corporation.

Figure 1.8 Growth rate of bank lending
Source: Bank of Japan 2008c

not keeping any risk on their balance sheet, releasing the capital that would otherwise be required.

It should be noted that this new business model flourished partly because of the failure of the Japanese banking system. Some financial experts and academics attributed the reason for the Japanese banking system being so problematic to there being so much risk concentrated in it. If banks can identify and break down the risk of loans they originate, and then sell securitized products backed by these assets to widely dispersed investors, with the risk sliced and diced to suit many varied investors in line with their risk appetites, the risk can relatively easily be assumed by the system as a whole. In this system, the risk is diversified among many investors, so the financial system was supposed to be able to overcome even the serious nonperforming loan problem experienced by Japan. (The IMF (2006) called this model the "twin-engine model," in contrast to the "single-engine model" of the Japanese banking system).

It is indeed an irony to note that lessons the system learned from the previous crisis have now caused another crisis. This irony should be a caution in reviewing this new business model. Fixing the current system could in the same way sow the seeds of another crisis, which might occur in another 10 or 20 years. To consider this possibility, the next chapter looks at the big picture of the current crisis and breaks it down into major elements, while chapter 3 discusses how regulators, banks, and others reacted to these elements.

CHAPTER 2

Overview of the Financial Crisis

BREAKDOWN OF FACTORS IN THE CURRENT CRISIS

As stated in the previous chapter, the current financial crisis contains various issues to be discussed. Although this book focuses on the weaknesses highlighted by the crisis and the countermeasures against them in the areas of banks' risk management or the stability of the financial system, there are many other topics to be considered. Discussing all these issues one by one at random might risk getting lost in the woods or not having a big picture of the crisis.

To avoid this risk and to capture the big picture of the current financial crisis, I first define the financial crisis as being a phenomenon associated with the burst of a financial bubble. First, the creation of a financial bubble is defined to be a phenomenon in which "typically against a background of long-lasting monetary easing, an excessively optimistic view of the future economy allows asset prices to continue rising, and subsequent positive effects on the macroeconomy further boost the economy to a level that cannot be sustained for long." Then the bursting of a bubble for whatever reasons entails the phenomenon of increasing losses for financial institutions and expanding distrust of the system that supports financial activities, together leading to a destabilization of the financial system. This phenomenon as a whole is called the "financial crisis" in this book.

Based on this definition, I break down the factors that materialized in this process into three different categories: 1) factors that created the financial bubble and those that triggered its burst; 2) factors that enabled the financial bubble to grow over a long period; and 3) factors that amplified the impact of the financial bubble bursting. Also, I try not to be consumed by the conventional idea of risk categories such as credit, market, operational, and liquidity, and instead focus on the economic causes behind the risk materialized.

CREATION OF THE FINANCIAL BUBBLE AND THE TRIGGER FOR ITS BURSTING

Many experts have different views on the initial causes of creating financial bubbles in the US. As in the case of Japan, they might be an overconfidence in innovative factors that justify high economic and asset price growth, or the failure of the central bank, which long continued its policy of monetary easing partly because it lacked the clear policy objective of keeping asset prices stable. Also, a demographic factor, the emergence of the economies of China and India (in particular in the area of manufacturing) might have had some effect in creating the bubble. The long policy of extreme monetary easing conducted by the Bank of Japan might have affected liquidity around the world, leading to benign conditions for taking risks in the US and other countries. This book, however, will not go too far into this discussion. This sort of macroeconomic discussion clearly goes beyond the scope of this book, so it is left to future discussions by experts in macroeconomics.

The periodic creation of a financial bubble itself, however, should not be seen as a surprise given the current incentive structure of financial institutions, which is strongly influenced by externalities and an environment that creates moral hazard. This was indicated by many academics, including recently Kashyap, Rajan, and Stein (2008), or as a more visceral example, Bookstaber (2007).

Financial institutions naturally fall into moral hazard so long as the authorities guarantee the payment of deposits (deposit insurance). It is also true if the systemic risk (or externalities) that could materialize as a result of the failure of big financial institutions is too big to be ignored by the authorities. To minimize this moral hazard, regulators normally require financial institutions to satisfy various regulations, including Basel II. Still, so long as financial institutions have incentives to capitalize on the externalities, they always seek the chance to take advantage of the new system in a legal way. This finally results in another financial bubble. This factor is closely related to the system that should replace the current one, so it is discussed later in this book.

Once a certain size of financial bubble is created, another question to be answered is whether its bursting is stochastic or deterministic. If we side with the latter camp, the most remarkable factor in the current crisis might be the increase in the delinquency ratio of US subprime loans. Behind the phenomena we have discussed we can easily find an excessive loosening of discipline in loan origination (failure of due diligence) from the microeconomic point of view. Meanwhile, from the macroeconomic point of view, the monetary tightening that started in June 2004 in the US after a benign environment for risk had long continued, with ever-rising asset prices, can be seen as a major factor.

In this regard, the trigger for the financial bubble looks quite similar to that in the Japanese banking crisis. In both cases, a small sign of failure of the system arising from the long-continued loosening of diligence had given market participants at the peak of credit cycle a good excuse to stop dancing and leave the party of "irrational exuberance."

FACTORS THAT ENABLED THE FINANCIAL BUBBLE TO GROW FOR A LONG PERIOD

The Rampant O&D Model

In highlighting the unique features of the current financial crisis, it might be more important to identify and study the various institutional factors that enabled the financial bubble to grow for a long time, than to study the factors that triggered its bursting. More concretely, these are the factors that changed a problem in the US local subprime loan market in a blink of the eye into a problem for globally active major banks and for the global financial system itself. As explained in the previous chapter, securitization based on the O&D model played a very important role in this process. In the following, I will discuss why it aggravated the problem.

The traditional business model of banks is to originate loans and keep them on their balance sheet up to maturity. During this process, banks are supposed to manage risks associated with these loans. This model is the so-called "originate and hold (O&H) model." By contrast, the O&D model is first to originate loans but then to pool them, so that they can be sliced and diced according to the risk preference of markets, and then to distribute them to market participants such as institutional investors (see figure 2.1). With this model, banks could profit from commissions related to loan originations while transferring the loans' risk to other parties.

The greatest merit of this model is to enable the risk existing in the financial system to be transformed through securitization into transferable small pieces with various risk characteristics in accordance with various needs and capacity for risk taking of economic entities. Previously, the bank had held all the risks arising from loans. Even if other parties took on the risk of loans originated by the banks, the banks simply sold the loans to them without any transformation of the risk characteristics.

This new business model could satisfy the various risk appetites of non-banks or third parties, including institutional investors. For example, certain investors might hope to take on smaller risks in a certain industry than those involved with bank loans. For this type of investor, securitization could pool the loans extended to the industry, keeping the characteristics of risk of this industry (in terms of correlation with other industries) but

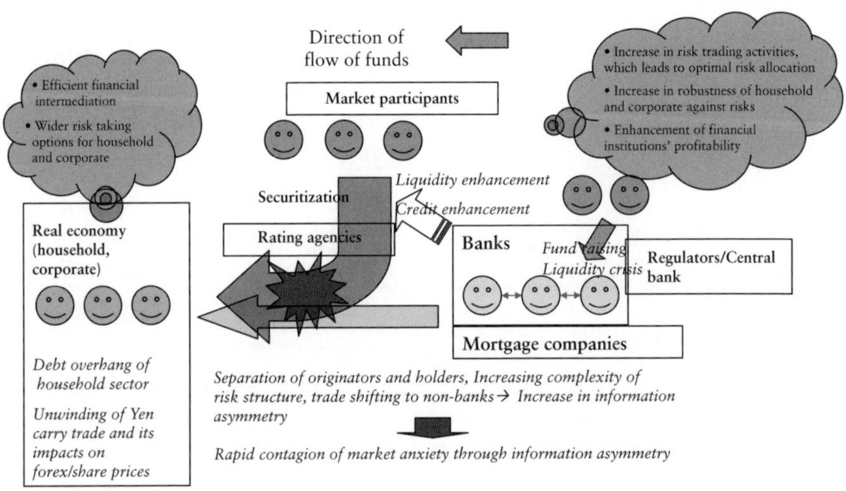

Figure 2.1 The O&D model

tranched them into different risk categories (e.g. in terms of probability of default), thereby creating a modern monster with, for example, characteristics of the credit risk of the real estate industry, but with a lower probability of default than would be typical of loans to this industry.

Furthermore, loan pooling could reduce the size of risk compared with a simple aggregation of the risk of each loan. This is because the probability of simultaneous default is generally supposed to be very minimal. In particular, if we can capture the default correlation, that is, the probability that the default of a certain loan occurs simultaneously with the default of another, we can use this pooling effect in an efficient way to reduce risk.

Consequently, the O&D model dramatically increased the system's ability to take on risk. Owing to securitization, the risk previously taken principally by banks was transformed into small parts with various risk characteristics, so that many investors could take only their preferred type and amounts, leading to a system that could take a bigger risk as a whole than before.

There are few academic studies that analyzed the positive impacts of this business model on the macroeconomy but, for example, Hamilton, Jenkinson, and Penalver (2007) cited the following points:

- Benefits to the corporate sector:
  - an increase in the number of corporations that could directly access financial markets (see figure 2.2);

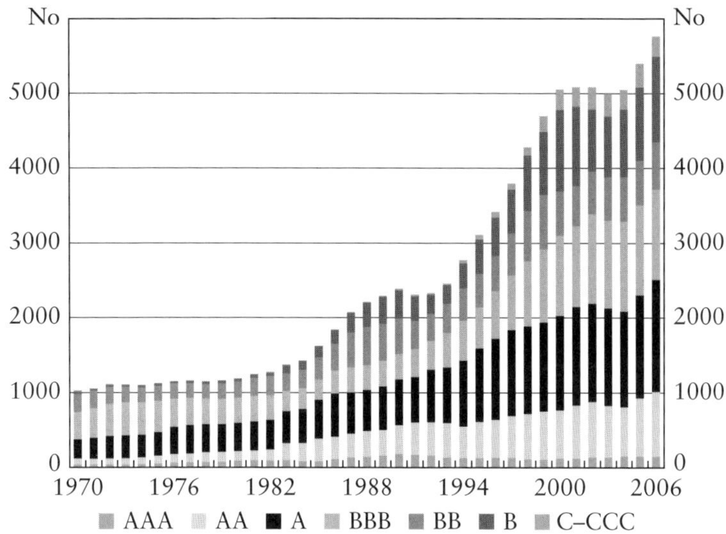

Figure 2.2 Number of corporates assigned ratings
Source: Hamilton, Jenkinson, and Penalver (2007), based on material from Moody's

- easier access to the long-term credit market;
- easier control of risks through various derivatives;

- Benefits to the household sector:
  - an increase in alternative mortgage loans and the increase in the maximum loan amounts that can be borrowed thanks to the advancement of banks' risk management techniques;
  - expansion of access to various credit markets (see figure 2.3);
- Benefits to the macroeconomy:
  - higher growth rate of the financial sector in major countries and a subsequent increase in the share of the financial sector in the economy. (As an example, this ratio increased in the UK from 5 percent in 1985 to 7 percent in 2006.)

So the O&D model was generally accepted as a symbol of financial and macroeconomic development that could never be reversed, particularly in countries such as the US and UK, where this model was rampant. Also, the basics of this idea itself have been retained in many countries, even after some large financial institutions collapsed and the authorities of many US and European countries were forced to inject public money into the banks.

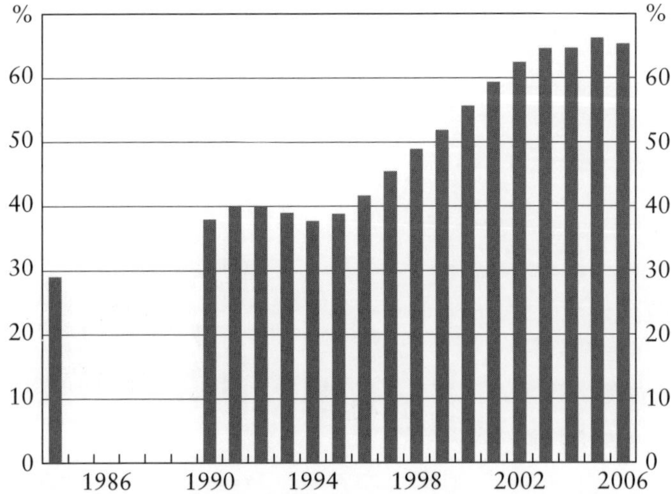

Figure 2.3 The share of individuals who hold credit cards in the UK in credit outstanding

Source: Hamilton, Jenkinson, and Penalver (2007), based on material from the Association for Payment Clearing Services, Bank of England, National Statistics

Failure of the O&D Model: Expansion of Information Asymmetry

The next question naturally is why such a rosy model eventually caused the current financial crisis. The answer is simple; it is mainly because major economic entities such as banks, investors, rating agencies, regulators, and the government failed to share information on the risk.

As stated, the O&D model expanded the number of entities that could share the risk, which was previously taken only by banks, increasing all of society's capacity for risk taking. An important element in this model's performance, however, is whether the risk information is properly transferred when the risk is transferred, or whether this model is properly equipped with a system that enables this risk information to be properly transferred.

In other words, this is a question of the degree of tradability of risk or of socialization of risk. Tradability of risk here indicates a situation in which sharing risk information among market participants widely facilitates stable transactions in the market, and socialization of risk indicates the situation in which a certain well-established consensus exists in the society on how to share risk information among concerned parties.

Needless to say, finance is the business of dealing with information asymmetry among various economic entities. Information asymmetry is defined in economics as "a situation in which the parties engaged in a certain transaction have different levels of information about the transaction." The party with inferior information might act with an increase in uncertainty because of the lack of information (if it recognizes this situation), which might lead to the failure of the transaction or a price far away from the one that would be obtained without any information asymmetry. This is one typical cause of "market failure."

A typical example of asymmetry in the banking business is that which arises between banks and obligors in information on the obligors' creditworthiness. Particularly, obligors with bad creditworthiness have an incentive to hide this inconvenient information from banks when they borrow money from them. For this reason, banks naturally need to devise measures to reduce this information gap, or to set up lending conditions that discourage obligors from abusing the asymmetry.

Similarly, information asymmetry occurs between originators and investors in the process of securitization. Originators have an incentive to transfer bad-quality products to investors, capitalizing on their advantage in information. Ordinarily, the rating agencies' examination of the securities and assignment of ratings to them, or disclosure of information related to securitizations, or various conventional practices and regulation and supervision by the authorities are expected to contain the possibility for abuse. Tradability of risk or socialization of risk is only ensured by establishing a mechanism that supports the proper functioning of all these means of containment.

In the current financial crisis, this containment failed to function well for various reasons, thus leaving the crisis to go out of control. Why could they not work to stop the fire from spreading? An answer can be found in the speed of the expansion of information asymmetry in the past few years, which was too rapid for these means to contain.

A typical example of this expansion of information asymmetry is the introduction of highly complex securitization products. For example, resecuritized products with underlying assets that are themselves securitization products, such as ABS of CDO or CDO squared, became popular and consequently have been sold widely in the market in recent years (see figure 2.4). The risk associated with these products, however, was estimated on the assumption that the risk associated with the underlying assets was correctly understood. In this process, there seems to have been no validation of the

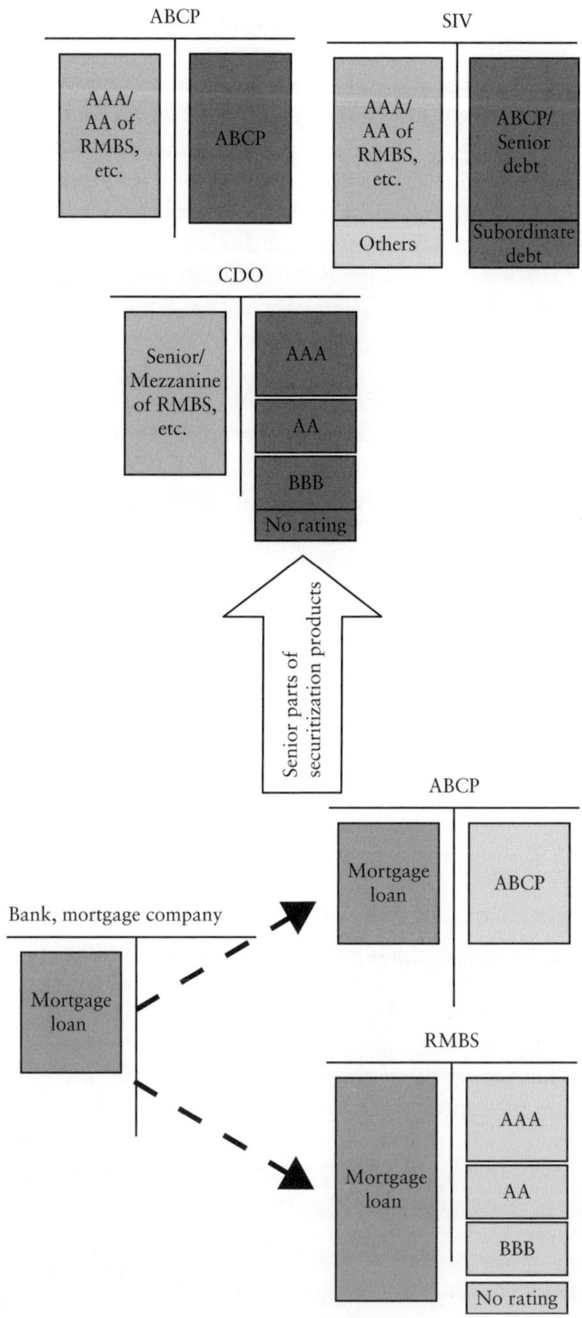

Figure 2.4 The resecuritization process

risk associated with the underlying securitization products and no consideration of model risk.

Generally speaking, any estimated risk tends to be quite sensitive to a variation in assumptions, so some model risk is hard to avoid. This type of risk can sometimes be quite substantial, so a capital buffer is set aside for it. The risk of securitizations of securitized products is likely to be underestimated if no model risk is considered. In other words, ignored model risk is multiplied with each increase in layer of securitization. In the current financial crisis, these securitizations were the ones that suffered most.

Another aspect of the expansion of information asymmetry in the recent securitization market is the increasing share of non-banks in the US mortgage market. Also in Japan, we have seen some non-banks recently entering this market, but in the US they started to enter it in the early 1980s. Particularly in the US subprime loan market, non-banks had already become a major player. For example, Norinchukin Research Institute (2002) indicated that the share of deposit-taking financial institutions in the mortgage loan origination market was about 70 percent in the early 1980s, but fell to about 50 percent at the end of 1990s. Meanwhile, in the same period, mortgage companies' share increased from about 20 percent to about 50 percent. Furthermore, deposit-taking financial institutions' share of mortgage loans held after origination dropped to about 30 percent in recent years (see figure 2.5).

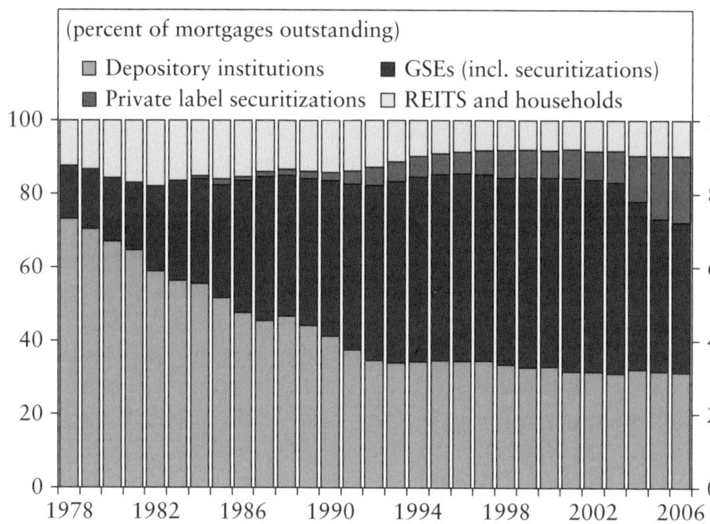

Figure 2.5 Declining mortgage holdings of deposit-taking financial institutions in the US

Source: FRB

An emerging concern in this environment is the expansion of information asymmetry between the authorities and non-banks on the non-banks' origination practices. Unlike banks, non-banks were not usually subject to direct supervision by the authorities, so it was hard for the authorities to monitor them, even if there had been a significant loosening of origination standards. Moreover, the authorities might have faced difficulties in conducting macroprudential policy without having the correct micro-information. To be sure, US regulators had already published their warning about excess loosening of loan conditions in the subprime loan market in March 2007 (OCC 2007). In hindsight, however, this did not have enough impact on fixing the problem.

The Mythification of Risk Management

The second cause behind the development in the O&D model that led to a serious crisis lay in the overconfidence in various risk management techniques to overcome the information asymmetry that arises in securitization transactions. This overconfidence led to many oversights of serious risk management weaknesses.

In the previous section we observed a recent rapid increase in information asymmetry in the securitization market. We then need to consider how the concerned parties deal with the risk associated with this information asymmetry. For example, financial institutions' risk management techniques were supposed to be sufficiently advanced to analyze the complex risk associated with securitization transactions precisely. However, when doing advanced risk management like this, we often forget the basics rather easily.

For example, model risk was often ignored when estimating the risk of securitizations of securitization products. Besides, although it is not only an issue of securitization, many financial institutions simply followed the outcome of VaR without asking further questions. VaR is supposed to indicate the probability of occurrence of huge losses using a statistical model based on the volatility of risk factors observed during a certain period.

This issue related to VaR will be discussed more in detail in chapter 4. The one thing to be noted here is that VaR itself is not problematic, but this way of using it is. Even though there are many assumptions in a VaR calculation, many experts easily forgot them and simply used its outcome as an unequivocal answer. This behavior caused the problem.

Also, many financial institutions and investors buying securitized products substantially outsourced their own risk analysis of these products to third parties, that is, rating agencies. In other words, they simply followed the ratings assigned by rating agencies in assessing the risks of these products and decided their investments on that basis.

This type of investment style itself cannot necessarily be blamed. Rather the issue is whether investors managed the "risk of outsourcing" well, or whether they were well prepared for the situation in which the outsourcee made the wrong decisions. Unfortunately, many investors, including large financial institutions, tended simply to follow the judgments of rating agencies and failed to review their assessments for themselves. This can be seen as a result of them putting too much stock in the rating agencies' capability to assess risks.

FACTORS THAT AMPLIFIED THE IMPACTS OF THE BUBBLE BURSTING

Malfunction of the Market Infrastructure and System that Support Marketization and Socialization of Risks

We have looked at the factors that generate bubbles and trigger their bursting. Then we have looked at the factors that enabled financial bubbles to expand for a long period before bursting. Finally, in this section, we will look at the factors that amplify the impact of a bubble bursting. These factors reflect that there remain many unexpected weaknesses in the market infrastructure or business practices that support the marketization and socialization of risks.

As discussed, the expansion of information asymmetry and the failure of risk management associated with it led to oversight of the risks and losses to be recognized. Financial institutions needed to revise their understanding of the risks and losses in line with the realities.

The financial turmoil had not ended at this point, however. The issues that emerged in the later stage can be characterized as an issue of failure of market infrastructure and system that support marketization and socialization of risks. This refers to the infrastructure or system that controls information asymmetry. Failure to establish this framework caused volatile movements in risk and loss amounts, which did not only include undervaluation, but also overvaluation or overshooting.

Marketization and socialization of risk, on which the O&D model strongly depends, require many economic entities to share risk information and thereby smoothly form a consensus on "price." For this purpose, we need a market infrastructure, business practices, and institutional system that enable the formation of such a consensus. This is a main difference from the traditional financial model.

The traditional financial model was a bank-centered O&H model. This business model required only a few parties, that is, banks and obligors as directly concerned parties, or banks and shareholders and regulators as indirectly concerned parties, to share views and form a consensus on the risk. Academics have actually long discussed how to overcome information asymmetry among these concerned parties (see, e.g., Freixas and Rochet 1997).

So what is the most important difference between the new business model of marketization and socialization of risk, and the traditional business model (O&H)? It is the number and the diversity of parties involved in the transactions, which are significantly higher. As a result, the complexity and diversity of the information asymmetry can also increase dramatically in the O&D over the O&H. Therefore, the consensus formation process could also be very different between these two business models.

Since the O&D is a business model based on market transactions with potentially huge information asymmetry, it naturally needs some risk-mitigating mechanism to contain the fear arising from this huge information asymmetry. The reality is that in recent years there has been only lip service paid to such a mechanism.

In the following, I will discuss more specifically the issues of market infrastructure and system that support marketization and socialization of risks, focusing on five areas: accounting, disclosure, liquidity, general risk management, and macroprudential policy. (I will also discuss these issues in more detail in chapter 4.)

Accounting

Among the most serious accounting issues highlighted by the current financial crisis is how to consider the impact of market liquidity in assessing fair values of transactions. How should we evaluate financial products that cannot be priced because of the evaporation of their market? Also, how should we draw the line between banking and trading transactions from the accounting point of view? For example, when there are no more trades in the market, should we change how we evaluate transactions or transfer them from trading to banking accounts?

Global accounting standards do not yet have answers to these questions. For example, in the US, all financial assets put into trading accounts and regarded as AFS (available for sale) in banking accounts are required to be assessed based on fair value. According to AFS 157, which defines the fair value applied to various transactions, this is "the amount of cash to be received as a result of sale of assets, or to be paid as result of transferring liabilities as of measurement date, among market participants in the ordinary market" (Yoshii 2007). It is also based on the exit price that would be received when selling assets, rather than the entrance price paid when buying them.

There is also a hierarchy, such as level 1, 2, and 3 corresponding to the degree of reliability of inputs for estimating fair values. At level 1 are public prices at which certain assets and liabilities are actively traded in the market. If this price is available, this should first be used. Level 2 are prices of certain assets or liabilities that could be either 1) disclosed prices of similar products traded actively in their markets, 2) disclosed prices of similar products that are not actively traded, 3) disclosed prices based on information on dominant factors in the formation of their prices, and 4) estimated prices using some observable market data such as correlations. Finally, at level 3 are prices that are estimated where none of the preceding information is available, so that they are based only on information collected on a best-efforts basis. This level 3 would mainly be model-inferred prices.

Under this accounting framework, we actually observed a massive shift of evaluation methods from level 1 to level 2 or level 3 by many financial institutions from 2007 to the summer of 2008 because liquidity dried up in some trading markets (see figure 2.6). Consequently, auditing firms warned that their definition of "dried-up market liquidity" or "valuation methods under level 3" were too vague or too loose.

For example, the Center for Audit Quality, which represents the interests of auditing firms in the US, published a white paper in October 2007 on the estimation of fair value of products lacking market liquidity. The Global Public Policy Committee, which represents the interests of global auditing firms, published a similar paper in December 2007. These papers requested financial institutions not to ignore so easily market prices or any market information that looked like outliers. Instead, they requested financial institutions to make more efforts to extract information from market prices such as liquidity risk premium and use it as a factor in evaluating prices.

Upon the request of auditing firms, financial firms were again forced to review the classification of level 1, 2, and 3. These back-and-forth irregularities led to never-ending disclosures of huge losses in quarter after quarter, amplifying the concerns of the market. The general trend observed up to the summer of 2008 was that halfway measures agreed upon by both financial institutions and auditing firms in a highly uncertain environment became more and more conservative under strong pressure from the market.

This trend, however, was completely reversed in the fall of 2008. First, the Emergency Economic Stabilization Act passed by the US Congress included an unexpected item reviewing fair value accounting. More concretely speaking, the act clarified the authority of the Securities and Exchange Commission (SEC) to stop the application of SFAS 157. Besides, the SEC published a paper called "SEC Office of the Chief Accountant and FASB Staff Clarification on Fair Value Accounting" on September 30, 2008 (SEC 2008). In this paper, the SEC clarified its position that trading prices in an inactive market could not constitute fair value, and therefore permitted the use of theoretical values including each firm's judgments. This could be seen

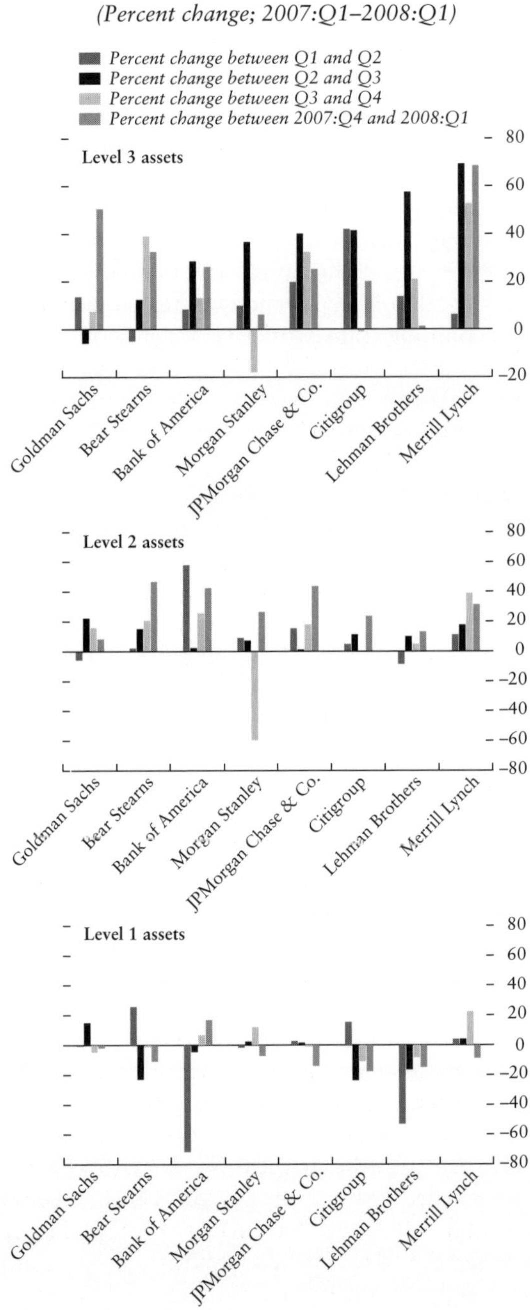

Figure 2.6 Changes in the outstanding of assets classified by level 1, 2, and 3 held by US financial institutions

Source: Disclosure reports of the concerned financial institutions

as a sea change from the previously published views. Previously, the authorities tended to interpret quite narrowly the wiggle room for using level 3, but then suddenly changed to be more flexible.

Similarly, the International Accounting Standards Board (IASB), which has a strong influence over European banks, published a very similar paper on October 13, 2008. This paper also showed that IASB would be more flexible in allowing the reclassification of financial products from the trading account to other accounts without requiring the use of mark-to-market accounting (i.e. loan and receivable accounts and accounts for products held to maturity). Finally, also in Japan, the Accounting Standards Board of Japan published a document on December 5 that allowed firms to reclassify the holding of financial products from "available for sale" to "held to maturity" with some conditions.

How to incorporate various elements (e.g. the liquidity risk premium) observed in markets when market prices have clearly deviated from fundamental values is indeed a big challenge. For example, pricing of elements such as liquidity risk premiums might vary significantly among financial institutions depending on the size of exposure to a certain risk. Arbitrage between market participants with different risk appetites will not necessarily be perfect. In this case, the possibility of different pricing outcomes because of differences in the size of risk exposures could be an important issue to be considered.

Besides, we also have to consider whether we should allow different ways of incorporating market elements between trading and banking account transactions. As stated, trading account transactions should assume "marketization and socialization of risks." In other words, they are the transactions that are supposed to accept the prices agreed by various market participants. So even when fundamental values have deviated from market prices, this is not enough to justify the use of different prices (e.g. fundamental values) that are not shared by market participants.

Meanwhile, banking account transactions do not accept the idea of "marketization and socialization of risks." Even in this case, market prices can be important in deciding prices. The most important element, however, is the consensus view among the limited number of concerned parties (e.g. bank, transaction counterparty, shareholder, and regulator). If this consensus price is closer to fundamental values, there should be no surprise, even if financial institutions use a price that has deviated from market prices.

Disclosure

The issue of disclosure is closely related to the aforementioned issue of accounting. For example, improvements in disclosure concerning the risk profile of securitized products (disclosure mainly of the risk of transactions), or the disclosure concerning each financial institution's risk exposures to such assets (disclosure mainly of the risk taken by each financial institution) can contribute to reducing the costs of increasing asymmetry of information that is associated with marketization and socialization of risks.

To improve disclosure, we should care about what constitutes truly meaningful information. If the analysis of disclosed information with reasonable costs could lead to a significant difference in investment performance from the long-term point of view, market participants would be naturally motivated to analyze this type of information. In other words, disclosed information could help smooth the formation of a consensus on transaction prices among the greater number of stakeholders due to marketization and socialization of risks. For this purpose, we should first understand what information is really required by market participants.

Liquidity

Liquidity of the short-term money market, where banks trade their funds, can be an important element that supports marketization and socialization of risks. It is also the mirror that reflects its malfunction. The concerns about excessively expanded marketization and socialization of risks can amplify distrust among market participants and consequently disrupt short-term money market transactions. This situation was most obvious in the short-term money market just after the collapse of Lehman Brothers, or the collapse of the myth of "too big to fail" in September 2008. In the case of Japan's banking crisis, this was obvious in the market just after the first defaults happened, that is, on the collapse of Sanyo Securities and Yamaichi Securities.

It may be too optimistic to suppose that this type of liquidity "panic" could be avoided merely by improving market infrastructure, because the source of the problem lies in asymmetry of information on the counterparties' financial conditions and also in the manner the authorities reacted to this situation of gridlock. In the current crisis, however, we could not neglect the aspect that poor market infrastructure fueled the problem associated with market liquidity drying up. On this point, the focal issue should be what tools central banks could employ to provide liquidity smoothly to a market in which participants had lost confidence in their counterparties.

The liquidity problems of the current financial crisis became serious around the summer of 2007, and after some amelioration and worsening, finally fell into a crash in later 2008. Behind the sudden increase in demand for liquidity during the summer of 2007 and subsequent drying up of liquidity in the money market was the return of assets to balance sheets that had previously been detached by securitization, because of the collapse of securitization markets and materialization of reputational risk. As a result, the major banks' liquidity demand increased significantly in a short period. Also, because of the failures of the German IKB and British Northern Rock, the uncertainties surrounding the soundness of the balance sheets of banks, including global top banks, abruptly heightened and led to a panicky situation in the market.

In the past, financial institutions facing liquidity problems had usually showed some signs of problems, such as piling up nonperforming loans, and the market needed some time to digest the information. It was also true of the Japanese banking crisis, in which the banks attacked in the market tended to be the same ones that had been long rumored to have huge nonperforming loans. In this sense, at that time in Japan, it was a surprise to see failures of big security houses and banks, but not necessarily a surprise to see which ones.

In hindsight, it was the market that pushed dithering regulators to make decisions on disposing substantially failed financial institutions with deep troubles of nonperforming loans. History showed that this market judgment was not wrong. During the Japanese banking crisis, we did not see a situation where the Japanese banking industry as a whole suffered from a shortage of liquidity, so long as the Bank of Japan supplied enough liquidity to the market, at least in Japan. Although the market transaction volume of the call market (in particular, the noncollateral call market) dropped significantly, the market still kept functioning in bridging gaps in the demand and supply of liquidity.

In the current crisis, however, we have seen a situation in which all the counterparties in the market, including major ones that had long been believed to be triple "A" looked suspicious without showing any clear signs, such as the amounts of nonperforming loans seen in Japan before. Of course, there were some signs of problems. The financial institutions that were first targeted by the markets were those with huge amounts of securitized assets, or the ones with huge credit default swaps (CDS) arranged by the former financial institutions. The next targets were those that adopted a business model that depended for liquidity on the wholesale market (such as investment banks like Lehman Brothers).

This way, in the current financial crisis, many financial institutions were not attacked by the market because their real capital ratios fell into the negative based on the fundamental value (assuming that they hold them to their maturities) of their assets held. Rather, many attacks were justified by self-realizing factors, such as financial institutions' net value based on fair value or drying up of liquidity in the market. In this sense, the financial institutions looked like they had lost their once established anchor, that is, fundamental value, and were now at the mercy of speculation by investors, including hedge funds.

Fair value is an issue of the accounting system, so the room for central banks to improve liquidity conditions might be constrained. Meanwhile, central banks have tools to work against the speculative movements that were agitating the liquidity crisis. In this financial crisis, however, these central banks' tools to provide liquidity did not work effectively, which worsened the problem.

Among representative problems was the so-called "stigma" problem. In this, financial institutions are discouraged from using the central bank's standby scheme even if they suffer from liquidity shortage because they fear that they could be labeled by the market as troubled if they do. Market participants, when locked in mutual distrust, will use any minor information, so long as it has some content to distinguish themselves from their counterparties. The stigma problem, in this sense, could be seen just as a reflection of information shortage among market participants. Having said so, still there should have been some room for central banks to mitigate this stigma problem beforehand.

There were also other issues faced by central banks in this crisis, which ranged from how to grasp the information on daily demand and supply of short-term funds among financial institutions to how to provide liquidity to non-banks, the range of eligible collateral for credit, and the provision of liquidity of foreign currencies. In particular, the liquidity provision to non-banks and provision of liquidity for foreign currencies were important in terms of the marketization and socialization of risk.

General Risk Management

To develop marketization and socialization of risks smoothly, it is necessary for financial institutions to introduce corresponding risk management, and also for supervisors to introduce corresponding supervisory measures. The following is a brief note on this issue, which will be expanded on in chapters 4 and 5.

I have already noted that excessive confidence in the capability of risk management may have deepened the root of the problem. In the same context, I have also emphasized the importance of understanding the limits of VaR. They are particularly important when we discuss the issue of securitization, which was highlighted in the current crisis.

Risk management can surely vary between the micro and macro level. For example, how to precisely measure risk to support marketization and socialization of risks could be a good issue to consider on the level of each financial institution (micro level), but would not sufficiently cover the issues to be discussed on the macro level. Besides, it is necessary to clarify how society should share the responsibilities for risk management or risk itself, particularly financial institutions and the authorities. In ordinary situations, the risk to be managed by financial institutions should be the risk taken by financial institutions voluntarily, and there is no room for the authorities to intervene in this area. Also, even if the losses are not the result of risk intentionally taken by financial institutions and instead are the result of financial institutions' underestimation of risks, they are expected to manage the losses by themselves.

Some of the risks that were taken unintentionally, however, might be difficult to attribute only to financial institutions' misjudgment. For example, we could not expect that each financial institution could react in a perfect way to the results of policy failures by the government or the central bank, or to the damages caused by so-called "perfect storm" conditions as in the current financial crisis. In this case, the issue to be considered is how we should draw the line between the risk to be managed by each financial institution and the risk that is beyond financial institutions' capability to manage and must therefore be managed by the authorities. Furthermore, we should discuss how we should express "this line" so that all concerned parties can reach a consensus view on it.

Furthermore, to make various risk measurement methods, including VaR, complement each other efficiently, we need to clarify the types of risks to be captured by financial institutions or by supervisors. More concretely speaking, we need to develop new communication tools to define clearly the risk factors, risk concepts, risk quantification, and risk appetite.

Many readers might think that all these questions should have already been answered. To be sure, in the world of economic capital management, risk factors are usually defined as the common causes of losses behind loss events, while quantified risk is defined as the outcome of VaR, and risk appetite is defined as the confidence interval used in VaR. Even taking the case of risk quantified by VaR, however, it should be noted that VaR methodologies can significantly vary among different risk categories (such as market risk, credit risk, and operational risk).

The same can be applied to the complementary relationship between VaR and stress testing. Moreover, the current definition of risk category, such as market, credit, and operational, which are mainly based on transaction types or organizational sections to deal with, might have already become outdated as financial transactions became more and more complicated. Keeping the conventional risk management system surely has a lot of merit. For example, it is the system that many employees in the organization are already familiar with, so it enables them to reach a consensus relatively easily. This also may be true of communication between financial institutions and outside stakeholders. In an environment where reality began to devaite more and more from established systems and practices, however, we could not ignore this gap of changing realities forever.

Macroprudential Policy

Finally, the current financial crisis has highlighted some weaknesses of the macroprudential system, which was expected to mitigate the limits of market function (market failures) and thereby smoothly support the marketization and socialization of risks. One example is various safety nets, including the deposit insurance system, which assumes that systemic risk cannot be sufficiently managed by individual banks alone.

For example, the UK discussed the issue of deposit insurance and also how to dispose of insolvent financial institutions in an intensive way after the occasion of Northern Rock's failure. Meanwhile, the US discussed and has partly implemented ways to provide liquidity to and supervise "non-banks," and also ways to inject public funds into financial institutions or to provide guarantee over their assets. Furthermore, many European countries followed the US by implementing an increase in the limits of guarantee by deposit insurance, and various rescue measures for financial institutions, including injection of public funds into those facing liquidity shortages and solvency problems after September 2008.

In addition to these issues, how to manage the credit cycle of the macroeconomy emerged as another issue that is beyond the capability of the market. In an ordinary situation, monetary policy deals with this. The recent credit cycle, however, is not necessarily represented by price index, the typical target of monetary policy. A typical example is an asset bubble.

Some indicators, which are supposed to represent the movements of a new credit cycle, such as credit spreads, actually signaled the underestimation of risk or the bursting of the financial bubble long before the current crisis. Unlike in the area of monetary policy, however, there is no consensus among the authorities on how to conduct macroprudential policy. More specifically speaking, we need to answer the questions: 1) which indicators should be targeted; 2) which authority (bank regulatory agency or central bank) should conduct this policy; 3) which measures (monetary policy, or any measures that directly control credit amounts provided by financial institutions) should be used; and 4) what type of credit cycles should be made smooth.

Also, we need to discuss more the possible procyclicality of the current macroprudential framework, including Basel II.

CHAPTER 3

First Reactions: Countermeasures and Recommendations

RECOMMENDATIONS FOR THE CRISIS: ONE HUNDRED FLOWERS BLOOMING

There is no doubt that the authorities have not just stood by and watched as all these events occurred one after another. As explained in the previous section, some international organizations and regulators already issued warning messages of a possible underestimation of risk in global financial markets as early as early 2006 (see table 3.1). Likewise, US regulators issued a statement in March 2007 that warned of excessive loosening of discipline in loan origination in the subprime loan market.

Moreover, against the liquidity crisis that emerged during the summer of 2007 and another serious one after September 2008, the central banks of major countries acted jointly by providing further liquidity and went so far as to conduct coordinated monetary easing. Also, each central bank eased the conditions on its standby facility, and expanded the range of participants that could use this facility during this period. Also in the UK, the authorities reviewed the deposit insurance scheme in the aftermath of Northern Rock's failure, and the US authorities announced a series of public rescue plans for large financial institutions.

After August 2008, when the crisis spread to Europe, European authorities also started to take various initiatives to mitigate the problems associated with the liquidity shortage and insolvencies faced by large financial institutions. When the US adopted policies such as injections of public funds into banks, an idea that has long been seen as a kind of taboo in the US to contain market fears, this was soon followed by major European countries. All these policy reactions, however, looked haphazard, rather than well-prepared policy measures.

In addition to these reactions by individual countries' regulatory agencies and central banks, various international regulatory groups consisting of

Table 3.1 Financial System Stability Assessment by IMF and BOE

IMF/GFSR	BOE/FSR
(October 2006) Favorable global financial market conditions appear to be consistent with the macroeconomic prospects of continued solid growth and contained inflation despite a modest rise in financial market volatility. Major risk factors are as follows: • An intensification of inflation pressures and subsequent monetary policy tightening • Pronounced economic slowdown in the US • Amplified reaction of financial markets under the current benign conditions to unexpected materialization of these risks • Some emerging economies' reliance on investors' capital inflows to cover large current account deficits	(June 2006) The profitability of the UK financial system remains high helping to underpin its resilience to future disturbances. But the risks associated with the key vulnerabilities, while remote, have increased somewhat and remain significant. Main vulnerabilities are as follows: • The unusually low premia for bearing risk • Large financial imbalances among the major economies • Rapid releveraging in parts of the corporate sector globally • High UK household sector indebtness • Rising systemic importance of large complex financial institutions • Dependence of UK financial institutions on market infrastructures and utilities
(April 2007) Favorable global economic prospects continue to serve as a strong foundation for global financial stability. However, some market developments warrant attention. Short-term risks are as follows: • Deepening and spread of US subprime market turmoil to other markets • A substantial rise in leverage in the acquired firms in equity buyouts • A rapid rise in capital inflows to some emerging markets • A possible disorderly unwinding of global imbalances Meanwhile, long-term risks are as follows: • A sharp increase in cross-border capital inflows which contributed to rapid credit growth and asset price inflation in some countries • Vulnerabilities in expected cross-border diversification effects owing to the potential for increases in linkages among markets and activities	(April 2007) The UK financial system remains highly resilient. But further extension of risk-taking with low compensation has increased the vulnerability of the system as a whole to an abrupt change in conditions. Main vulnerabilities identified in the previous report remain important. • The stress testing results suggest that if these vulnerabilities were to crystallize individually, they would be unlikely to erode to any significant extent the capital base of the UK banking system, but vulnerabilities in combination could have a more material impact.

the representatives of major countries, such as the Financial Stability Forum (FSF), which is a group of treasuries, bank regulators, and central banks; the Basel Committee of Bank Supervision (BCBS), which consists of bank regulators; the Joint Forum (JF), which consists of regulators of bank, security, and insurance industries; the Senior Supervisors Group (SSG), which consists of senior supervisors of the countries hit most severely by the current crisis; and also the Institute of International Finance (IIF), which represents the interests of the international banking industry, analyzed the background of the current crisis, and made recommendations to tackle the weaknesses of the financial system and risk management of individual firms. Table 3.2 summarizes the reports made by all these organizations chronologically.

The following is an overview of the recommendations made by these reports, and also some of the measures actually taken by central banks after the emergence of the crisis, and then classified into the type of weaknesses, which we have already seen in the previous chapter, ensuring the coverage and tendencies of these recommendations vis-a-vis the vulnerabilities highlighted by the crisis. Also, this chapter will discuss the implications of these recommendations in terms of financial system stability as well as of risk management of individual firms.

It should be noted that the following discussion does not cover every major report published by international organizations or individual countries' authorities. For example, the CEBS, which is the group of EU members' bank regulatory agencies, published reports on the issue of liquidity risk, valuation of complex and illiquid financial instruments, and disclosure in June, 2008. Also, IOSCO published a report on the role of credit rating agencies (CRAs) in structured finance markets in May 2008. They are not covered by the following discussion, however, mainly because the content overlaps somewhat with that in other reports. Meanwhile, various measures (particularly the measures to set up a new framework for financial stability) taken by individual agencies, and recommendations for macroprudential policies will be touched upon in the concerned sections.

OVERVIEW OF THE RECOMMENDATIONS MADE BY INTERNATIONAL ORGANIZATIONS

Statement Made by US Bank Regulators (March 2007)

All US bank regulators, including the OCC and Federal Reserve System, issued the statement titled "Subprime Mortgage Lending" in March 2007. This was the first official warning message against the excessive loosening of loan origination standards observed in the subprime loan market.

Table 3.2 Crisis reports published by major international organizations

Timing	Organization	Report title
March 2007	US bank regulators	Subprime Mortgage Lending
March 2008	SSG	Observation on Risk Management Practices during the Recent Market Turbulence
March 2008	UK Financial Services Agency (FSA)	FSA Moves to Enhance Supervision in Wake of Northern Rock
April 2008	UBS	Shareholder Report on UBS's Write-down
April 2008	FSF	Report on the Financial Stability Forum on Enhancing Market and Institutional Resilience
April 2008	BCBS	Basel Committee on Banking Supervision Announces Steps to Strengthen the Resilience of the Banking System
April 2008	JF	Cross-Sectoral Review of Group-wide Identification and Management of Risk Concentration
May 2008	International Organization of Securities Commissions (IOSCO)	The Role of Credit Rating Agencies in Structured Finance Markets
June 2008	BCBS	Principles for Sound Liquidity Management and Supervision. (This consulting paper was finalized in September 2008.)
June 2008	Committee of European Banking Supervision (CEBS)	Second Part of CEBS's Technical Advice to the European Commission on Liquidity Risk Management
June 2008	CEBS	Report on Issues Regarding the Valuation of Complex and Illiquid Financial Instruments
June 2008	CEBS	CEBS Report on Banks' Transparency on Activities and Products Affected by the Recent Market Turmoil
July 2008	Committee of Global Financial Stability (CGFS)	Ratings in Structured Finance: What Went Wrong and What Can Be Done to Address Shortcomings?
July 2008	CGFS	Central Bank Operations in Response to the Market Turmoil
July 2008	IIF	Final Report of the IIF Committee on Market Best Practices: Principles of Conduct and Best Practices Recommendations
October 2008	IMF	Global Financial Stability Report

In this statement, regulatory agencies showed special concerns over, for example, the loans that intended at their outset to be temporary credit accommodations in anticipation of early sale or refinancing (i.e. assuming a continued increase in real-estate prices) that may exceed the borrower's ability to service the debt without refinancing or selling the property, ARM products for which initial payments are based on an introductory rate that is considerably lower than the fully indexed rate, or for which risk information is provided to borrower only in an inadequate way.

This statement, however, was applied only to financial institutions that were subject to these agencies' regulations and therefore could not influence the behavior of many non-banks, which were then the main originators in the subprime loan market.

Senior Supervisors Group Report (March 2008)

Senior supervisors gathered from the hardest-hit five countries (the US, the UK, Germany, France, and Switzerland) drafted a report titled "Observations on Risk Management Practices during the Recent Market Turbulence," which contains various recommendations to tackle the weaknesses highlighted by the crisis, published in March 2008. This is the first report made by the bank regulatory agencies on sound risk management practices to be introduced to deal with the problems.

This report actually described best and bad bank practices to deal with the problems triggered by the subprime loan turmoil, which regulators found in the interviews with large financial institutions. The following are the main findings of the report.

Concerning the firmwide risk management practices, there are the following four areas that differentiated their performances:

- *Effective firmwide risk identification and analysis:* Some firms under top group management leadership were able to identify the sources of the crisis very early, and had as much as a year to evaluate the magnitude of those risks and to implement plans to reduce exposures. Meanwhile, other firms, business lines, and senior managers did not promptly discuss among themselves and with senior executives the firm's risks in light of evolving conditions in the marketplace, and made isolated decisions.
- *Consistent application of independent and rigorous valuation practices across the firm:* Some firms had established rigorous internal risk valuation processes and were skeptical of rating agencies' assessments of some products. Meanwhile, firms relied too passively on external views of credit risk from rating agencies.

- *Effective management of funding liquidity, capital, and the balance sheet:* Some firms aligned treasury functions more closely with risk management processes, and had created internal pricing mechanisms that motivated business lines to manage liquidity based on the premium required by the market. Meanwhile, other firms had weaker controls over their potential balance-sheet growth and liquidity and insufficient information sharing among multiple concerned sections.
- *Informative and responsive risk measurement and management reporting and practices:* Some firms had management information systems that assessed risk positions using tools that draw on differing underlying assumptions, or more adaptive risk measurement processes and systems that could rapidly alter underlying assumptions in risk measures to reflect current circumstances. These firms used VaR and stress testing, understanding their weaknesses, and thus complemented each other.

FSF Report (April 2008)

FSF is the organization established on the occasion of the Russian Crisis in 1998 to coordinate major countries' reactions during periods of financial crisis. Members are major countries' (G7+five countries and some international organizations) finance ministry and bank regulatory agencies. The report was published in April 2008 to show the authority's views on the background of the current financial crisis, and also policy actions of G7 based on this analysis. The following are the main contents of the report, which is so far the most comprehensive among various published reports particularly on financial institutions' risk management practices. Some information in this report came from findings of previously introduced reports by SSG.

- Raise Basel II capital requirements for certain complex structured credit products, trading book transactions, and liquidity facilities to off-balance sheet conduits.
- Issue supervisory guidance for the supervision and management of liquidity risk.
- Develop guidance for supervisory reviews under Basel II, which will strengthen oversight of 1) banks' identification and management of firmwide risks, and 2) banks' stress-testing practices for risk management and capital-planning purposes, and also require banks to manage soundly and to report off-balance-sheet exposures.
- Encourage market participants to act promptly to ensure that the settlement, legal, and operational infrastructure for over-the-counter derivatives is sound.

- Encourage financial institutions to make robust risk disclosures using the leading disclosure practices, and issue further guidance to strengthen disclosure requirements under Pillar 3 of Basel II.
- Improve and converge financial reporting standards for off-balance-sheet vehicles, and develop guidance on valuations when markets are no longer active, and encourage market participants to expand the information provided about securitized products and underlying assets.
- Rating agencies should manage conflicts of interest in rating structured products and improve the quality of the rating process, differentiate ratings on structured credit products from those on bonds, and expand the information they provide.
- A college of supervision will be put in place by late 2008 for each of the largest global financial institutions.

Reports of BCBS, April and June 2008; JF, April 2008; CGFS, July 2008

BCBS started the work of reviewing many areas of banks' risk management, including Basel II itself, based on the lessons learned from the current financial crisis. And its overall roadmap was published in April 2008 under the title of "Basel Committee on Banking Supervision Announces Steps to Strengthen the Resilience of the Banking System." As of December 2008, however, the paper that was published by the BCBS focusing on banks' risk management practices was limited only to "Principles for Sound Liquidity Risk Management and Supervision," which was published in June 2008 as a consultation paper, and then finalized in September 2008.

The JF, which was jointly set up by BCBS, IOSCO, and the International Association of Insurance Supervisors (IAIS), published a paper titled "Cross-sectoral Review of Group-wide Identification and Management of Risk Concentrations" in April 2008. The drafting of the paper itself was not necessarily initiated by the crisis, but it happened to deal with issues closely related to the ones that materialized in the current crisis.

Meanwhile, CGFS, the group of G10 central banks, published in July 2008 a paper titled "Ratings in Structured Finance: What Went Wrong and What Can Be Done to Address Shortcomings," which dealt with the issue of ratings in structured finance and discussed measures to tackle their shortcomings.

The following are the main recommendations made by each report.

"Basel Committee on Banking Supervision Announces Steps to Strengthen the Resilience of the Banking System":

- Reviewing part of the Basel II framework (mainly leading to higher capital requirements), including the capital treatment of complex structured

credit products, liquidity facilities to support ABCP conduits, and credit exposures held in the trading book;
- Strengthening global sound practice standards for liquidity risk management, stress testing, off-balance-sheet management, and valuation, and also the Pillar 2 process, including the management of firmwide risks, banks' stress-testing practices, and capital planning, and the management of off-balance-sheet exposures and associated reputational risks;
- Monitoring the procyclicality impacts of Basel II;
- Increasing market discipline through better disclosure and valuation practices.

"Principles for Sound Liquidity Risk Management and Supervision":

- A bank should establish a robust liquidity risk management framework that ensures it maintains sufficient liquidity. Supervisors should assess the adequacy of both a bank's liquidity risk management framework and its liquidity position, and should take prompt action if a bank is deficient in either area.
- A bank should clearly articulate a liquidity risk tolerance, and senior management should develop a strategy to manage liquidity risk in accordance with the risk tolerance. A bank should explicitly incorporate liquidity costs, benefits, and risks into the product pricing.
- A bank should have a process for identifying, measuring, monitoring, and controlling liquidity risk, and should actively manage liquidity risk exposures and funding needs within and across legal entities, business lines, and currencies, taking into account boundary limitations to the transferability of liquidity.
- A bank should establish a funding strategy that provides effective diversification in the sources and tenor of funding, and also regularly gauge its capacity to raise funds, and identify the main factors that affect its ability to raise funds. A bank should actively manage its intraday liquidity positions and collateral positions.
- A bank should conduct stress tests on a regular basis for a variety of institution-specific and marketwide stress scenarios, and also should have a formal contingency funding plan. A bank should maintain a cushion of unencumbered, high-quality liquid assets to be held as insurance against a range of liquidity stress scenarios.
- A bank should publicly disclose information on a regular basis on its liquidity risk management framework and liquidity position.
- Supervisors should regularly perform a comprehensive assessment of a bank's overall risk management framework and liquidity position, and should supplement this assessment by monitoring some combination of

internal reports, prudential reports and market information. Supervisors should intervene to require effective and timely remedial actions by a bank to deal with deficiencies.

- Supervisors should communicate with other supervisors and public authorities to facilitate effective cooperation.

"Cross-sectoral Review of Group-wide Identification and Management of Risk Concentrations" (JF):

- Risk concentrations refer to exposures with the potential to produce losses large enough to threaten a financial institution's health due to their high sensitivity to single or closely related drivers of risk.
- Risk concentrations at most financial conglomerates are still chiefly identified, measured, and managed within separate risk categories and within business lines (so-called "silo management"), making it hard for a financial conglomerate to capture firmwide risk exposures.
- Because of the development and tremendous growth of risk transfer markets and increased interactions between market and credit risks in recent years, management of concentration risks becomes highly important for a financial conglomerate.
- Obtaining a groupwide view of risk beyond silos is a priority for entities' risk concentration management. The economic capital framework provides a useful tool to introduce a common risk denominator for integrated firmwide risk management, but has limitations including difficulty in capturing hidden risks, second-order effects, and dependencies under stressed conditions. In this sense, some conglomerates use stress testing as a complementary risk measurement methodology for the management of risk concentrations across a financial group.

"Ratings in Structured Finance: What Went Wrong and What Can Be Done to Address Shortcomings" (CGFS):

- Investment fund trustees and managers should review their internal procedures and guidelines concerning how ratings information on structured products is used in their investment mandates and decisions.
- Rating reports should be presented in a way that facilitates comparisons of risk within and across classes of different structured products.
- Rating agencies should provide clearer information on the frequency of rating updates.
- More user-friendly access to CRA structured finance models and their documentation should be provided.

- CRAs should document the sensitivity of structured tranche ratings to changes in their central assumptions regarding default rates, recovery ratio, and correlations.
- CRAs should clearly and regularly disclose to investors their economic assumptions underlying the rating of structured products.
- Where only limited historical data on underlying asset pools are available, this should be clearly disclosed as a source of model risk.
- CRAs should monitor more intensively the performance of the various agents involved in the securitization process (from origination to sale and subsequent servicing and administration).
- CRAs should periodically consider the wider systemic implications of a rapid growth of similar instruments of vehicles.
- CRAs should consider how to incorporate additional information on the risk properties of structured products into the rating framework.

UBS Report (April 2008), Report of IIF (August 2008)

Two reports were published from the industry side. The first one is the report titled "Shareholder Report on UBS's Write-Downs," which was reported to its shareholders by UBS, a large Swiss bank, and another one is the report titled "Final Report of the IIF Committee on Market Best Practices: Principles of Conduct and Best Practice Recommendations," which was published by the IIF, the group representing the interests of the global banking industry.

The contents of the UBS report tended to overlap with those of the previously mentioned SSG report, and these similarities sometimes went so far as to make us wonder whether the Swiss regulators mainly drafted the SSG report. So here I have just limited myself to giving some of my impressions of this report.

It was a little surprising to find that there was no limit system or clear policy on risk assets or balance-sheet control in this top-tier global bank. This is certainly a serious problem for the bank, but should also be the serious problem of supervisors which long overlooked this poor risk management.

The fact that the group's top management could not control (and subsequently allow the aggressive risk taking of) a newly established strategically important section, that is, Dillon Read Capital Management, which specialized in alternative investments, is noteworthy. This might imply the existence of an optimal size of organization in terms of corporate governance. In other words, once the organization size and complexity go beyond this threshold, control expectation covering the whole group deteriorates significantly.

The main recommendations made by the IIF report are as follows. Some of them are policy recommendations made for the authorities, but they are not included here so as to avoid overlap with those made by other reports.

- Embedding a firmwide focus on risk, developing a robust risk culture throughout firms.
- Articulating the firm's risk appetite, considering all types of risk, involving finance and treasury functions, as well as risk management, in monitoring the overall risk.
- Strengthening risk management organization structures, ensuring independence of the chief risk officer and its influence over the firm's risk level.
- Strengthening risk management tools and framework by using multiple methodologies, understanding the limitation of single risk measurement approach, eschewing the silo approach, improving stress testing.
- Strengthening the risk management tools and frameworks of securitization and complex structured products.
- Base compensation on risk-adjusted performance, aligning incentives with shareholder interests and long-term, firmwide profitability.
- Strengthening the liquidity risk management, including the strategy for day-to-day liquidity risk management, granular management, for example, by currencies, effective internal transfer pricing, consideration of market liquidity, and so on.
- Maintaining robust valuation processes, having an appropriate governance framework for valuations, inputs from as broad a range of sources as possible, ensuring model validation, and so on.
- Applying the same credit due diligence standards regardless of whether assets are to be held on the books or distributed, appropriately monitoring them, and disclosing their performances.
- Increasing transparency at the structured product level.
- Establishing the Market Monitoring Group (MMP), which will serve as a forum to monitor global financial markets for early detection of vulnerabilities having systemic implications, to examine market dynamics, which could lead to financial market strains and to discuss ways to deal with such risks.

UK FSA Report (March 2008)

The UK FSA is so far the only regulatory agency to have published its analysis of its own failure of supervision. It was carried out by its own internal auditing division, and focused on the case of Northern Rock. Main points are as follows.

- Major factors behind the failures:
  - a lack of sufficient supervisory engagement with the firm, in particular the failure to follow up the business model vulnerability arising from changing market conditions;

- a lack of adequate oversight and review by FSA line management on the quality, intensity, and rigor of the firm's supervision;
- inadequate specific resources directly supervising the firm;
- a lack of intensity by the FSA in ensuring that all available risk information was properly used to inform its supervisory actions.

- Main features of supervisory improvement program:
  - A new group of supervisory specialists will regularly review the supervision of all high-impact firms to ensure procedures are being rigorously adhered to.
  - The number of supervisory staff engaged with high-impact firms will be increased.
  - The existing specialist prudential risk department of the FSA will be expanded following its upgrading to divisional status.
  - Supervisory training will be upgraded.
  - The degree of FSA senior management involvement in direct supervision and contact with high-impact firms will be increased.
  - There will be more focus on liquidity.
  - Emphasis on assessing the competence of firms' senior management will be raised.

IMF's GFSR (October 2008)

IMF biannually publishes the GFSR to monitor the stability of the financial system from a global point of view. The one published in October 2008 summarized the policy recommendations made for the authorities of their reactions to the financial crisis. Main points are shown in the following five principles the report established:

- Employ measures that are comprehensive, timely, and clearly communicated. They should encompass the principal challenges arising from the strains of deleveraging, cost, and maturity to stabilize balance sheets, injecting capital to support viable institutions, and so on.
- Aim for a consistent and coherent set of policies across countries to stabilize the global financial system.
- Ensure a rapid response on the basis of early detection of strains.
- Assure that emergency government interventions are temporary and taxpayer interests are protected. Accountability of government actions is important.
- Pursue the medium-term objective of a more sound, competitive, and efficient financial system.

More concrete actions in line with the above guiding principles are as follows:

- *Capital:* The GFSR estimates some $675 billion in capital would be needed by the major global banks over the next several years to keep private-sector credit growing while strengthening bank capital ratios. The authorities may need to inject capital into viable institutions.
- *Assets:* The use of public-sector balance sheets (e.g. government purchase of problem assets) can help prevent firesale liquidations that threaten to reduce bank capital. Allowing for a greater degree of judgment in the application of mark-to-market rules may avoid accelerating capital needs.
- *Funding:* Financial institutions that rely on wholesale funding, especially in cross-border markets, have faced severe and mounting refinance risks. Central banks are exploring more ways to extend term financing to meet the funding needs of institutions. Under extreme circumstances, deposit insurance could be expanded beyond normal limits, and guarantees could cover senior and subordinated debt liabilities temporarily.

Liquidity Provision by Major Countries' Central Banks (Since the Summer of 2007)

After reviewing various reports, we now turn to see actual reactions of central banks of major countries against drying up of liquidity in short-term money markets in the midst of the crisis.

Central banks of the US and European countries had not only significantly expanded their provision of funds to short-term money markets plagued by liquidity shortage, but also had introduced many measures that enabled them to expand their provision since the summer of 2007.

Moreover, according to the Bank of Japan (BoJ), Money Market Department (2008), the FRB, BOE, and ECB implemented the following measures that enabled them to provide enough funds to financial institutions since the summer of 2007. They include: 1) increasing the use of overnight lending starting on the same day; 2) lengthening the term of money market operations or making them more flexible; 3) providing dollar funds against eligible collateral in domestic markets; 4) expanding the scope of eligible collateral for market operations; 5) easing the so-called stigma impacts; and 6) expanding the type of institutions with which central banks could directly deal (see table 3.3).

For example, concerning (3), major countries' central banks, including the BoJ, simultaneously provided a massive amount of funds to markets in September 2008 to contain the shock from the failures of Lehman Brothers.

Table 3.3 Changes in the central banks' way of providing funds to money market

Action	FRB	BOE	ECB
Increase in overnight lending starting on the same day	Continuously implemented since August of 2007	Implemented frequently, particularly after 2008	Same as BOE
Lengthening or making flexible the term of market operations	Emphasized the need to contain liquidity crisis in the term markets in its statement	Same as FRB	Same as FRB
Provision of dollar funds against domestic collateral	Provided dollar funds to other countries' central banks using currency swaps. First started with ECB and SNB (Switzerland), and expanded to BoJ, BOE, and BOC	Agreed swap agreement with the US in September 2008	Agreed swap agreement with the US in December 2007. Then expanded its amount
Expanding the scope of eligible collateral	Expanded significantly the scope of eligible collateral to include securitized products. Also implemented a bond lending scheme against the collateral of securitized products that suffered a lack of liquidity in the markets	Same as FRB	No special measures taken
Containing stigma impacts of the use of standby facility	Reduced the penalty margin of stand-by facilities and lengthened its application period. Encouraged financial institutions to use the scheme	Encouraged financial institutions to use the scheme	No special measures taken
Expanding the type of financial institutions with which the central bank directly deals	In addition to deposit-taking institutions, included primary dealers by establishing a new lending scheme. Also announced the scheme to buy out CP issued by corporations to help their liquidity management	No special measures taken	No special measures taken

Source: Financial Market Department, BoJ (2008b)

It was reported that the amount of funds that they provided on September 15 and 16 reached $360 billion (*Nihon Keizai Shinbun*, September 17, 2008). Furthermore, on the next day (September 18), the central banks of the US, Japan, Europe, the UK, and Switzerland announced an emergency measure that provided $180 billion in each domestic market. This was a measure to counter the shortage of dollars in non-US markets. It was actually the first time the BoJ had provided dollar funds directly mainly to foreign banks using a currency swap (total amount is $60 billion) concluded with the US.

In addition to these measures, central banks in the US and European countries, for example, introduced measures to guarantee banks' exposures against other banks in the money market.

CLASSIFICATION OF THE RECOMMENDATIONS MADE BY INTERNATIONAL ORGANIZATIONS

As seen in the previous section, international organizations and the authorities of major countries already announced a variety of measures, which actually covered most of the issues indicated in the previous chapter. For example, the SSG report, a harbinger of a series of reports, encouraged financial institutions to reconsider the firmwide risk management framework to be established. Then the FSF report considered wider issues, which do not only cover risk management of financial institutions but also issues facing other main players in the financial market, such as rating agencies, regulatory agencies, and central banks.

Furthermore, the reports issued by BCBS, JF, and CGFS discussed in more detail the issues such as liquidity risk management, risk concentration, and rating of structured products. They were emphasized again by private institutions or industry group despite some nuances mainly because of the difference in positions as regulators and as regulatees.

Meanwhile, the UK authority's self-review of its failures and corrective actions was quite exceptional. It emphasized the weakness of the existing supervisory framework from the authority's point of view. (However, the report indicated only the weaknesses of supervision on business risk and liquidity risk and stopped short of recommending exact measures to be taken by supervisors to assess those risks.)

Finally, massive liquidity provision by major central banks was associated with various measures to correct the defects of the framework of liquidity provision, which were highlighted by the financial crisis.

In the following, I summarize the recommendations and sometimes the measures made by various organizations against the issues indicated in the previous chapter.

Risk management of individual financial institutions:

- Improvement of governance over risk management (SSG, FSF, IIF);
- Improvement of enterprise-wide risk management and breaking down risk management silos (SSG, FSF, JF, IIF);
- Review of the excessive dependence on VaR and the use of effective stress testing (SSG, FSF, IIF);
- Improvement of liquidity risk management, including the consideration of market liquidity, effective stress testing, and the use of internal pricing of liquidity (SSG, FSF, BCBS, IIF);
- Review of the comprehensiveness of risk coverage including reputational risk (SSG, FSF, IIF);
- Review of the risk management of securitized products (SSG, FSF, CGFS, IIF);
- Tackling the excessive dependence on the ratings assigned by rating agencies (SSG, FSF, CGFS, IIF); and
- Review of the compensation mechanism of financial institutions (SSG, FSF, IIF).

Regulatory and supervisory framework:

- Clarification of the definition of the ratings given by rating agencies and of the differences among the ratings of different products, improvement in the governance of rating agencies (FSF, SEC, CGFS);
- Improvement of disclosure of the risk associated with securitization products and of the risk profile of individual institutions (FSF, CGFS);
- Review of a part of Basel II (FSF, BCBS);
- Review of the authority's supervisory framework (UK FSA);
- Review of the tools of providing liquidity to the markets (major central banks);
- Review of the deposit insurance system (some European countries); and
- Introduction of the framework for injecting public funds into banks' capital (US, and many European countries).

As summarized here, many issues highlighted by the financial crisis were already noted and considered in various reports. This may imply that only if each responsible entity implements these recommendations, we will never see the same kind of crisis in the future, even though we need to manage the repercussions of the current crisis for the next few years. Is it, however, really true?

EVALUATION OF THE RECOMMENDATIONS—DÉJÀ VU?

After the overview of all these recommendations made by various organizations, some readers might note an interesting fact. That is, most of them are actually the ones that have long been noted as the elementary risk management problems to be solved by financial institutions. A big question is why problems that have long been recognized remained to be solved before or even during the crisis.

We have not yet seen a thorough analysis of this point. For example, we have not yet seen the answers to many questions, such as why CEOs were not involved enough in risk management in global financial institutions, why stress testing outcomes were not used in an effective way, and why the board allowed certain sections to take excessive risks.

Many US and European financial institutions, which suffered huge losses during the financial crisis, were regarded as the most advanced in the area of risk management. They often behaved themselves as though they were models to be followed by the other financial institutions and even by supervisors up to early 2007. Thus, many financial institutions were believed just up to early 2007 to be dealing perfectly with the risks that materialized in this crisis. Then why did they find themselves facing tremendous problems and in the end publicly declare that they failed to implement elementary risk management processes?

Moreover, most of these financial institutions were subject to the supervision of the supervisory agencies. And some of them were actually qualified by the authority for the advanced approach under the Basel II. The advanced approaches of Basel II request banks to establish various quantitative and qualitative risk management methods, which should have resolved the problems that materialized in the crisis.

In the next chapter, we will see why many global financial institutions, which were even qualified for the advanced approaches of Basel II by the authorities, have to admit that they were not necessarily good at risk management a few months after these qualifications.

CHAPTER 4

Various Issues Highlighted by the Financial Crisis

WHY WERE THE SAME MISTAKES REPEATED?

In the previous chapter, we have seen that most recommendations made by many international organizations and individual country's authorities were not necessarily new, but rather ones that have long been recognized as issues to be tackled. In addition, many financial institutions have tried in vain to deal with these issues with seemingly highly sophisticated risk management tools. How could this happen?

In the following, I note four factors that explain why these efforts failed. The first three concern the difficulty in forming a consensus on the risks to be prepared for by financial institutions. The last concerns the issue of incentive compatibility, or whether the current financial system adequately motivates financial institutions to prepare for risk.

The first factor is the difficulty that even internal parties find in ensuring the effectiveness of the core part of risk management. For example, even before the current financial crisis, no financial institutions denied the importance of senior managers' deep involvement in risk management. Furthermore, most global financial institutions devoted pages of their annual reports to explaining how the CEO or board members frequently discuss and examine the risks facing these institutions, and reflected these insights in their risk-taking policy.

That emphasis notwithstanding, the current crisis simply demonstrated that senior manager involvement was not sufficient in those financial institutions. This fact clearly showed that risk management is a kind of art, which consequently is very difficult to judge as good or bad only based on descriptions of a risk management framework or guidelines in documents. And a more serious issue is that the authorities as well as the financial industry had given up at a very early stage on developing a way of more precisely evaluating the "artistic" part of risk management.

The second factor is intentional government ambiguity over the line between risk to be absorbed by financial institutions and that to be absorbed by the government. For example, the report published by SSG picked up best practices that were observed among investigated financial institutions and then contrasted them with bad practices observed from the same sample. This benchmarking methodology implicitly assumed the existence of financial institutions that behaved smartly during the crisis.

Some other reports that reflected the situation in 2008, however, indicated that almost all global financial institutions, with exceptions in performance, failed to deal with huge losses from the latter half of 2007, and subsequently faced a liquidity crisis. Also, the reports published by the industry group indicated that there may be some limitations to private financial institutions absorbing all the losses in such a stressful environment. So what are indeed the risks that could not be well managed by all global financial institutions? Are even these losses expected to be absorbed by these financial institutions? They are the questions to be reconsidered.

The third factor is closely related to the first, which is that the countermeasures against this type of crisis tend to focus only on consequent events, and therefore do not go beyond dealing with the exact events that have already occurred. In other words, they did not analyze the root causes of the events, nor did they deal with the stress events that were triggered by causes that were similar but not identical to those that had already occurred.

This tendency was observed in the current crisis too. For example, many recommendations indicated that financial institutions have not used stress testing outcomes well in their reaction to risk management. These observations, however, led only to the conclusion that "financial institutions should use more stress testing in their risk management." No one has yet posed to financial institutions the question of why financial institutions did not prepare and use stress testing well in advance. So while the currently recommended measures might prevent the exact same stress events in the future, they do not help prepare for similar ones in a proactive way.

Similarly, the measures against the crisis tended to be short-sighted and the measures to deal with the institutional framework and infrastructure tend to be put on ice for reasons of limited time and political unpopularity, even though they are often more important in preparing for a future crisis. This sequence could cause a problem, however, if the effects of countermeasures with a short time horizon conflict with those of countermeasures with a long time horizon.

For example, an unprincipled government rescue package for troubled financial institutions might help overcome the crisis temporarily but also could produce a moral hazard on the private side and thereby jeopardize the stability of the financial system from a long-term point of view. Moreover, in the case where specific financial products such as subprime loans and securitization products were especially highlighted, we often see discussions that try to seek a scapegoat, that is, a specific regulation or specific type of risk management.

This is indeed a process that first names easily identifiable scapegoats, and then concentrates the authorities' criticism on them, and finally just makes the scapegoats stop doing the same thing. This is surely easy for the general public to understand, so it tends to be politically well accepted. If the policy recommendations focus only on ease of understanding and short-term effects, however, they might discourage the authorities from facing structural issues requiring long-term solutions, even though they understand that they are the core issues to be resolved.

The final factor, as indicated in chapter 2, is embedded in the very structure of the current financial system itself. Financial institutions naturally have the temptation of a moral hazard so long as the authorities guarantee their deposits through deposit insurance. Furthermore, if the systemic shock (externality) caused by its own failures could be too big to be left without any rescue action by the authorities, the concerned institutions could also fall into a moral hazard situation.

Therefore, the current financial system will always be accompanied by a moral hazard by financial institutions. In other words, we should assume that financial institutions will "rationally" seek the chance to benefit in the form of a moral hazard so long as the current system is in place.

A possible reaction to this moral hazard issue is to increase monitoring to become aware of the risks taken by financial institutions and increase regulations to close loopholes. Our history shows, however, that increasing regulations would surely produce financial innovations to get around them. Meanwhile, it is also difficult to expect that financial institutions and market discipline voluntarily tackle the above issues through the process of Pillars 2 and 3 of Basel II.

After all, all the preceding discussion shows that we have to establish a new incentive mechanism to contain the moral hazard of financial institutions (see figure 4.1).

In the following, I will discuss the four factors I noted in a more specific way.

CONFUSION IN THE RISK CONCEPT: THE MEANING OF VAR

The Assumptions of VaR

The term "risk" can be interpreted in a variety of ways, even in financial institutions. However, the most common factors among the interpretations might indicate the idea of the frequency being "unexpected" or "a rare occurrence," or limited to concepts regarding severity of damage such as "the losses would be huge if the risk comes to pass." So risk, in a broad

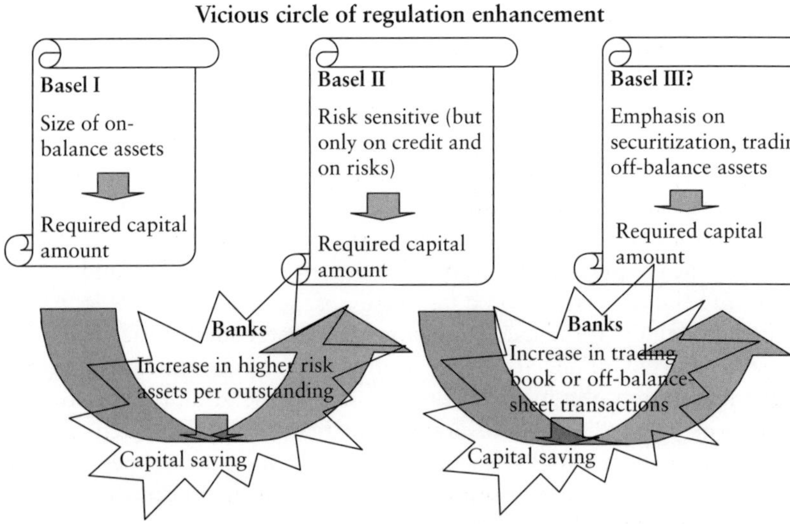

Figure 4.1 Vicious circle of improved regulation

way, could be defined as an event that will only rarely occur but causes huge losses once it does. The real issues to be considered, however, start from this point. The first question is how we should define "rare" occurrence. In the world of VaR, this rare frequency is often defined in terms of confidence level. VaR is an idea that quantifies the risk amount. Detailed explanations can be found in more specialized books (e.g. McNeil, Frey, and Embrechts 2005), but its essence is as follows (see figure 4.2).

The method is first to collect the frequency data of values of specific risk factors during the specific period and then measure the parameters of, say, a standardized normal distribution, assuming that the change in values of this risk factor basically follow this distribution. In this case, a confidence level of 99 percent indicates the value on the distribution, which matches the largest amount of loss just below the amount with the probability of 1 percent. The maximum loss amount could be too huge to be managed but in this case, we use a 1 percent margin and this width of margin actually constitutes the concept of "rare" in the world of VaR.

Another important assumption of VaR aside from the confidence level is the "holding period." In other words, it is the assumption of how long the exposures to the risk are fixed. For example, in the case of transactions where exposures can change relatively easily through market transactions, this holding period can be very short, such as 10 days, or a month, depending on the capability to change positions.

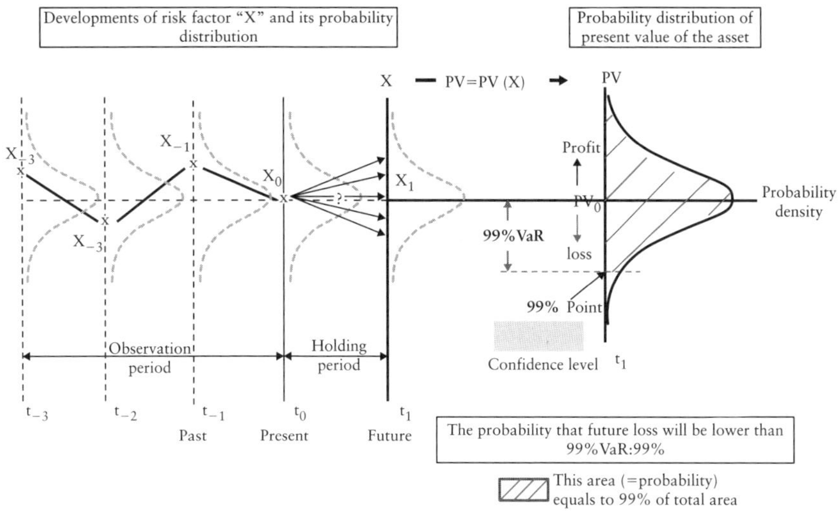

Figure 4.2 Concept of VaR
Source: Tachibana (2008)

It should be noted that this holding period reflects not only the market liquidity factor, but also the policy of concerned financial institutions regarding the frequency of portfolio review. Meanwhile, in the case of corporate loans, many financial institutions simply set one year for their holding period. Because the maturity of most corporate loans is more than one year, some argue for a longer holding period to be set. However, because we can also suppose that changes in capital (e.g. raising capital from the market or just adding profits over this period) correspond to an increase in risk over a time horizon of more than one year, many financial institutions just use one year as a holding period in the case of corporate loans.

It should be noted that some financial institutions have recently started to set their holding period simply at one year for every transaction, including market transactions, in the framework of an integrated risk management system. This idea emphasizes frequency in reviewing investment strategy and capital policy, and also integration of various risks for economic capital management reasons.

The World Assumed by VaR: the Meaning of Stability of the External Environment

In the integrated risk management framework, financial institutions integrate the amount of various risks that are quantified by VaR and then compare it with the amount of capital, and thereby assess the adequacy of capital. The holding period that is assumed for this purpose is usually set at one year, considering the frequency of capital adjustments and of revising the accounting information. In this case, if we use a 99 percent confidence level for risk quantification by VaR, we often say that the quantified risk is equal to that which could occur once in every 100 years.

This expression itself is faulty in many ways. First, from the technical point of view, a 99 percent confidence level does not exactly correspond to a loss that could happen once in every 100 years, but is just below that level, or the maximum amount below the amount that could happen once in every 100 years. This expression, however, might be accepted as a way to explain the concept of VaR easily to laypeople.

Instead, a more serious problem arises from the very concept of "the loss amount that could occur once in every 100 years" (or an amount commensurate with that which could occur only once in every 100 years). The reason is that a very important assumption for VaR is the stability of the external environment for the concerned risk factors.

This assumption is important in obtaining a stable model. If we put the information of factor movements under the variant external environments (or during a long observation period) together in a model with a single factor distribution, we might only see its poor performance to predict near future factor volatility. For this reason, in the case of market risk measurement, for example, the observation period of the data tends to be limited to one year in the past or at longest three years. Even in the case of credit risk, risk measurement often excludes data from extremely stressful periods.

However, the risk amounts obtained this way are only from stable external environments. In this sense, the loss amounts that could happen once in every 100 years (or just less than this amount) should always be accompanied by the (very unlikely) assumption that the external environment will be stable over the coming 100 years. So an expression like "the loss amount that could happen once in every 100 years" (or just less than this amount—in the following, I will not repeat this remark for convenience—but it should be understood) is very misleading to understand the real meaning of the risk amount measured by VaR.

The Meaning of Two Horizons for Measuring the Degree of Stresses

In the current financial crisis, the problems of VaR have often been discussed. For example, the FSF and IIF reports, which were introduced in the previous chapter, also highlighted the issues. I myself have long insisted that the risk corresponding to 99 percent of VaR should be expressed as "the loss amount that could happen at one bank among 100 (similar) banks every year" instead of "the loss amount that could happen once in every 100 years." And I name the concept of the first frequency as the "horizontal frequency," and the second as the "historical frequency" (see figure 4.3).

The reason the horizontal frequency (or the expression of "the loss amount that occurs at one among 100 banks every year") is better than the conventional historical frequency for representing the confidence level of VaR is that the former is more consistent with the VaR's assumption of a stable external environment. If we can suppose that the length of an observation period is inversely proportional to the stability of the external environment, the expression using the shortest observation period could be more appropriate.

This issue is more strongly highlighted by using the case of a 99.9 percent confidence level of VaR. Many Japanese banks use 99 percent for their confidence level of VaR, but many US and European banks use 99.9 percent or higher for this purpose. In this sense, 99.9 percent looks more like a global standard, although this does not necessarily mean it is better than 99 percent.

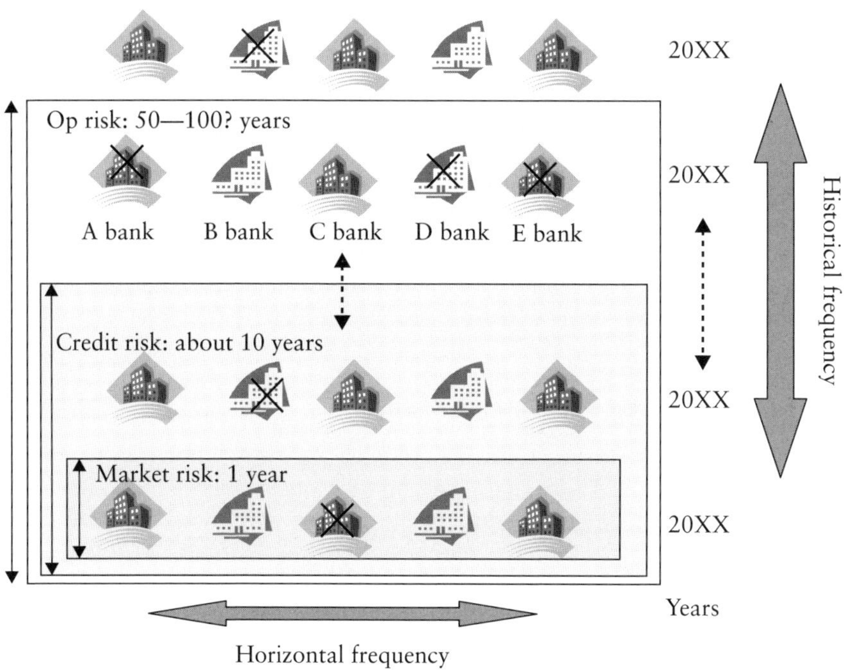

Figure 4.3 Two different frequencies

If using the idea of historical frequency, this 99.9 percent can be expressed as the loss amount that could occur once in every one thousand years. One thousand years ago, Japan was in the Heian Era. If, for argument's sake, a bank had been established at that time, this bank would have surely experienced a whole series of extreme stresses in the ensuing years, which even the state could not absorb.

Even before discussing the capability of VaR to capture such stresses, we would find that an expression like "the loss amount that occurs once in every one thousand years" would break down as a communication tool. The only exception might be the case of an earthquake for operational risk quantification, where the concerned parties could make a kind of consensus of loss amounts with this historical frequency.

On the other hand, if we use the idea of horizontal frequency and say that the risk of a 99.9 percent confidence level is equal to "the worst loss amount that could occur at one among 100 banks over the coming 10 years", it might be much easier for us to conceptualize. Also, 10 years might be accepted as a period during which we can realistically expect external environments to remain relatively stable. My use of the expression "over the coming 10 years," however, does not necessarily intend to combine the idea of historical frequency with horizontal frequency. I just simply supposed that the stability of external environments can be imagined even during a period of 10 years. The reason I did not use an expression like "the worst loss amount that can occur at one among 1,000 banks every year" is the difficulty in finding 1,000 similar banks even globally not to mention domestically.

Of course, in these so-called "dog years," even 10 years would not strictly satisfy the assumption of a stable external environment. Still, I believe that this could serve as a "communicable" expression. In the future, we might have more objective yardsticks to measure the stability of external environments, such as some econometric ideas including "stationality" or "structural breaks."

The Impacts Provided by Different Horizons

Behind the current financial crisis may exist an overconfidence in a magic number such as 99.97 percent. No one seriously believed that the risk amount measured by VaR could really reach the once in every 1,000 years or 10,000 years level. But the regulators as well as financial institutions might still find it easy to believe that their measured risk and consequently prepared capital should be big enough to overcome the class of maximum stresses after the Second World War.

Indeed, the risk amount measured by horizontal frequency and by historical frequency could be very different. In the following, I introduce the case of major Japanese banks, shown in Oyama (2007). Figure 4.4 indicates the estimate of risk amount taken by major Japanese banks using the method of VaR with some specific assumptions, and then compares that with their Tier 1 capital. Here I use the assumption of a 99 percent confidence level. The chart shows you that total risk amounts recently tend to go below the level of Tier 1 capital. Meanwhile, in table 4.1 I selected the representative risk factors for different risk categories including credit, market, equity, and op risks, and then estimated the loss amounts caused by the worst number during the past 20 years for comparison with their Tier 1 capital (as in table 4.1).

Table 4.1 shows a very different picture from figure 4.4, indicating that the risk amounts are still much larger than Tier 1 capital. So the risk amount measured by VaR, which often refers to the loss amount that could occur

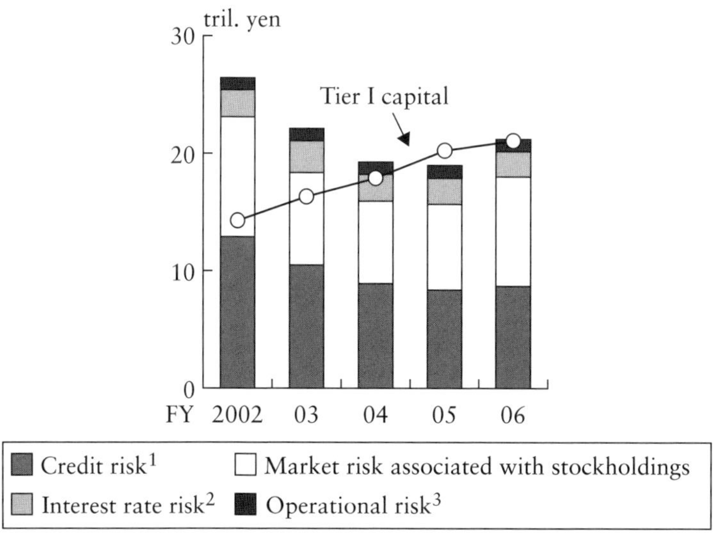

Notes: [1]Credit risk is calculated by subtracting the expected loss (EL) from the maximum loss (EL + Unexpected Loss [UL]) based on the Basel II risk weight formulas with a confidence interval of 99 percent. In the estimation, borrowers classified as requiring "special attention" or below (in terms of credit quality) are considered to be in a state of default.

[2]Interest rate risk is limited to yen-denominated bond portfolios

[3]Operational risk is defined to be 15 percent of gross profits based on the Basel II basic indicator approach.

Figure 4.4 Risk amounts faced by major Japanese banks
Source: Adapted from Bank of Japan (2007)

Table 4.1 Loss amount estimates based on the worst experiences after the debacle of the financial bubble

Asset type (risk type in parenthesis)	The worst loss ratio/the size of loss for op risk (recorded fiscal year in parenthesis)	The amount of losses of Tier 1 capital (I)	The amount of risk (figure 4.4) of Tier 1 capital (II)	(I)/(II)
Loans (credit risk)	Credit cost ratio: 47% (1998)	55.6%	41.3%	1.4
Equity (equity risk)	Total profit/loss ratio: −61.4%(1991)	70.8%	44.2%	1.6
Governmental bond (market risk)	Total profit/loss ratio: −1.3%(2005)	4.3%	10.2%	0.4
Op risk	The loss amounts associated with misplaced order of stocks made by M securities: 400 million yen(2005)→its ratio against group total Tier1: little less than 1%	1.0%	4.9% *%1.3%*	0.2 *0.8*
Total		131.7%	100.6% *97.0%*	

Source: Oyama (2007)

Remark: In the column of risk amounts of Tier1 capital, there are some italic numbers for op risk, which represent the estimated VaR-based risk amounts. See more details in the following paragraph.

once in every 100 years, is very likely to go below the worst numbers over a span of only 20 years.

It is interesting to note some features of different risk categories. The far right column gives a comparison of the worst loss numbers over the past 20 years with the risk amount obtained from VaR at a 99 percent confidence level. Only op risk shows two numbers because the op risk numbers indicated in Bank of Japan (2007) that I used here were not based on VaR but on 15 percent of gross profits, taking the Basic Indicator Approach (BIA) of Basel II. Here, I used the following method to transform this BIA number into the approximate VaR numbers.

First, I used the figure 4.5 from Nagafuji (2008). This was the analysis based on Japanese banks' op risk Loss Data Collection Exercise. With the assumption that Japanese banks' losses follow the power law (a linear relationship between the squared number of loss events and squared number

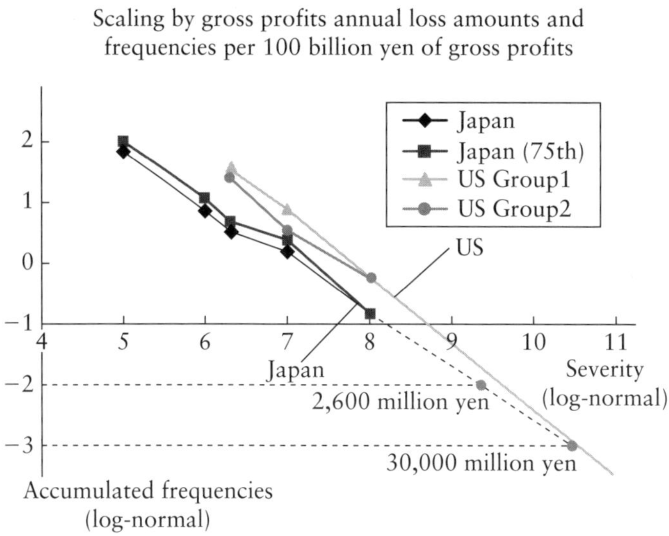

Figure 4.5 Estimates of op risk amount using LDCE data
Source: Nagafuji (2008)

of loss amounts), I first estimated the risk amount corresponding to a 99.9 percent confidence level, which is generally assumed in the Basel II. This amount is ¥316 million. Meanwhile, the op risk amount under the BIA of Basel II is ¥150 million if gross profit is ¥1 billion, which is assumed in figure 4.5. So the risk amount calculated by using the power law could be much higher (more than double) than the number under the BIA.

Then I adjusted the risk amount from a 99.9 percent to a 99 percent confidence level because the other risks are quantified based on the 99 percent confidence level. This process reduced the op risk amount to ¥26 million or one-sixth of the amount under the BIA. I used this risk amount here.

The comparison of quantified risk amounts by different risk category shows that the ratio of (I)/(II), or the ratio of the worst losses over the past 20 years against the risk amount with a 99 percent confidence level tends to become smaller in the order of equity, credit, and op risk (I intentionally excluded the market risk from this comparison because its risk factor is limited only to interest rates of government bonds). As I will show later, this phenomenon actually reflects that even the methodology of VaR can differ significantly among different risk categories, particularly in a way that considers the historical frequency of risk events.

In this financial crisis, we have already observed losses that reached a level that would ordinarily be incredible, such as more than 10 sigma in some securitization markets. From a historical horizontal point of view, these losses should occur only once in every million or so years. Because such losses actually occurred frequently, it is very natural for many to lose their confidence in a VaR-type risk quantification model.

However, as noted, this is not necessarily a problem of VaR itself, but rather of how to use it. VaR is just a risk quantification method with many specific assumptions that should be used with a consideration that they are assumptions or are limited in performance. For example, as noted, the frequency represented by the confidence level in many cases assumes a stability of the external environment, and this assumption is not consistent with the expression of risk amount referring to historical frequency.

In addition, in the environment before the burst of the financial bubble, in which a long credit risk-benign condition continued, the risk amount based on VaR reflected only the observation data during this euphoric period. VaR is indeed a very objective method for measuring risk amount, but at the same time it is a very backward-looking method.

CONFUSION IN THE RISK CONCEPT: THE LIMITS AND THE POSSIBILITY OF STRESS TESTING

The Salvation of VaR-Centered Risk Management: Mounting Expectations on Stress Testing

As a supplement to the limits of VaR, many advocated an active use of stress testing and also for it to be improved in this financial crisis. This type of argument, however, has been heard in every financial crises in the past. Each time, regulators and financial institutions confirmed the importance of stress testing and advocated its clearer position in the risk management framework. In this sense, the only difference in the current crisis from previous ones may be the exact events that are happening now, implying that adding another story to the stress scenarios might be sufficient for many regulators and financial institutions.

It is true, however, that the current financial crisis highlighted more than ever before the importance of stress testing in terms of its role in supplementing VaR, or the need for a clearer relationship between VaR and stress testing in an integrated risk management framework. It is partly because many regulators and financial institutions have just recently started to believe that the result of VaR (or the risk amount measured by VaR, which is often called "economic capital") was robust enough to be compared with the capital amount and consequently to be used to assess capital adequacy. The shock of this crisis puts this belief very much into question.

Once we have determined that VaR as a sole tool is not necessarily reliable enough to assess the adequacy of capital, what alternative measures could fill the vacuum? Stress testing has emerged in this context. This may be slightly different from the case of past crises, in which stress testing was highlighted, for example, as a tool to supplement the data shortage problems of VaR for some risks in marginal markets.

Classification of Stress Testing Concepts

Stress testing might be defined in a variety of ways depending on who is using it. So the term "stress testing" contains a variety of concepts. I will show some representative ones in the following.

The most common factors found in this variety of definitions for stress testing seems to be the method, which first defines the stress event and then looks at the impacts of its materialization. This method can be classified into smaller groups by focusing on 1) the perspective to define the stress events or the type of stress events, 2) the scope of the stress events, and 3) the way of using the outcome.

For example, stress events can be captured with a macro perspective and with a micro perspective. The former is often called macro stress testing to be distinguished from the latter. This macro stress testing is often used by the authorities, including central banks, to see the impacts of specific macroeconomic shocks on the macroeconomy. For example, stress testing that assesses the impact of the current financial crisis on the stability of the financial system could be classified as macro stress testing.

Meanwhile, stress testing that is conducted by ordinary financial institutions is to see the impact of the current financial crisis on the P/L and balance sheets of the concerned financial institutions. As I note later, most of the current stress testing tends to stop at seeing the first direct impact. In order to consider the repercussions of the initial impact among different entities and different markets to assess the second and third effects of the initial ones, we need to introduce an element of macro stress testing.

The scope of stress events to be captured is another yardstick to classify stress testing. Stress events can generally be classified into 1) events that actually occurred in the past (or slightly revised for contemporary context), 2) events based on a combination of the worst records of risk factors, 3) events represented by multiplied sigma or confidence levels based on expert judgments, 4) hypothetical events that could be caused by macroeconomic disequilibrium, which share the same root causes of past crises, but do not look the same or even similar to past crises.

Finally, the use of stress testing can be classified into two types. The first is similar to contingency planning, and is designed to allow the concerned

Table 4.2 Features of stress testing

Perspective to capture stresses	Macro Micro
Scope of stresses	Historical events (or slightly revised for contemporary context) Combination of the historically worst numbers of risk factors Multiplied sigma and confidence levels based on expert judgments Hypothetical events that share the root causes of disequilibrium with past crises
Use of stress testing	Contingency planning Confirming the adequacy of capital

institutions to react to the stress event in a smooth way once it actually occurs. Another is to assess the adequacy of capital once the stress events occur and consequently cause huge losses.

In table 4.2, I summarize the types of stress testing based on this perspective.

What Went Wrong with Stress Testing?

One of the biggest claims about financial institutions' stress testing that came from the regulators in this crisis concerns the stress scenario itself. In other words, they questioned why financial institutions did not assume the type of stress scenarios we have already seen in the current crisis. These are events in which prices in some securitization markets dropped significantly, or where the assets that had been once detached and transferred to structured investment vehicles (SIVs) then returned to their own balance sheets. Furthermore, they are also the events that explicitly consider the risks that have not been well recognized before, including market liquidity risk, second effects, or the repercussions from the initial macroeconomic shocks, and model risk concerning the risk of securitization products. According to the authorities, they have seen that the degree of stresses were generally not enough even when these risks were considered in financial institutions' stress testing.

However, the supervisory agencies were also supposed to supervise those financial institutions' stress testing through on-site inspections or off-site monitoring. In this sense, the claims from the authorities might not be clear even to the authorities before the crisis. In this connection, it is interesting to see the outcome of a horizontal study of stress testing, which was published by the UK FSA in October 2006. In this publication, the UK FSA clearly concluded that the degree of stresses that financial institutions actually used was not enough. This indicates that some authorities had already recognized the insufficiency of stress scenarios in financial institutions' stress testing but had not fixed them in the period leading to the financial crisis. This fact might lead us to conclude that the relationship between supervisors and financial institutions should also be considered. I will discuss this issue further later.

In addition to the contents of stress scenarios and degree of stresses, the regulators' claims concentrate on the use of stress testing for management judgment. They saw that the stress testing outcomes might be used to assess risks in the risk management section, but might not be fed back to senior managers as elements to influence their business decisions. They also observed that the stress testing outcome did not necessarily constitute an integral or effective part of ensuring capital adequacy.

These were actually areas in which the major global financial institutions had long boasted of their own practices as being world best, showing us how difficult it would be for a third party to judge whether some banks' risk management is better than others.

DEGREE OF STRESSES: ARGUMENTS OVER "HORIZONTAL FREQUENCY"

What Degree of Stresses Should Financial Institutions Absorb?

In the arguments over stress testing, the authorities have not yet clarified their expectations of the degree of stresses to be absorbed by financial institutions. For example, no experts, including the authorities, at the beginning of 2007 could predict that this type of financial crisis would come. Even if some perceived the risks that had materialized in the financial crisis at that time, it would have been very difficult for them to make a persuasive case for this risk materialization against other arguments.

Meanwhile, after the crisis, the conduct of ordinary stress testing could be expected to assume scenarios like the current crisis, and the preparation of capital based on this stress testing could lead to the situation where financial institutions always maintain huge capital to brace themselves for a perfect storm. In the case of Japan, for example, you could have a situation in which financial institutions always keep enough capital to survive in a macroeconomy with significant negative growth, consecutive huge drops in real estate prices, and a fall in stock prices. Is this really a desirable picture for the financial system?

There should be some conservatism required for financial institutions but also some limits to be understood. So long as financial institutions are privately owned, they have to seek efficiency as well as be conservative. Then the issue to be considered is how we should strike the right balance.

My view is that this balance should be decided on the regulators' side. Financial institutions are supposed to be the agencies that consider the needs of different stakeholders and then try to satisfy them as much as possible. If a stakeholder does not clearly show its expectations, however, financial institutions are naturally biased toward the expectations of other stakeholders (e.g. shareholders). In this situation, financial institutions might be perplexed if the authorities, just from hindsight, remark that their risk management was not conservative enough to reach the level of the authorities' expectations.

So what degree of stresses should banks be set for from the authorities' point of view? There are two difficult issues on this point. One is the difficulty of measuring the degree of stresses, and another is the difficulty of judging the absolute level to be required.

Degree of Stresses in VaR

I have already stated that VaR and stress testing are supposed to complement each other. Particularly in this financial crisis, many expect that stress testing would support the limits of VaR, which has long played a major role in risk management. Under this environment, the degree of stresses to be expected in the stress testing should not be independent from the degree of stresses to be expected in VaR. Therefore, in the following, I will first discuss the degree of stresses, which have generally been expected in VaR.

Concerning the minimum requirements of the degree of stresses or risk amounts in VaR, banks and the authorities had already established a kind of consensus. This is represented by an important assumption of VaR, that is, confidence level. In this case, it is 99.9 percent or 99.97 percent for many global banks in the world, and is 99 percent for most Japanese banks.

Of course, these are not official numbers offered by the authorities. For example, even if a Japanese bank uses a confidence level of 95 percent in its economic capital management, the supervisors would not complain about this level itself. However, it may be natural for supervisors to pay special attention to this level, which is much lower than those used by other institutions. This is the natural outcome of the authorities often using an inspection methodology of so-called "benchmarking."

So we can find a kind of consensus on the level of "horizontal frequency" among banks, among the authorities, or between banks and the authorities.

The reasons are not necessarily clear but there may be some influence from regulation, and also from rating agencies. In the Basel Accord, the concept of VaR was, for the first time, introduced in the market risk framework in 1998, when the confidence level to be used was set at 99 percent.

In the case of market risk, another assumption of VaR is that the holding period tends to be very short (e.g.,10 days for the Basel Accord). So it may be a little difficult to compare the case with the time horizon of one year, but here we simply assume that this risk amount (10-day VaR) would not change even in a world of the one-year time horizon. Furthermore, we assume that this idea can be applied to other types of risks, say, credit risk. In this case, with a confidence level of 99 percent, the authority might encourage banks to contain their annual default probabilities to less than 1 percent, assuming that loss given default (LGD) equals 100 percent.

This confidence level used for risk measurement, however, has been changing in the process of introducing Basel II. In the credit risk management framework, called IRB, and also in the operational risk management framework, called Advanced Measurement Approach (AMA), a confidence level of 99.9 percent was basically used. In other words, the VaR standard increased tenfold if compared to the level for the market risk framework, which was introduced in 1998.

The premium for deposit insurance in Japan, for example, is set at 0.108 percent against outstanding demand deposits, and 0.081 percent against outstanding term deposits. This premium level might imply that the confidence level of 99.9 percent is appropriate if the LGD is close to 100 percent. Also, in the case of foreign countries, the average deposit insurance premium is roughly 0.1 percent even though more and more countries have introduced a variable premium according to the soundness of bank balance sheets.

Basel II, however, basically left the market risk framework of Basel I untouched, and consequently there remain two different confidence levels in capital adequacy regulation, 99 percent and 99.9 percent. Some do try to justify this seemingly double standard. Often an explanation heard is that the market risk measurement is supposed to be more accurate compared to credit and op risk measurements, so the difference in confidence level between market and credit and op risks resides in the difference in model risk. In the case of market risk, the number of outliers found in its back testing determines the level of the multiplier (three to four), which was imposed on the original VaR number with the confidence level of 99 percent. Some argued that this level, after being increased by a multiplier, could be more or less equal to VaR with a confidence level of 99.9 percent.

Meanwhile, among financial institutions, a confidence level of 99.97 percent in economic capital management has long been believed to be a very artificial requirement for earning a double "A" rating from the rating agencies. In other words, if financial institutions have capital that is higher than risk amounts measured by VaR with a confidence level of 99.97 percent, they qualify for a double "A" rating. The rating agencies deny that they make this type of mechanical judgment, but it is possible that in the past this type of implicit agreement has actually existed between banks and rating agencies.

Confusion About the Confidence Level in Economic Capital Management

In the preceding chapters, I have shown that a kind of consensus has been emerging on the horizontal frequency to be assumed by banks. Having said so, it is still true that the required horizontal frequency could vary among different risk categories and different countries. Now I would like to draw on the background of the remaining differences among banks and countries even after the formation of this consensus.

For example, most European and US major banks use a confidence level of 99.97 percent or so for their economic capital management. Many banks in Asian countries seem to prefer a level of 99.9 percent. Meanwhile, most major Japanese banks use a level of 99 percent, although some have recently started to use the level of 99.9 percent. What do these different practices indicate?

As stated, the confidence level of economic capital management should be equal to the risk appetite of banks, or an indicator of the risk tolerance level that is shared by senior managers. If this is the case, the lower confidence level of Japanese banks compared to that of foreign banks might indicate Japanese banks' more aggressive stance toward risk taking. But is that really true?

Of course, we can make a case that the risk amounts taken by Japanese banks compared with their capitals tend to be larger than those of banks of other major countries. It should also be noted that the type of risks taken by Japanese banks and foreign banks differ significantly. In the case of European and US banks, major risks mainly consist of 1) credit risk from retail lending (according to the QIS5, or the impact study for the Basel II implementation, the share of risk associated with retail lending is quite high at more than half the risks associated with corporate lending), and 2) business risk and op risk mainly from their active businesses in the area of investment banking.

On the other hand, in the case of Japanese banks, most of their risks arise from corporate lending (see figure 4.6). This difference mainly comes from the different business models between European/US banks and Japanese banks.

It has long been discussed but is still not so clear whether Japanese banks from the profitability point of view can really justify a business model

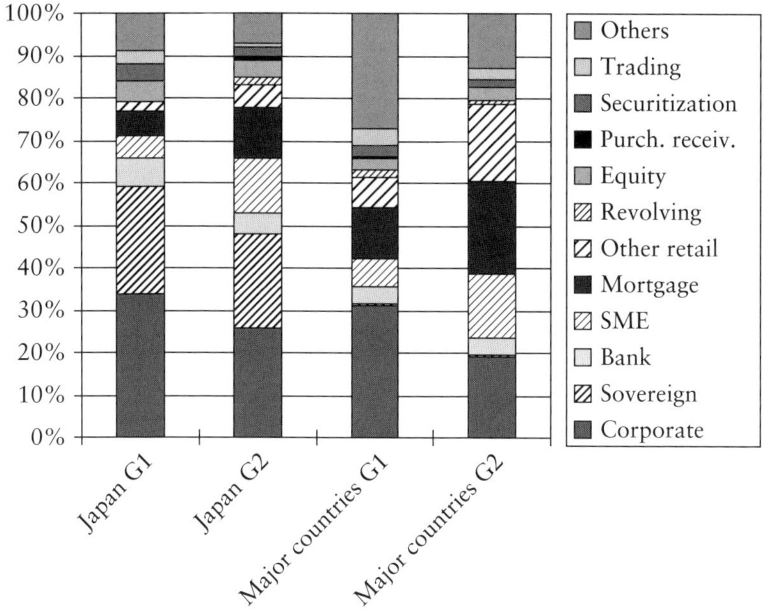

Figure 4.6 Outcome of QIS5
Source: Sato (2008), BCBS (2006a)

supported by holding equity in their obligors. The business model supported by holding equity in banks' obligors is closely associated with the main bank system. In other words, banks hold their obligors' equity for the purpose of showing a strong commitment to their management, establishing a long-term relationship with these obligors. This is actually the business model that had long supported the continued high growth of the Japanese economy after the Second World War.

In the process of a rapid decline in stock prices after the bursting of the financial bubble at the beginning of the 1990s, however, this business model had to be reviewed (see Shiratori and Oyama 2001). In other words, some essential elements for the success of this business model were simply lost during this process. They were 1) the continuous increase in stock prices as a trend, 2) the continuous high growth of the Japanese economy, which allowed banks to absorb the risks of obligors over business cycles, and also 3) various social infrastructure, including the accounting system (such as accrual-based accounting, or the system allowing the existence of latent profits or losses) that had allowed banks to make a long-term commitment to obligors.

These conditions changed dramatically after the burst of the financial bubble because stock prices had continually dropped, and the economic growth rate went down. Moreover, the accounting system has changed to one emphasizing the importance of fair value, or the consensus of stakeholders over the relatively short time horizon. Under this environment, the picture of Japanese banks still holding huge obligors' equities and consequently taking huge risks might subsequently lead to their "unintentionally" aggressive risk taking.

However, it may be a little risky to judge the risk appetite of banks only based on horizontal frequency in the form of VaR confidence level. This is because they may include a margin of error that does not sufficiently reflect the perspective of historical frequency. The attitude toward the perspective of historical frequency varies among banks, and some put aside additionally conservative capital as a buffer against this risk while others do not.

In some cases, the confidence level of VaR considers historical frequency as well as horizontal frequency. The degree of this consideration, however, can vary significantly among different risk categories. I will draw on this issue later but, generally speaking, market risk, which tends to use observation data from a short period, rarely considers historical frequency while credit risk, which uses data over several business cycles, considers it somewhat. Meanwhile, op risk tends to consider this element using external or scenario data, or both.

This observation indicates that op risk amounts measured by VaR consider the element of historical frequency the most, followed by credit and market risks. In other words, market risk is very unlikely to capture the stress event impact due to the changes in external environments. This might be well evidenced by the fact that the risk amounts measured by VaR with a confidence level of 99.97 percent were easily toppled by the actual loss numbers in this financial crisis.

It may be interesting to think of a case where different risks are measured by VaR with a specific confidence level and are aggregated into one with some assumptions of correlation among them in an integrated risk management framework. This methodology naturally leads to a certain optimum composition of risk. In this case, the larger the confidence level is, the larger the composition of market risk is, or the smaller the composition of credit risk is. It is because the tail part of loss distribution of market risk tends to be thinner than that of credit risk because the former considers the element of historical frequency less. Therefore, there might be some room for Japanese banks that use a confidence level of 99 percent to take some credit risks, whereas it becomes theoretically much harder for US and European banks that use the confidence level of 99.97 percent to take credit risks (see figure 4.7).

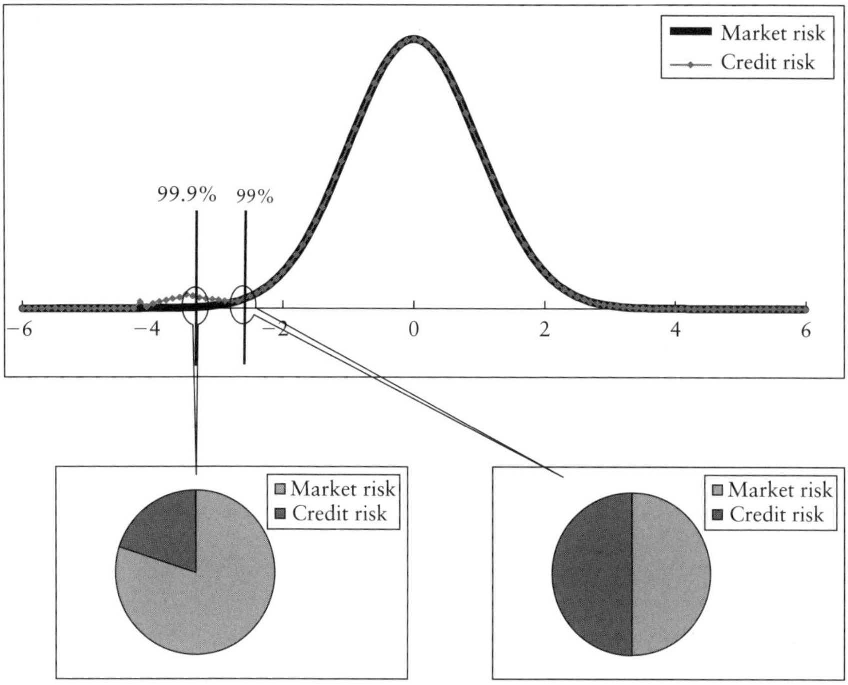

Figure 4.7 Impacts of the selection of confidence level on the optimum mix of risks

This indicates that the selection of a certain confidence level could significantly affect the optimum composition of risk. In other words, this risk composition, which is determined by risk quantification in the process of integrated risk management, tends to be strongly biased by varying degrees of considering the elements of historical frequency among different risks. The effects of this bias could become bigger as the confidence level becomes larger.

This factor might also have influenced the recent trend of US and European banks up to this crisis to move from the previous O&H to O&D business model, or shift emphasis from corporate lending to retail lending and trading transactions.

In this environment, Japanese banks' stance of using a lower confidence level for risk quantification and for deciding the optimum risk composition, and then adding more capital as a buffer looks quite reasonable. That said, a confidence level of even 99 percent could never be exempt from the bias problem. In addition, the extra capital needed for more than a 99 percent level has to be agreed upon among different stakeholders. This issue will be discussed later.

DEGREE OF STRESSES: ARGUMENTS OVER THE "HISTORICAL FREQUENCY"

The Search for the Appropriate Degree of Stress from the Viewpoint of Historical Frequency

As noted, the banks and the authorities have striven to find a kind of consensus on the confidence level of VaR, that is, the degree of stress of horizontal frequency, although its meaning is not necessarily so clear. The introduction of Basel II itself might also be regarded as a part of these efforts. Although different confidence levels are still in use among countries and risk categories, these differences are often understood. Meanwhile, we have not yet reached any consensus on the degree of stress for historical frequency. This is a factor that further complicates the problem.

It goes without saying that historical events are not the only factors that determine the degree of stress. In this sense, some readers might find the term "historical" frequency odd. "Historical frequency," however, tries to capture an extended meaning. Here I use an expression like "once in every XX years" or "historical," because that more readily conveys a sense of the degree of stress. I expect that an expression like "once in every XX years" could lead scenario makers to imagine that a worst event could happen not only in the "past" XX years but also in the "coming" XX years based on various information. In this sense, historical frequency can be defined as the degree of stress that is mainly driven by the elements of historical events, but also considers recent changes in the external environment.

Actually, there are many descriptions in Basel II concerning the degrees of stress in the stress testing that are expected by authorities. In Basel II, there are the stress testing requirements under Pillar 1 and also under Pillar 2. Concerning credit risk, the former requests banks to assume mild recessions, and the latter requests banks to assume some shocks caused by structural changes in the economy. From the viewpoint of historical frequency, the former corresponds to "once in roughly five years," because the business cycle is usually a cycle of four to five years. The latter may correspond to once in every 10 years or 20 years, depending on how often significant shocks caused by structural changes can occur.

The degrees of stress implied by this were not so helpful to preempt, at least, the current financial crisis. It is true that many countries have just recently started Basel II, and might not have yet well prepared the supervisory review and evaluation process (SREP) under Pillar 2. Even discounting this point, however, it might have been difficult for Basel II to have preempted the current crisis.

The first reason is that the main arguments over the stress events in the context of Basel II mainly concentrate on the impact of the business cycle on "credit risk." This is because market risk is not the main focus of Basel II, and many regulators might find that stress testing was already well established in the area of market risk, and therefore it is not necessary to request banks explicitly to assume the specific type of stress testing for market risk in Basel II. Also, in the case of op risk, stress scenarios are requested to be incorporated in VaR calculations directly, and in this way, stress testing is substantially requested for op risk in Basel II, even though we do not call it stress testing (however, I will argue later that there is no consistency in Basel II between op risk and credit risk on this issue).

The second reason is that while the required assumption under Pillar 1 (i.e., mild recessions) was clearly defined as being zero GDP growth over two consecutive quarters (even though this case was cited just as an example in Basel II, this has already become a kind of rule in many countries), the structural stresses that are required to be assumed under Pillar 2 are quite opaque.

However, the government of one country had already introduced a clear concept of this historical frequency: the UK FSA. It defined it as an event that could occur once in every 25 years, and then required banks to assume this in their stress testing not only for credit risk, but also for other risk categories. The other agencies in other countries, however, have not yet introduced such a clear definition of historical frequency. They provided banks with only a vague idea that banks need to assume such an event occurring once about every "10 years" only for credit risk.

So as a tool for expressing the degrees of stress, while there is a kind of consensus of the degrees of stress and of the scope of application for horizontal frequency, we have not yet reached a stage determining the scope of application nor the degrees of stress for historical frequency.

Difficulty in Forming Consensus on Historical Frequency

One of the reasons we have faced difficulties in forming a consensus on historical frequency among different countries is the difference in the histories of financial crises that each country has experienced. In the case of the UK, for example, it is said that the government selected the number of "25 years" partly because they had to go back 25 years to cover the last major financial crisis that they experienced. The UK experienced the bursting of a real estate bubble at the beginning of the 1980s as well as at the beginning of the 1990s, both of which entailed some instability in the financial system.

After the latest one, however, the UK had enjoyed its longest expansion period up to the current crisis (see figure 4.8).

Needless to say, this type of country-specific experience cannot be applied to other countries. For example, Japan experienced its worst banking crisis just 10 years ago, so regulators might reasonably judge that the historical horizon of 10 years is enough for Japan.

Therefore, it may not be so easy to form a consensus on the right historical frequency among different countries unless we can easily find a common cycle, as we can with the business cycle. It is actually very difficult to form a consensus on the frequency of financial shocks caused by structural problems in the economy or the bursting of financial bubbles, because they have country-unique features. We need to make more efforts to extract more common factors from various countries' experiences of financial crises for this purpose.

Even in the current financial crisis, for example, some people say that it corresponded to a shock that could occur once every 50 years, and others say that it is every 100 years. The former might come from the idea that it is the worst event since the Second World War, and the latter from the idea it's the worst event since the Great Depression. Meanwhile, some others say that this type of shock might attack our economies more frequently than before because the bubble formation process is deeply embedded in the

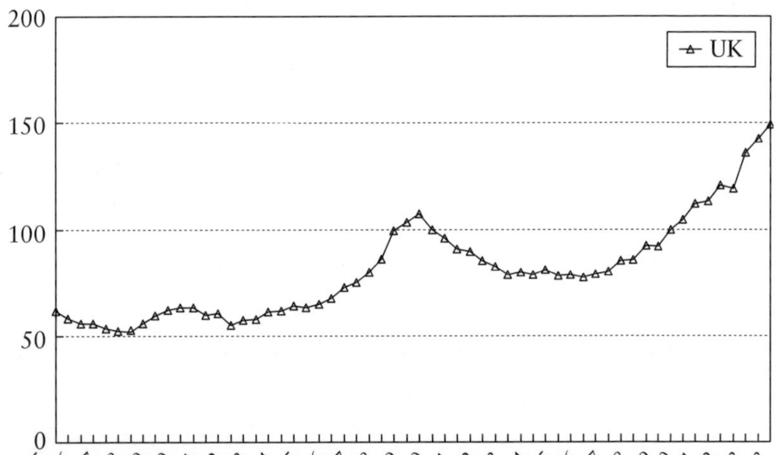

Figure 4.8 Developments in real housing prices in the UK
Source: Ishikawa (2004) based on material from UK National Statistics, *Blue Book*
Note: Scaled by the level of March 1990 (=100)

structure of the current economy. If this is the case, the current crisis might need to be regarded as an event that could occur once every, say, 25 years, rather than the mass-media-favored 100 years.

Moreover, there might be differences in government philosophies concerning the degrees of stress to be absorbed by banks in different countries. In other words, it is the issue of whether governments should request banks to always put aside capital sufficient to manage a crisis of a magnitude occurring "every 25 years." Using the analogy of monetary policy, this may be similar to the argument that central banks should always conduct ultra-tight monetary policy to preempt inflationary risk on a magnitude of "every 25 years" at the cost of slow growth of the macroeconomy.

Many readers are likely to say "no" to the second question. We could easily guess the possible outcome of ultra-tight monetary policy that is set for inflationary pressure with a magnitude of occurring "every 25 years." That would cause constant deflation. If that is the case, what should we think about an ultra-tight prudential policy with a magnitude of occurring "every 25 years"? The answer might depend on the reader. Some might suspect that it would be so excessive as to entail a constant credit crunch. Some might argue, however, that we should at least consider an event possibly occurring once every 25 years if the current crisis, as pointed out by many in the mass media, could correspond to an event that could occur once every 100 years.

Difference Between Monetary Policy and Macroprudential Policy

One of the main differences between monetary policy against inflation and macroprudential policy against a shock to the financial system is the targeted cycle. The former deals with the relatively stable business cycle over four or five years, while the latter deals with the so-called financial asset (or financial bubble) cycle over more than 10 years. It is certainly very difficult to identify the latter cycle beforehand.

Though not necessarily widely shared among concerned parties, there might be an implicit burden sharing between monetary policy and macroprudential policy to stabilize the macroeconomy. In other words, monetary policy is used for dealing with a shorter cycle and macroprudential policy for a longer cycle. The tool of monetary policy had already been long established (even though there are still many big questions posed about its effectiveness, particularly in the current crisis), so it might be possible to do fine-tuning of the impacts if the targeted cycle is stable. Meanwhile, there is not yet a widely shared consensus on the tools of macroprudential policy. For example, we find, after a great struggle, a moral suasion by supervisors to request banks to put aside more capital when some indicators including the outcome of stress testing imply that credit risk is very likely to be underestimated. Besides, there are any methods to do fine-tuning of the impacts of a cycle that has not been established yet. For this reason, while monetary policy is often proactive, macroprudential policy cannot be but passive against the shock.

While the interest rates of monetary policy can be seen as drastic medicine that will have a direct impact on some final demand components, such as capital investment and household consumption, the adjustment of required capital for banks can be seen as a much milder form of medicine that affects final demand indirectly only through changes in bank attitudes toward risk taking. The latter, however, sometimes needs more decisive actions because once many large banks face a shortage of capital as a result of a financial shock, the engine of the macroeonomy, that is, the function of financial intermediation, could almost stop.

It might be possible for monetary policy to deal with financial bubbles, which are here expected to be dealt with by macroprudential policy. History, however, should incline us to be somewhat skeptical about this expectation. Consequently, a conservative capital adequacy policy might be requested as a failsafe for monetary policy. In other words, the degree of confidence in monetary or fiscal and other policies as a measure to preempt a financial bubble could consequently influence the degrees of stress that is expected in macroprudential policy. Further studies and the formation of global consensus are needed in this area.

DIFFERENCES IN HOW RISK IS CAPTURED BY DIFFERENT RISK CATEGORIES

Differences in Stress Testing Among Different Risk Categories

I have thus far discussed the potentiality and weaknesses of stress testing in terms of its expected role in supplementing the weaknesses of VaR, and also the lack of consensus on the degrees of stress from the global point of view, and background. Indeed, the use of this stress testing varies significantly among different risk categories. I will discuss this issue in this section.

Typical books on risk management tend to argue that techniques of stress testing are most advanced in the area of market risk management, partly owing to its long history compared to the other risk categories, such as credit and op risk management (see, e.g., CGFS 2005). This may be true in some senses. In the area of market risk management, risk managers have long struggled with the limitations of VaR, so they naturally have a longer history of creating helpful stress scenarios and of discussing them with senior managers. Compared to market risk management, stress testing in other risk management areas definitely has a shorter history and consequently less diversity in scenarios, and is of less use for their businesses.

Implementation of Basel II, however, might have changed this landscape. For example, if we evaluate stress testing in terms of consistency with other risk management methods, such as VaR, and transparency, objectivity, and comprehensiveness, we now find that op risk management is the most advanced, having established its framework first. Meanwhile, market and credit risk management were remarkably behind in this area. In the following, I will argue how differently stress testing is used among op, market, and credit risk management.

Op Risk Quantification Under Basel II

Here first I would like to discuss the type of risk quantification required for op risk under Basel II before going into a discussion of elements of stress testing for op risk.

As is well known, the advanced approach of Basel II requested that op risk as well as credit risk be quantified to assess banks' capital adequacy. One of the difficulties for quantifying op risk, however, is a lack of real loss data. This is an area that is very different from the case of market and credit risks. In the case of market risk, we can observe the movements of risk factors even on a daily basis. Also, in the case of credit risk, because banks started to collect loss data in a systematic way from the beginning of the 1990s under the framework of an internal rating system, they have quarterly data for at least 10 years.

Meanwhile, in the case of op risk, it was just at the beginning of the 2000s when many banks started to collect loss data in a systematic way. Also, it is often indicated that there are two different types of losses for op risk, that is, one is high-frequency, low-severity losses and another is low-frequency, high-severity losses. The latter is more important for quantification of op risk, but quite hard for individual institutions to collect enough numbers for risk quantification.

So it is very difficult to estimate the op risk amount accurately based only on observable real loss data. Because of this, the AMA of Basel II requests that banks use four elements for op risk quantification, which include external data, scenario analysis, and business environment and internal control factors, as well as internal data, and thereby capture the fat tail part of loss distribution. In the following, I will discuss the other elements more than internal data.

The first candidate for supplementing the lack of internal data is external data. External data might be judged to be second most important after internal data. They include pooling data collected by member banks of the consortium, and also databases made by vendors, which collect loss data from various sources.

External data, as in the case of internal data, are the loss cases that actually occurred, and are associated with high objectivity. Also, even though they are not the data of the banks' own experiences, pooled data based on various bank experiences should be expected to capture the important features in the tail of the op risk loss distribution, which banks generally face. Besides, external data include forward-looking information, such as cases that have not yet happened at one's own bank, but could occur any time in the future. Because of this feature, external data are also often used for making scenario data.

Meanwhile, the weakness of external data is that they could be loss cases that occur at banks whose risk profiles are very different from the bank's own. In such a case, banks need some adjustment of external data before using them for op risk quantification. Furthermore, we have to admit that even the use of external data often cannot provide enough loss data necessary to quantify the risk amount corresponding to a 99.9 percent confidence level.

Scenario data based on scenario analysis form the third important element after external data to supplement the lack of data for the tail of the loss distribution, and the backward-looking feature of internal data. However, its weakness is in the difficulty of gaining comprehensiveness and objectivity comparable with internal and external data.

Business Environment and Internal Control Factor (BEICF) is the last element, and this is required because of the very special nature of op risk. This special nature mainly comes from the wide scope of op risk management, including changes in the external environment (e.g. changes in banking businesses, in work ethics of employees, or in general public risk tolerance against firms' op risk events). This also comes from the endogenous nature of op risk, where its profile could be changed by the bank's own efforts to contain risk. BEICF covers this special nature of op risk.

Among the four elements, scenario analysis and BEICF are particularly special. Because a main purpose of scenario data is to supplement the lack of real data over the tail of the loss distribution, it is very natural to suppose that such scenario data are more or less the same as the data called stress scenarios in other risk categories. (Of course, this does not exclude the scenarios of cases with high frequency.) In other words, in the op risk area, stress scenarios themselves are input into the risk quantification model. It is indeed a unique feature of op risk, which is not observed in market or credit risks.

Moreover, op risk losses with low frequency and high severity often occur during significant changes in the external environment. For example, it would be a little difficult to imagine the recent high-severity op risk loss cases a few years ago. This issue is not limited to banks, but issues such as camouflaging of product quality or leakage of personal information are very closely associated with a decline in society's general tolerance of op risk events and the widespread use of the internet. Also, an increasing complication of banks' business, globalization and deregulation, associated with a general decline in work ethics, partly because of the collapse of the lifelong employment system in Japan, presented financial institutions after the 1990s with very different risk conditions from the years before. In a few years, we might also see that the rapid increase in litigation costs and consequent op risk losses in the US would occur in Japan, too.

So how to capture the high severity low frequency cases becomes critically important for measuring op risk under the AMA of Basel II. And it should be noted that the stability of external environments, which is an important assumption for other risk categories, was intentionally not assumed for this op risk measurement. It is very clear because BEICF was included as one of four elements for AMA calculation. This is another big difference between op and other risk categories.

Degrees of Stress to be Assumed for Op Risk Quantification

We would naturally wonder whether regulators give any benchmark for historical frequency (the 99.9 percent confidence level is required under the AMA of Basel II) as well as horizontal frequency for op risk quantification. In this area too, there remains an important issue to be solved.

We sometimes see that some financial institutions try to look for events that occur once every 1,000 years based on the idea of horizontal frequency. This may be possible for natural disaster cases such as earthquakes, but next to impossible for ordinary op risk loss events. Experts at financial institutions in general often recognize that the limitations of imagination stop them at 100 years using the yardstick of a historical horizon, which is actually often used in their op risk scenario making. Even this number, however, is not widely shared in the industry or between banks and the regulators, indicating that we are still in search of a consensus on the historical frequency of op risk.

In figure 4.5, for example, I measured the op risk amount corresponding to a 99.9 percent confidence level based on the idea of the power law using the loss data collected by LDCE. This outcome indicates that the op risk amount could be double the outcome of the BIA, or about 30 percent of gross profits. Very interestingly, the US LDCE data also indicate a similar outcome. In the case of the US, while an op risk amount (in terms of gross profit) corresponding to the 99 percent confidence level is significantly higher than the amount for Japanese banks, its amount (in terms of gross profit) at the 99.9 percent confidence level turned out to be more or less the same for Japanese banks. If this comparison between the op risk amount based on the power law and the outcome of BIA could be regarded as a comparison between the AMA and the BIA outcomes, in the future we might have discussions of the adequacy of 99.9 percent level itself as well as the adequacy of the scaling ratios of the BIA (or the Standardized Approach) when reconsidering revisions of Basel II.

As explained, the degrees of stress for op risk measurement tend to be stronger than in other risk cases. Risk that could materialize once every 1,000 years is surely out of scope even for op risk, but some risks that would be way out of the question in other risk categories are included in op risk. And if we try to incorporate this idea into risk quantification for other risks, the amount of these risks and consequent amount of required capital could be very much higher than today's.

So why is there a significant difference in the degree of stresses assumed for risk measurement between op and other risks? The reason is not necessarily clear, but I suppose that the difference in stakeholders that drove the risk management development in the past is likely to influence it. In other words, in the area of market risk, the perspective of the front business line has been emphasized in the process of risk management, leading to more emphasis on VaR with horizontal frequency and less on stress testing with historical frequency. Stress testing tends to be regarded just as a supplement to the VaR, so the degrees of stress tend to be set to produce less risk amounts than in the case of VaR, or regarded simply as a brainstorming exercise to prepare for stress cases.

After this privately driven development, the Basel regulations were surely introduced into market risk management, but mainly taking after practices that were already developed by the private sector. This allowed banks' risk management to be aligned with regulations, which is the core idea of the so-called "use test," motivating banks to advance their management further even under the regulatory framework. If the private sector and regulators do not necessarily share a similar risk appetite, however, this framework risks being biased toward the private sector at the expense of regulators' risk appetites.

Meanwhile, op risk quantification was mainly driven by Basel II. To be sure, a few banks had already initiated projects for quantifying op risk around the end of the 1990s, but my impression is that the overall framework itself was first established by the authorities. In this case, more emphasis was put on a framework that could well reflect the risk tolerance shared by regulators. The historical background seems to have consequently required banks to assume a higher standard, even in the area of historical frequency in op risk than in other risks. So we need to consider such a difference in the history of risk management development to understand the reasons behind the different degrees of stress used between op and other risk categories.

Securing Comprehensiveness and Objectivity of Stress Scenarios

Another unique feature of op risk management is to require scenario data to be associated with high levels of comprehensiveness and objectivity as is the case for real data. It is partly because of the Basel II requirement for the use of scenario data for op risk quantification. Indeed, banks have long sought a way to establish an op risk management framework to secure comprehensiveness and objectivity. As noted, the weakest point of scenario data in comparison with real data is the lack of comprehensiveness and objectivity. Meanwhile, because banks usually depend heavily on scenario data to quantify op risk, it becomes naturally a kind of requirement for them to establish the framework to secure comprehensiveness and objectivity of data.

To secure comprehensiveness of data, banks actually started to take various measures, including 1) securing the comprehensiveness of a variety of expertise in human resources from various sections to make scenarios, 2) ensuring the adequacy of loss amounts of scenarios by benchmarking with estimates by external data or using the power law, and 3) ensuring the adequacy of scenarios by being compared with the actual events that occurred in other banks using external data.

To secure objectivity of data, in addition to the above measures, banks also have introduced measures to identify and correct various biases that could occur during the scenario-making process, using behavioral economics. Table 4.3 summarizes the examples of various biases and their correction measures with external data used in op risk management, which I made partly using information in Harvey (2008).

Such a framework that brings in objectivity and comprehensiveness into stress scenarios has not yet been observed in risk management areas other than op risk. Many stress scenarios were actually made in market and credit risk management, but their degrees of stress, and also their comprehensiveness and objectivity, tended to depend solely on the expert judgment of scenario makers. In this case, it is next to impossible to ensure whether the current stress scenarios cover all the possible risk cases sufficiently, or whether the degrees of stress assumed in the scenarios are in line with the firm's risk appetite. So the experiences of op risk management could also be helpful for improving stress scenarios for market and credit risk management.

There is also an important difference in recognizing the risks between op risk and other risk management. This is the "scope" of risk category and will be discussed later in this chapter.

Table 4.3 Various biases and their corrective measures

Name of bias	Nature of bias	Corrective measures
Reporting bias	This bias is produced by the data collection policies of financial institutions (e.g., threshold of data collection) and the type of transactions (for example, insurance contract) that produce losses to be reported. Generally speaking, low-severity losses are not comprehensively reported if compared to high-severity ones.	Assume the frequency distribution of the pattern of financial institutions to set different thresholds. Correct the biases found in selected samples.
Control bias	This is bias that is produced by the influence of different levels of op risk management between sections and financial institutions.	Identify any scores or indicators that represent different levels of op risk management.
Scale bias	This is bias that is produced by the difference in size of business sections and financial institutions.	Identify the business size indicators that are closely associated with op risk cases.

DEGREE OF STRESSES: LIQUIDITY RISK

The Arguments Over the Burden Sharing of Liquidity Risk Management Between Authorities and Banks

I have already argued that we have not yet seen any consensus on the risk appetite or the degrees of stress to be assumed, particularly in terms of historical frequency, between authorities and financial institutions. I have also discussed elements to consider the degrees of stress to be withstood by individual financial institutions. In the following, I will discuss the remaining issue concerning risk management sharing between authorities and banks: sharing liquidity risk management between individual banks and central banks.

In this crisis, liquidity risk, in particular, market liquidity risk and banks' risk of raising funds in the short-term money market were highlighted. I already provided an overview of this issue and central bank reactions in chapter 3, so I will try to avoid repeating those discussions here. It should be noted, however, that I have not yet seen a conclusion on what extent individual banks should be ready for a market wide liquidity problem.

Should banks really manage liquidity risk by being prepared for a paralysis of whole markets and the drying up of liquidity? To take an extreme example, the event that occurred in the securitization market in this crisis was a situation in which the market perception could suddenly change, even in a market that was reasonably liquid under ordinary conditions, leading to the evaporation of market liquidity or plummeting prices. This analogy could lead to a situation in which banks are always required to assume a significant market liquidity discount for almost all market transactions, with a few exceptions such as governmental bonds.

If this possibility is within the risk appetite of each bank (or within the confidence level [99–99.97 percent] of VaR from the viewpoint of horizontal frequency, and once in 10–25 years from the viewpoint of historical frequency), these losses are supposed to be reflected in the required minimum capital calculations. For example, considering that the prices ABX–AAA fell to 40 against par even in the case of triple "A," and to less than 10 in the case of triple "B," the capital requirement treatments for them might be nearly equal to the deduction of their exposure from capital. If this is the case, this type of risk management could do fatal damage to the market that trades these financial products.

Issues Related to Fair Value Accounting

To consider the issues raised in the previous section, I would like to discuss first the current way that financial institutions recognize liquidity risk. This discussion will be helpful because this also affects the various measures for sharing the stresses between the public and private sectors. While there is a way that the two sides share the risk quantified by the specific methods, there is another way that the public sector adjusts the recognition of losses, and consequently influences the loss shared between the two sides. For example, the issues concerning fair value accounting belong to the latter. So I will first provide an overview of the issues of fair value accounting here.

The risk that has arisen from the drying up of liquidity in the market is closely associated with the methods of estimating the prices of products. As indicated in chapter 3, the regulators and banks have already discussed this issue a lot, and are also preparing many recommendations to tackle it. One of these hot topics is the definition of fair value to be applied to the assets with drying liquidity. In this case, it may be clear to use market prices that reflect the liquidity premium sought by the market for trading account transactions, but not so clear for "available for sale"(AFS) products booked in the banking book.

How should we distinguish trading book transactions from banking book transactions for pricing purposes? Moreover, is there any room for using different fair values for the same assets but with different trading purposes? For example, if we hold securitization products for long-term investment purposes, their prices might be supposed not to be influenced by the short-term liquidity situation of the markets, or, at least, to be equal to fundamental values to be realized at their maturity. After September 2008, when the financial crisis was intensified, the argument appeared for stopping the application of fair value accounting in the US, and some of this idea was reflected in the Emergency Economic Stabilization Act, which was approved by US Congress in September 2008. This type of measure could be understood to reduce the stresses to be shared by banks by adjusting accounting valuations, because the net values of banks at bankruptcy (that is, the values to be presumed by the FDIC) could be much reduced because of this treatment.

Issues of Market Liquidity Risk Management

Market liquidity risk tends to be captured in the quantified risk amounts by being reflected in the holding period of VaR for market risk, as well as being considered in stress testing. Generally speaking, in the world of VaR, the assets booked in trading accounts assume a much shorter holding period for VaR calculation than do the assets booked in the banking account. This just reflects the purpose of trading book transactions, that is, high turnover in a short period. This holding period, however, usually does not well cover evaporation of market liquidity (this then tends to be expected to be reflected in stress testing).

Meanwhile, the risks of the assets booked in the banking account are usually measured using a half- or one-year time horizon of VaR because of their investment policy. At once, the same prices used for trading account transactions are often used for banking account transactions regardless of the differences in investment purpose. In this way, the prices used for banking account transactions could sometimes reflect a huge liquidity risk premium. Unlike the case of trading account transactions, unrealized gains and losses of securities booked in the banking account do not directly affect the P/L, but only influence the assets outstanding (and thus net capital) on the balance sheet. Because risk management focuses, however, on whether banks have sufficient capital against their holding risk amounts, it also covers events that could directly influence net capital beyond the P/L.

In the current financial crisis, it became clear that banks and regulators did not recognize clearly the market liquidity risk for the trading account transactions, which are supposed to be the most vulnerable to this risk.

In particular, it was confirmed that some important features of assets booked in the trading book account were not well understood by market participants. For example, they have such a structure that once the prices went under a certain level, the forced sale of underlying assets was triggered, or that funding liquidity risk faced by financial institutions accelerated the fire-selling of their holding assets. Because financial institutions whose main business is trading tend to depend heavily on fundraising through selling their holding assets, drying up of market liquidity would naturally cause serious trouble for their own liquidity. At the same time, as a result of accounting arguments of hierarchy of fair values, it also became clear that the assets booked in the banking account could also be influenced by the market liquidity situation.

In the following, I would like to discuss the issues of market liquidity risk in terms of 1) how to assess the impact of this risk, and 2) reactions to the outcome of this assessment.

As for the issue of the assessment of impact, individual institutions often face difficulty in its estimation because these are marketwide events. For this, financial institutions may use the methodology or the outcome of macro stress testing conducted by the authorities if they are available. Of course, this does not mean that banks should be forced to use this outcome. However, as a starting point for thinking about marketwide stress testing, it is helpful for banks to use the outcome often published by central banks in their financial stability reports, and thus facilitate a discussion of stresses between banks and regulators (or other stakeholders), or among banks. This may be similar to the situation in which the official data on the impact of big earthquakes helped Japanese banks make their own earthquake scenarios for their op risk management. This way of sharing information might also be helpful in conveying in an implicit way governments' expectations of the degree of stress to be assumed by banks.

On the other hand, it should be noted that the above process can also increase the herd behavior of banks as a result of increasing the similarity of scenarios on market liquidity assumed by banks. Indeed, we have already seen the arguments that the increase in similarity of the risk management framework did this.

For example, a sudden drop in government bond prices in Japan in 2003, the so-called "VaR shock," reminded us of this possibility. In the "VaR shock," the long-term interest rate shot up from 0.430 percent to 1.550 percent from June to August 2003. At that time, many banks simultaneously introduced a similar limit structure on the amount of risks based on VaR around 2000, which led to the similar reactions of selling bonds by many banks once market volatility reached a certain level.

The authority and banks should consider in advance how to react to such a situation. In the first place, the authorities should decide their expectations of the reactions of major market players, and answer questions such as "should financial institutions follow the outcome of stress testing or the risk management principle, and consequently try to retreat from the market as soon as possible, minimizing their losses regardless of the disastrous marketwide consequences? Or should they behave as a guardian of the market to resist the seemingly temporary overreaction of the market particularly from the long-term point of view?"

Of these two extreme options, I believe central banks tend to support the latter while regulatory agencies tend to support the former. In this case, we must consider how the authorities as a whole should deal with this issue consistently. How this issue will be resolved remains to be seen.

What of the reactions to the outcome of impact assessment? If assets are held for trading purposes, banks need to consider the impact of market price volatility on their own funding, as well as on the losses of these assets. The issue is how banks could effectively integrate their fundraising liquidity risk into market risk management. In this case, part of the liquidity risk is materialized in the form of market risk. In this sense, if banks put aside enough capital for market risk, the banks' frequently observed arguments that the capital requirement for this liquidity risk can be seen as double counting of risks seems to be reasonable. However, the part of market losses caused by the firesale of assets because of banks' own fundraising difficulty cannot be estimated unless they can assess the impact of their own fundraising liquidity management. So the information feedback from the liquidity management section to the market risk management section, focusing on the required capital, becomes very important.

Issue of Fundraising Liquidity Risk

Unlike market liquidity risk, fundraising liquidity risk is a classical risk management issue for banks. This financial crisis, however, reminded us that there is also room for further improvement in this area.

Securing enough capital against possible losses and securing enough liquidity against its shortage are the main drivers of bank risk management, and integrating the latter into the former is, as indicated, a little difficult. It is also true, however, that many authorities have long requested banks to consider the latter using stress testing and qualitative assessment. So we might wonder why the authorities' concerns could not be transmitted into bank risk management successfully.

On this issue, the banks' carelessness of their own liquidity owing to the long-continued ample liquidity situation and the way of providing liquidity to the short-term money market by central banks have often been noted. For example, the latter includes the issue of cooperation between the regulatory agency and the central bank, and the variety of the central bank's tools to provide liquidity to the market.

The issue of cooperation between the regulatory agency and the central bank might be highlighted partly because this was the first financial crisis faced by the UK and Europe after the separation of the functions of central banks and the banks' regulatory agencies. Meanwhile, the variety of the central bank's tools to provide liquidity to the market was closely associated with the failure of central banks to reconsider their schemes of liquidity provision to the banking system in corresponding to the significant changes in asset types held by the financial industry since the end of the previous century. Moreover, it might be influenced by the confidence in the regulatory capability of assessing solvency issues of banks, partly owing to the implementation of Basel II and the consequent belief that the liquidity issue is no longer essential to central banks. The solvency issue denotes a situation in which bank capital (or sometimes the net value of banks) goes under the minimum regulatory requirement because of deterioration in the quality of their holding assets. Banks could, for various reasons, face liquidity problems even when they do not have any solvency problems. However, if a central bank is expected to provide liquidity to banks in trouble with liquidity but without any solvency problems, it might find it difficult to reject the idea of providing liquidity to a bank that has already implemented Basel II because it was supposed to have had its solvency problem, if any, addressed by the regulatory agency. This, in other words, might imply that the authority now has better information on the bank's solvency than the market, which shows its judgment in the form of a "bank run" or "cutting the line of transactions in the money market." This leads to the argument that a central bank should have no reason to stop rescuing banks in liquidity trouble with doubts that the bank has a solvency problem that should be left unsolved, rather than a liquidity problem to be rescued.

Major Differences in Approach Between European, US and Japanese Central Banks

On this point, the Bank of Japan (BoJ) looks unique compared to its peers in Europe and the US. As indicated by the paper titled "The Turmoil of the Short-Term Money Market Caused by the Current Financial Crisis and the Reactions by the Central Banks," which was published by the BoJ in July 2008, on first appearance their policy framework looked very similar. Meanwhile, there were actually big differences in how the frameworks operated.

Regarding the framework of monetary operation, central banks usually have common tools for filling the gap between supply and demand of funds in every country, which are 1) reserve requirements, 2) open market operations, and 3) standing facilities. The term "operation" indicates that the central bank buys or sells financial assets with financial institutions to fill daily gaps between supply and demand of funds. These transactions can broadly be classified into two types: long-term operations using the assets such as governmental bonds to respond to the long-term trend of fund demands, and short-term operations using repo transactions to smooth short-term fluctuations of supply and demand conditions for funds. All these transactions are offered by the central banks. Meanwhile, the central banks also have a tool called the standing facility, in which they provide short-term funds with a predetermined interest rate based on the application of financial institutions.

This framework is more or less the same among major countries. The BoJ might have slightly more diverse operational tools than other countries because the fluctuation of supply and demand conditions in the short-term money market tends to be larger because of fiscal factors. The BoJ also accepts more diverse assets, including risk assets such as securitization products, as collateral for fund provision compared to other countries. Moreover, the types of assets for collateral are common between usual operations and standing facility in Japan, a feature that is not observed in the US or UK (see figure 4.9). As I will explain later, many of these Japanese unique systems can be seen as a legacy of monetary policy under deflation.

As noted, central banks in the US and Europe have also started to accept more diverse collateral for fund provision as a result of the financial crisis.

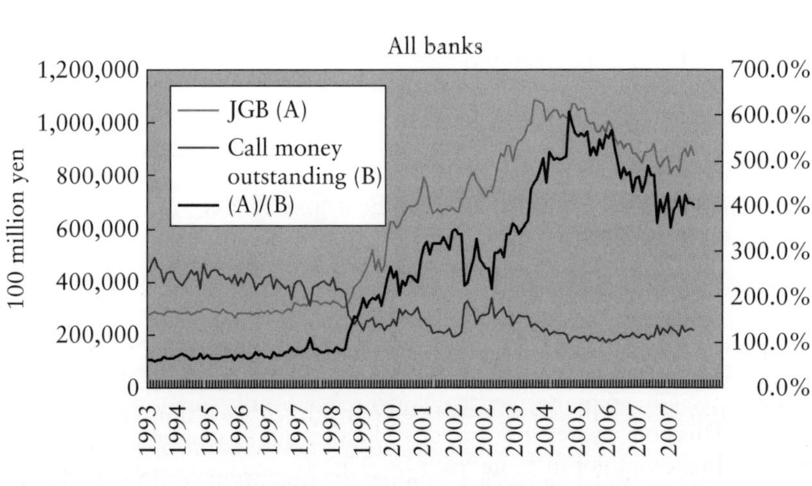

Figure 4.9 Comparison of eligible collateral for central bank operations
Source: Financial Market Department, Bank of Japan (2008b)

For example, the central banks in the US and UK expanded the range of collateral for market operations to include securitization products in the summer of 2008, and also introduced the security lending scheme, in which the central banks lend government bonds against the collateral of securitization products with declining market liquidity.

Finally, unlike the cases of the US and Europe, Japan did not experience the stigma problem in this crisis. One of the reasons is that the lending interest rate of standing facility is set at 25 basis points (bps) over the discount rate, so it has less feature of a penalty compared to the US and Europe (ECB, BOE: 100 bps, the US: 100 bps→50 bps<August 2007>→25 bps<March 2008>). It is also thanks to the BoJ's generous stance encouraging banks to use this facility even during an ordinary period. Indeed, many financial institutions actually used this facility so easily that some used it for the purpose of contingency planning. All these elements as a whole contributed to reducing the negative image of using the standing facility in Japan.

Now that we have confirmed the framework of the system, we will see the actual operations of the system in the following. Between Japan and the US and Europe, there are larger differences in operations (or the principles of operations) of the system, rather than their framework. In other words, unlike in the US and Europe, financial institutions' holding assets that could be used as collateral for borrowing funds from the central bank tend to move significantly over the minimum level for their liquidity in Japan.

For example, if you compare Japanese city banks' funding outstanding at the call money market with the amount of governmental bonds held by them, it was a little more than 100 percent around the end of the 1990s but then jumped to about 500 percent in 2005, and now is slightly down to about 300 percent (see figure 4.10). It should be noted that some of their holding governmental bonds cannot be used for collateral for call money market transactions, and that the conditions faced by each individual financial institution might be overshadowed by the aggregated numbers. Still, it is sure that there have been significant changes in the liquidity environment surrounding Japanese banks since the early 2000s, when the ratio of a little more than 100 percent caused concerns about the stability of the real gross settlement system among banks, which was introduced by the BoJ in 2000 (Bank of Tokyo Mitsubishi 2000).

This can be seen as a legacy of monetary policy during the deflationary era. During this era, financial institutions were forced to hold an amount of liquidity that was more than they needed, under the name of "quantitative monetary policy." This policy surely mitigated the liquidity crisis caused by the financial turmoil, but it was not its main purpose. That was to contain deflation.

This quantitative monetary policy ended in March 2006, when the monetary policy target changed from the reserve balance at the central bank

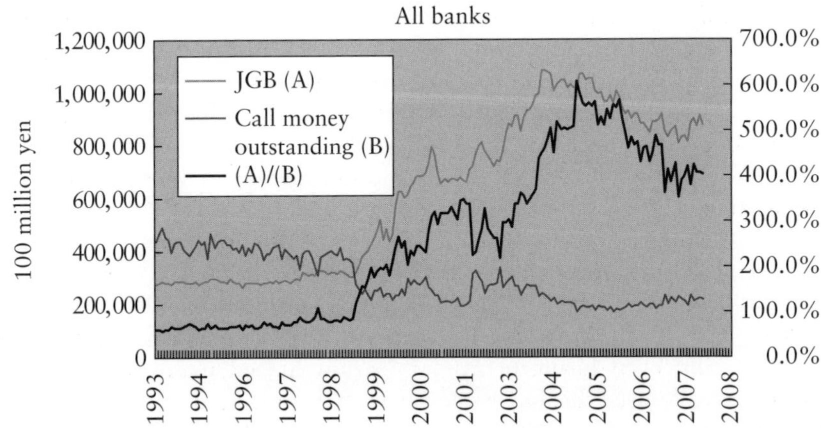

Figure 4.10 Development of Japanese city banks' funding outstanding at the call money market and their holding governmental bonds

to the call rate. An end to the "zero interest rate policy" was also declared in July 2006. Despite that, the excessive collateral situation has continued. The possible reasons are that 1) the interest rate in the money market is still very marginal, so opportunity cost is very low, and 2) the memory of the liquidity crisis during the banking crisis still remains vivid enough for many bank managers to conduct very conservative liquidity management.

At any rate, this conservatism might be appreciated in a sense that Japanese banks never felt the liquidity crisis seriously in this financial crisis. It is only some foreign banks that faced some difficulties in the Japanese money market. This Japanese way, however, definitely has a problem of efficiency of funds investment.

Another big difference between the US/European and Japanese situation is the relation between the central bank and the market. The BoJ has the framework to collect huge information on liquidity conditions of individual institutions daily or sometimes even hourly, and thus be well-prepared to recognize and react to the micro level liquidity stresses immediately. Even the US Fed may not have such huge amounts of liquidity information on individual institutions. Meanwhile, the ECB collects only aggregated liquidity information from the central banks of member countries and thus could collect much less micro information in a less timely manner compared to the case of the BoJ.

In this financial crisis, the amount of funds provided by the ECB looked particularly remarkable when compared to a normal size, and one of the reasons might be the shortage of micro information. In other words, it corresponded to the assumption that the ECB could not help but provide a lot of funds to the market without knowing exactly how much funding banks needed in which country.

This way of providing funds to the market based on estimates with low accuracy could increase uncertainty in the market, particularly during a stressful period. Besides, the central bank's provision of ample funds to the market could be seen by outside parties to represent the "size of the problem." Finally, the most serious problem is a possible conflict with the target of monetary policy. As the inflation rate is gradually ratcheting up and monetary tightening should have been expected under normal conditions, the ECB's provision of such abundant funds to the market could naturally entail concerns from a monetary policy point of view.

The next question is whether the ECB or even the US Fed should have followed the way adopted by the BoJ to minimize the possible conflict of interests and to stabilize the financial market. Take the case of the ECB first. Regardless whether the ECB should take this option, it could not. The reason is closely related to the process of European integration. In Europe, money markets among banks tend to be separated by borders even after the introduction of the euro. With this condition, it is politically as well as technically next to impossible for the ECB to adjust supply and demand in the money market of each member country based on information about individual banks' supply and demand conditions.

Also in the case of the US, it might be impossible for the Fed to collect all the detailed information on fundraising conditions of individual banks and confirm them over the telephone daily given the number of institutions to be checked. Moreover, there would be some arguments about whether the central bank should always keep a close eye on individual banks' liquidity conditions. This might entail a moral hazard for the banks because they could demand the central bank's rescue once they face any liquidity problems.

Besides, the market's excessive dependence on the central bank for adjusting supply and demand of the funds among financial institutions could discourage the incentive of the market to search for the equilibrium by itself. Whether markets should have this capability depends on the assumptions of the information shared by markets. If we can judge that the authority has more correct information on the solvency of financial institutions than markets have, then the BoJ approach could have more merit for bringing stability in the financial market. Meanwhile, the US or European approaches could have more merit in encouraging markets to have more self-adjustment capability and thereby have more innovation and cost-sensitive behavior in the long term.

Finally, it is better to think of whether central banks really have more information than markets have on the solvency of individual financial institutions.

This situation could also vary significantly among countries. For example, in the UK where Northern Rock was in deep trouble, it was indicated that there was a communication problem between the BoE and the UK FSA to deal with this case (House of Commons, Treasury Committee 2008). The same can be true of many countries where the central banks do not have the power of bank supervision.

The timely sharing of information on individual bank solvency between central banks and regulatory agencies is likely to remain a high priority. At one extreme, this issue can be translated into the politically delicate issue of whether a central bank and a bank regulatory agency should be separated. The argument for two separate entities reflects the political concern of excessive concentration of power in the politically independent central bank or of a possible conflict of interest between monetary and prudential policy. There seems to be a choice between efficiency or better governance and a diversity of views in the process of policy decision, and it is therefore difficult to say which is better.

On this aspect, the current relationship between the Japan FSA and BoJ is unique, because the Japan FSA plays a major role in bank regulation and supervision, but BoJ also conducts supplementary bank supervision. This does not necessarily make for a perfect solution, but it is second best.

ANALYSIS OF RISK FACTORS BEHIND STRESSES

Lessons from Op Risk Management

Up to now, a large part of the losses that occurred in the current financial crisis seem to have been classified under market or credit risk losses by banks, even though some have been classified under op risk losses corresponding to an increase in legal losses associated with subprime loan issues.

The main reason for this classification is quite simple. It is because the transactions were done at the trading section or loan section, or the transactions were already defined as market or credit-type transactions. So the risk factor classification heavily depends on the sections that deal with the transactions or their types. This is a somewhat strange phenomenon because this method of classification determines the type of loss distribution of the risk factor, which exists behind loss events. Classification into market or credit risk, of course, does not mean an attribution to a single factor. Still, even if we can attribute the causes of loss events to many factors, once we classify them into market or credit risk, this classification principally determines the basic feature of the risks behind the certain loss event. In other words, as already indicated in the section of VaR, they are a normal distribution, and from an intuitive point of view are market random walk and business cycle-driven losses.

Meanwhile, there is a big question whether we can really attribute the risk factors behind the loss events to the factors that we have noted. For example, the op risk factor, which is usually defined as the risk of losses resulting from inadequate or failed internal processes, people, and systems, or from external events, is usually considered to follow not the normal distribution but a fat-tail distribution. If such an op risk factor significantly influences the losses in the current financial crisis, the current classification of these losses mainly into market or credit risk is not appropriate for assessing the risk.

Indeed, some experts have already argued that the op risk factor might dominate the losses of the current financial crisis. For example, according to Rosengren (2008), 46 cases of more than $1 billion losses were reported by financial institutions globally from 2001 to 2007, and among them 14 cases occurred in 2007 alone. Also, all 14 cases were accompanied by litigation, indicating that the litigation ratio has become much higher than the period between 2001 and 2007 where 33 out of 46 cases were accompanied by litigation. In other words, most of the recent high-severity cases could be associated with the current financial crisis. Besides, Algorithmics (2007) also indicated that 83 percent of all losses related to the US subprime loan problem could be attributed to the op risk factor. This implies a need to place more focus on the "causes" behind loss events, rather than the consequent events, to assess the risks.

We have already seen economic and institutional factors behind the financial crisis in chapter 2. There, I indicated that the credit cycle, a major systemic factor influencing credit risk, can be seen as a factor that triggered the eruption. As I indicated, however, it is rather the institutional factors that influence the size of the "lava" (size of losses). For this reason, international arguments about risk management based on the lessons learned from the current problem also implicitly assume that internal processes, people, and system processes did not work properly to stem this crisis.

This suggests that it might be worth reanalyzing the factors behind the losses under the current financial crisis from an op risk point of view. It is particularly true of 1) the method of risk factor classification based on causes, and 2) the argument assuming the endogenic nature of risk.

The Method of Risk Factor Classification Based on Causes

Unlike credit and market risks, op risk is defined based on the features of its causes, even though it uses business type and event type when further classifying op risk into subcategories in the AMA (see table 4.4).

These categories may look a little superficial but that cannot be helped because we need more consensus among many countries on the criteria as an international rule. Some financial institutions that manage op risk following its original high-minded principles might prefer cause-based classification instead of event type-based classification, and this looks very reasonable to me. A difficulty is, however, in how we should set up the category based on causes that could be shared by many parties.

Table 4.5 gives some proposals for categorizing causes for classifying op risk losses.

There are many similarities between these suggestions and the event types of Basel II. Indeed, Alvarez (2001) noted that the classification item of Zurich IC corresponds item for item to the classification items of Basel II except "Clients, Products & Business Practices" and "Execution, Delivery & Process Management," and also insisted that if they further classify these two into more detailed subcategories, all the classified items could be associated with a certain causal type.

Table 4.4 Op risk classification under the AMA

Business lines	Loss event type
Corporate finance	Internal fraud
Trading and sales	External fraud
Retail banking	Employment practices and workplace safety
Commercial banking	Clients, products and business practices
Payment and settlement	Damage to physical assets
Agency services	Business disruption and system failures
Asset management	Execution, delivery, and process management
Retail brokerage	

Table 4.5 Cause items for classifying op risk losses

Muermann and Oktem (2002)	Zurich IC—Alvarez (2001)
Country risk due to severe changes in the political system	*Business process:* loss events arising from a firm's execution of business operations
Crime risk due to internal and external fraud	*Employee:* loss events resulting from the actions or inactions of a person who works for a firm
Legal and liability risk due to employment practices, workplace safety, or changes in the regulatory environment	*External:* loss events caused by people or entities outside a firm
Operational risk due to transaction failures, rogue trading, and so on	*Relationships:* loss events caused by the connection or contact that a firm has with clients, regulators, or third parties
Physical risk due to loss or damage of assets such as buildings or computers	*Technology:* loss events due to piracy, theft, failure, breakdown, or other disruption in technology, data, or information

If we follow this type of classification, we might end up classifying many loss cases in this crisis under the item "external factors." This might reflect that individual institutions could face difficulty in analyzing the systematic factors in further detail beyond judging them just as "external." However, if even large financial institutions will not make efforts to study the background of macro stress events further to classify them into more detailed subcategories, it is very likely that the financial system will not be robust enough to withstand stress events that could occur once every 10 or 20 years. Therefore, it is expected that, at least globally, active large banks that could be vulnerable to global systemic shock should further study this.

There are some academic studies already in this area. For example, based on qualitative information, E.P. Davis (2003) classified past macro stress events into three types: financial crises triggered by banks, market price, and market liquidity. Then he further classified them into ones triggered by globalization, currency crisis, individual institution failures, asset markets, commodity prices, and deregulation. Moreover, IMF (2008b) recently identified and classified various financial crises in the past based on objective indicators, and then analyzed them by focusing on their relation to subsequent business conditions. The principal categories of crises in this work look very similar to the classification done by Davis with one mainly related to the banking system, another mainly related to the security market, and one more mainly related to the foreign exchange market.

At any rate, the risks associated with these events are hard to express using only statistical analysis (including VaR) based only on past data, so we need a scenario analysis with some econometric elements. And in this area, too, the perspective of op risk management becomes very important.

Arguments Assuming Endogeny of Risk Control

Because AMA requested banks to consider BEICF as one of the four elements for op risk quantification, this aspect can be seen as a unique feature of op risk. Meanwhile, we have not seen many discussions of risk control assuming endogenic risks in the area of credit and market risks partly because they have features strongly influenced by exogenous factors.

In this financial crisis, however, even the losses that were classified under credit or market risks by conventional standards could often be caused by inadequate or failed internal processes, people, and systems. If this is the case, it may be necessary also for market and credit risk management to introduce the idea of endogenic risk, or the idea of a good or bad risk management process, which could surely influence the consequent risk amount. In particular, as we often discuss the area of op risk management and internal control, we need to establish the so-called PDCA cycle to keep a certain level of risk management quality in the area of market and credit risk management. It means that we have to consider why C (confirmation) and A (act) of the PDCA cycle did not necessarily work well in this crisis for market and credit risks.

ESTABLISHMENT OF A SUSTAINABLE REGULATION STRUCTURE

Required Reactions by the Authorities

As we have already seen in chapter 3, many international organization of regulators, central banks and banks, as well as regulatory agencies of some countries published various recommendations or implemented various countermeasures based on the lessons learned from the current financial crisis. Among them, some measures did not only require efforts on the part of the banks, but also the direct involvement of the authorities (i.e. revisions of existing regulations and the introduction of new ones). They can be classified into the following four types.

Review of Basel II/Pillar 1 As discussed in chapter 3, the BCBS was currently reviewing 1) an increase in risk weight of securitization products to be aligned with their actual risk amounts, and 2) an introduction of a formula for calculating trading transaction risk weight that is more conservative than those that had been considered before. These countermeasures directly deal with the defects highlighted by the current crisis.

Review of the Basel II/Pillar 2 The BCBS is considering a revision of Pillar 2, as well as of Pillar 1. One of the main topics is the improvement of the Internal Capital Adequacy Approach (ICAAP) and Supervisory Review and Evaluation Process (SREP), which mainly focus on the introduction of a robust framework for stress testing and the improvement of enterprise-wide internal controls.

Review of the Basel II/Pillar 3 The BCBS is also considering further improvement of banks' disclosure of the risk profile of securitization products, which are held or originated by banks.

Others For example, the BCBS is considering advising other rule-making bodies, such as the IASB, more actively so as to increase the stability of financial system.

These measures can be seen to react properly to risk management issues highlighted by the current crisis, at least from a short-term point of view. The reason I emphasized "short term" is that they do not seem to have necessarily paid enough attention to long-term objectives and measures that are effective in the short term can sometimes work against the long-term stability of the financial system. In a serious financial crisis, it is very natural for the public and politicians to seek solutions to problems that are laid before them. In this environment, it is a little difficult to persuade them to think of long-term issues, say those that will materialize in five years. Meanwhile, putting more regulatory burdens on financial institutions that were already severely injured and that understood their own failures might only aggravate the situation.

Also, in this financial crisis, while many US and European financial institutions suffered huge losses, many institutions in Japan and other Asian countries were not so damaged for reasons that I will mention later. Nevertheless, the new regulations under discussion are likely to be applied uniformly to Japanese and Asian banks, as well as to US and European ones. In this case, if these measures were designed mainly based on the short-term concerns of US and European regulators, and could therefore be harmful to the long-term stability of the financial system, the extraterritorial application of these regulations to Japan and Asia may just cause trouble rather than benefit the region.

In the following, I will discuss the possible adverse effects of the measures from a long-term point of view. Before going into this discussion, however, I will briefly overview the relationship between the current crisis and Basel II, because many newly introduced measures tried to change the contents of Basel II or change how it was implemented. So we can ask whether the current crisis can be seen as a failure of Basel II to contain bank risk taking, or whether we can see that Basel II could successfully stop a further expansion of financial shocks that otherwise could occur.

Financial Crisis and Basel II

One thing, to be sure, is that Basel II has been implemented since 2007 in some countries, including Japan. Most of the countries, including major European countries, started to implement the Internal Rating-Based Approach (IRB) approach for credit risk management only in 2008. In the case of the US, the earliest adopters are expected to start it only in 2009. In this sense, it is next to impossible to judge whether Basel II implementation affected the current crisis as far as US and European banks are concerned.

From the point of view of the panel data analysis, however, we can say that a few countries such as Japan and Hong Kong, which started the full-scale Basel II in 2007, tend to be less affected by the crisis. Indeed, even the Japan FSA emphasized that some regional banks significantly reduced their holdings of securitization products before this crisis because they wanted to contain the increase in risk assets because of their Basel II implementation. This surely affects the amount of losses suffered by Japanese banks, which was much smaller than losses of their US and European peers. Also, some bank analysts highly appreciated Japanese bank disclosure information of securitization products, which was requested in Pillar 3 of Basel II, to avoid unnecessary confusion in the market. Indeed, because Basel II reflects the authorities' concerns about bank regulatory arbitrage using securitization products strongly (BIS 1999), it is very natural that the implementation of Basel II resulted in the containment of losses associated with securitization products.

Still, if we pose the question whether the US and European banks could have averted the misery if they had actually implemented Basel II a few years earlier, the answer may be "no." However, this is not necessarily due to defects in Basel II. According to the author's view, it is rather due to the immature stage of establishing the know-how to implement Basel II. (Of course, Basel II itself has some room for further improvement, such as too low risk weighting of securitization products that underestimate their risks, or its excessive dependence on external rating agencies.)

In other words, as discussed so far, among major challenges highlighted by the current crisis, not a few were to be fixed by the dialogue between the authorities and banks under Pillar 2. And this dialogue had already started even before the starting of the Basel II in many countries. These major challenges are, for example, the adequacy of stress scenarios for stress testing and its use in business decisions or senior management involvement, the establishment of a groupwide risk management, and a breakdown of silo risk management so as not to allow oversight of risk between categories. All these were long recognized as major issues by the authorities and banks, and actually have been actively discussed. This situation could not be changed even if Basel II had been introduced a few years earlier.

Then why did the authorities and banks not correct weaknesses in their risk management, even though they recognized their importance? In this context, it is interesting to see the outcome of a benchmarking study of stress testing that was published by the UK FSA in 2006. The UK FSA actually indicated at this point that the degrees of stress assumed in many bank stress testing was simply not sufficient. This notwithstanding, only one year after this publication, many UK financial institutions suffered huge losses, and the medium-sized Northern Rock was virtually forced into default. The bottom line is that even the mighty UK FSA did not have enough power to change the degrees of stress assumed in stress testing by banks in the environment of long-lasting, benign credit conditions. This story illustrates how difficult it is for regulators to form a consensus with banks on the degrees of stress under the framework of SREP.

In sum, it is likely that Basel II cannot react well to many risk management problems highlighted by the crisis, not because it is lacking in regulation (with some exception), but rather owing to the lack of know-how to implement the regulation effectively. My next question is whether many recommendations and measures proposed by the authorities after the crisis would really be in line with this view. In the following, I will discuss this issue.

Evaluation of the regulatory reaction to the crisis: Pillar 1

The recent actions for reviewing a part of Pillar 1, that is, the risk weighting of some transactions associated with securitization products, just reflect the recognition on the part of authorities and banks of their underestimation of these risks. I have already indicated that with some exceptions, Basel II itself does not have serious problems. In this sense, we could judge it to be an appropriate reaction. However, it is also important that in the future a third party, separate from the BCBS, trace back past policy discussions and identify why they produced regulations that underestimated certain risks.

Securitization was the area in which many global financial institutions had long been aggressive in expanding their own businesses. So this intensified competition among banks may have biased the stance of the authorities toward the interests of their own countries' banks. So tackling only the problems highlighted by the crisis was not enough. Rather, we should review the global policy-making process, which led to this biased outcome. To be sure, this type of argument could be extremely difficult to be accepted from a political point of view. Still, if we cannot resolve this type of problem under ordinary conditions, this simply indicates that we have to wait for another crisis to address the potential defects of international regulation.

Evaluation of the Regulatory Reactions to the Crisis: Pillar 2

In the context of Pillar 2, encouraging banks to increase the perspective of group-wide risk management, stress testing in general, and liquidity risk management through identifying and tackling the weaknesses highlighted by the crisis can be seen as appropriate reactions. The only concern, however, is how the authorities request banks to improve these areas under Pillar 2, in which banks are basically "expected" to improve them voluntarily. The issues are "specificities" and "features of obligation" of these requests.

The very likely reaction of the authorities after a big financial shock is the so-called "Pillar 1-ization" of Pillar 2. In other words, they would first set up many very prescriptive regulations and then require banks to comply with them strictly. We should now be reminded of the reasons for introducing the idea of Pillar 2 into Basel II. It is because the authorities judged that innovation of financial products and their risk management by advanced financial institutions was just too fast and too diverse to be followed and uniformly regulated. This indicates that "Pillar 1-ization" of Pillar 2 would simply worsen the situations that Pillar 2 tried to resolve. In this context, we might better hear a criticism that the main interests of many financial institutions and the authorities concentrated on some technical issues of Basel II, including the parameter estimations for IRB and AMA. In other words, this excessive emphasis on technical issues diverted senior managers from more important issues such as an emphasis on the perspective of groupwide risk management and deep involvement of senior managers in this management.

Indeed, the internal auditing section of the UK FSA implied this point in its report that reviewed failed reactions to the Northern Rock case (FSA 2008). For example, this report indicated that "during 2006–07 a considerable supervisory effort on Northern Rock was expended on Basel work ... but risk indicators arising from that work ... do not appear to have been factored into the FSA's ongoing supervisory assessment nor strategy for the firm," or "[c]onsiderable emphasis was placed on stress testing as part of the Basel changes, and in particular in the Pillar 2 Internal Capital Adequacy Assessment Process. I recommend more work to challenge firms on the vulnerabilities of their business and strategic plans, in line with the 'Comprehensive Approach' set out in the FSA's 2005 Discussion Paper." These critical reviews also led to views that implicit priority ranks represented by the number after the Pillar should be exchanged between Pillar 1 and 2 (i.e. ICAAP and SREP should be regarded as the number one priority process and therefore be called Pillar 1, and this should be followed by a new Pillar 2, in which banks are requested to come up with a minimum required capital based on a standardized uniform formula). They are worth hearing by the authorities.

The core issues seem to be summarized as the following. They are: 1) in Pillar 2, how much degree of specificities and power of enforceability authorities need to bring discipline into advanced banks' risk management, and 2) whether it is, above all, possible for the authorities to depend on financial institutions' initiative and allow for diversity in their bank supervision. These issues are closely related to the moral hazard issues that are embedded in the financial system. It is definitely hard for the authorities to follow the speed of financial innovation in the private world, and also to do tailor-made supervision that corresponds to bank diversity. Therefore, the authorities have no option but to introduce a system that allows for voluntary actions and diversity of financial institutions to some extent, as in the case of Pillar 2 and 3 of Basel II. However, it should be noted that it is anyway impossible to expect financial institutions that always have incentives to take more risk than expected by the authorities to contain their risk-taking within the authorities' expectations. In this environment, what kind of measures are left for the authorities?

One thing of which I am sure is that we should not introduce specific requirements for stress testing and liquidity risk management on a global basis, although we should do so sometimes on a domestic basis. This is because sound practices in these areas could significantly vary among different countries. If the authorities try to regulate them in a uniform way, this would not only place huge costs on banks, but also discourage them from developing further innovation in their risk management. So what kind of measures are left? I will discuss this issue in detail in chapter 5 but I believe that at first the authority should give clear guidance on the degrees of stress to be managed by banks based on the idea of historical frequency, and then banks and the regulators should discuss the adequacy of this stress level. If the authority and banks reach agreement on scenarios with this degrees of stress (for instance, that the stress that could occur once every 25 years) or the required capital amount based on this scenario, the authority should share the losses that exceed the agreed level. More specifically speaking, the authority could inject public funds into banks to cover these losses without any managerial conditions.

Meanwhile, what could happen if banks do not reach agreement with authorities on the degrees of stress assumed in the stress scenario (in other words, banks will not put aside the capital that corresponds to the additional losses realized in this scenario)? This may be similar to the situation indicated by the stress testing benchmark study done by the UK FSA. In this case, the authority should not guarantee banks that it will share losses even if the stress that could occur once every 25 years actually happens.

The above system could be effective in fixing the problems of incentive structure in the current financial system since banks are motivated to agree with the authorities on the degrees of stress of a class occurring once every 25 years, and then put aside the capital for it. They are actually motivated by the insurance provided by authorities over losses that exceed the agreed level. Unlike the UK case, it is a little difficult for financial institutions to dismiss the authorities' view on the degrees of stress to be assumed by banks in this case. Besides, this system would also be effective in preventing moral hazard on the authority side, because the authority would be subject to public criticism over its assessment of risks in the case of their underestimation.

Therefore, with these policies, the degrees of stress to be assumed by banks is standardized, but the actual scenarios themselves are left to the discussions between regulators and individual banks. Of course, there may be many difficulties in actually implementing these policies (e.g. some might doubt that the authority and banks could really agree on the degrees of stress by using a historical frequency standard such as "once every 25 years"), and some of these issues will be discussed again in chapter 5. Moreover, as a tool to supplement the above policies, we could use a macroprudential policy that smoothens away the credit cycle impact more actively through adjustments of required minimum capital. This issue will be discussed in chapter 5.

Evaluation of the Regulatory Reactions to the Crisis: Pillar 3

The increase in Pillar 3 requirements to improve the Pillar 2 process should be positively accepted. In particular, the disclosures of transactions of securitization products are not enough even under the current Basel II, so this reaction could be judged to be appropriate.

However, it should be constantly noted that a cost/benefit assessment of the increase in the number of disclosure items should be required. Disclosure information that cannot be digested correctly or is misunderstood by the market might produce additional costs on financial institutions and sometimes negative effects on the stability of the financial system. A difficult issue related to the improvement in disclosure is that the type of information that could be properly digested by the market is not necessarily clear. Bank analysts and external rating agencies tend to prefer information that enables them to compare one bank to others. This is because their evaluation method itself uses benchmarking methodologies. Meanwhile, the provision of this type of standardized information requires banks to do additional work in changing their formats. Furthermore, some banks might be concerned that the information that is revised to the uniform format does not necessarily reflect the real risk profile faced by the banks.

Another issue is the appetite of the market, including bank analysts, for disclosed information coming from Pillar 3. The main text of Basel II stretches to 190 pages, and its contents are not easy reading. Besides, the market recognized that banks are now required to put aside capital that reflects their real risk amounts much more accurately under Basel II than under Basel I. Also, they know that regulators even watch banks' economic capital management under Pillar 2. Under this condition, it is very natural for the market to doubt that it could better judge the credit conditions of banks than the authorities based only on the disclosed information that can use much more and better information acquired through Basel II implementation. Indeed, there is a kind of tradeoff between the improvement of the contents of Pillar 1 (or the quality of information held by the authority) and market incentives to use the disclosed information under Pillar 3.

In this environment, how should we increase the amount of information to be disclosed under Pillar 3? One measure is to reduce the difference of information content between that held by the authority and that held by the market, thereby motivating the market to analyze the data better than the authorities do. The information required to calculate the required amount of capital under Basel II, at least, should be disclosed for facilitating benchmarking by the market. Also, to help the market's understanding, the authorities might be required to educate the market to some extent (in particular, on the mechanism of Basel II).

Finally, authorities should better convey to the market their concerns in a more active and concrete way so as to motivate the market to study the disclosed information further. This could allow the authorities' concerns to be conveyed to the market, increasing market pressures or market proposals to improve banks' risk management. Previously, I noted that the authorities' advice under Pillar 2 has not been persuasive enough for the banks to follow, but this situation might be changed by collaboration with the market as I propose. Of course, there are some reservations. First, we should note the possibility that authorities might lead the market in a direction based on a wrong judgment. Furthermore, there is a concern about a bigger overreaction from the market than expected by authorities, or reactions based on the wrong judgment of the market. In particular, there might be more possibility of the market's incorrect understanding if disclosed information simply increases without deep reflection over its content.

In addition, as indicated by the situation of a few years ago, in which the market in general underestimated credit risk, and only very weakly reacted to the authorities' concerns, if at all, the market might not be able to react well to systemic risk information, including credit cycles, although it can react well to idiosyncratic information. How we should react to this last point is closely related to the macroprudential policy dealing with credit cycles, which will be discussed in the next chapter.

Evaluation of the Regulatory Reaction to the Crisis: Accounting Rule and External Rating Agencies

Last, I would like to discuss regulatory reactions beyond the area of Basel II. In this area, accounting rules are most important. Bank regulators now face the big challenge of how they should exercise their influence. More specifically speaking, it is the issue of how regulators convey their messages on the use of fair value accounting to accounting rule-making bodies such as the IASB. On this issue, it is desirable, for example, that the BCBS and IASB discuss actively in the future how two communication tools of firms' financial conditions, accounting and risk management, should be coordinated and distinguished, also considering the procyclicality issues of fair value accounting.

An important issue could be to what extent the accounting side could incorporate positively the idea of the credit "cycle" moving against market sentiments of the time, or mean-reversion movements in the name of "forward-looking" evaluation. From the viewpoint of the accounting rule-setting body, current market conditions are most important, and not history that is not accepted by the current market. Meanwhile, the bank regulators and many other authorities believe that markets repeated the same mistakes, and that is the reason we have seen the credit "cycle" historically. They argue that accrual accounting based on book values or accounting based on fundamental values provide not a perfect but a second-best solution to this problem.

An important issue in this argument is to identify the needs of major stakeholders, which use communication tools such as accounting and risk management. The rule should never be determined only by normative ideas of the rule-setting body. Regardless of whether one is the accounting rule-setting body or the bank regulator, it should first confirm the needs of major stakeholders, and share their understanding with the public in more transparent way.

The governance of external rating agencies is another important issue. Above all, Pillar 1 of Basel II heavily depends on the judgments of external rating agencies on various aspects. This is not limited to the rating assigned to securitization products, but also extends to ratings assigned to corporate credits in the standardized approach, instead of internal ratings used in the IRB approach. In this sense, the validity of judgments by external rating agencies significantly influences the validity of Basel II. In this financial crisis, because this validity of rating agencies' judgments was questioned, whether we can tackle this issue also strongly affects the credibility of Basel II.

This issue is also closely related to Pillar 2. In other words, that Basel II allows for using the ratings assigned by external rating agencies, instead of providing another formula with financial institutions, might reflect the authorities' expectation of private discipline, as well as that these ratings were already widely used among financial institutions. The authorities expected that private agencies such as external rating agencies would work as quasi-regulatory agencies, improving the stability of the financial system without public intervention.

This expectation has just been betrayed, and the remaining vacuum needs to be filled. However, it is not yet clear whether this should be by a change in the structure of Basel II, which heavily depends on external rating agencies, or the introduction of supplemental measures to ensure the adequacy of external rating agencies' judgments (that is, supervision by regulations or regulatory agencies). Considering the general difficulty in realizing the first option, the answer to this question depends on the content of the second option. And this second option is now being considered by parties outside the BCBS, a situation that frustrates the BCBS.

CHAPTER 5

Reform of Risk Management Based on the Lessons Learned from the Crisis

OVERVIEW OF THE REFORM OF RISK MANAGEMENT

In this chapter, I will discuss how risk management can be improved by individual financial institutions, and also the macroprudential framework to be established by authorities based on the lessons learned from the crisis, which were discussed in the previous chapter. First, in this section, I will give an overview of my policy reform recommendations. This reform includes the reform of the macroprudential framework as well as micro-level risk management. This is because these simultaneous reactions on the micro and macro sides complement each other and are essential for avoiding future financial crises.

As I discussed in previous chapters, at the core of financial crises or creation and bursting of financial bubbles exists a structural problem such as the moral hazard of banks. In the following, I will show you the grand design of a policy that deals with this issue. This policy is supported by four pillars as follows:

- *Clarification of stress sharing*: The authority should clarify the border line for stress sharing between it and financial institutions, reducing the room for moral hazard on the part of banks and also of regulators.
- *Introduction of a credit-cycle-smoothing macroprudential policy:* The minimum requirement of capital or capital adequacy ratios should be variable corresponding to different phases of the credit cycle, reducing the procyclicality of the current prudential framework.
- *Introduction of stress-focused risk management at financial institutions:* Each financial institution should improve its risk management so that it can clearly capture the risks indicated by predetermined degrees of

stress, and manage them using tools that are currently being developed in the area of op risk management, enabling stress sharing between the authority and financial institutions.

- *Introduction of a compensation mechanism that induces management to work for the long term:* Senior managers of financial institutions should sell to authorities put options that are structured to pay a part of their compensation received during a certain past period to compensate financial support by the authorities during the stress period. This facilitates stress sharing between authorities and financial institutions.

It should be noted that the relation between the degree of stress required by the authority and credit-cycle-smoothing macroprudential policy should be similar to the relation between stress testing in the framework of ICAAP under Pillar 2 and minimum required capital under Pillar 1. Consideration of the stress testing outcome in ICAAP is basically voluntary depending on the intention to buy quasi-insurance from the authorities, and the minimum requirements are always determined by the capital adequacy ratio.

In the following, I will explain the grand design of the four pillars in more detail (see figure 5.1).

Clarification of Stress Sharing

1. The regulator clearly shows the degrees of stress to be absorbed and to be prepared for by each bank, using the historical frequency.

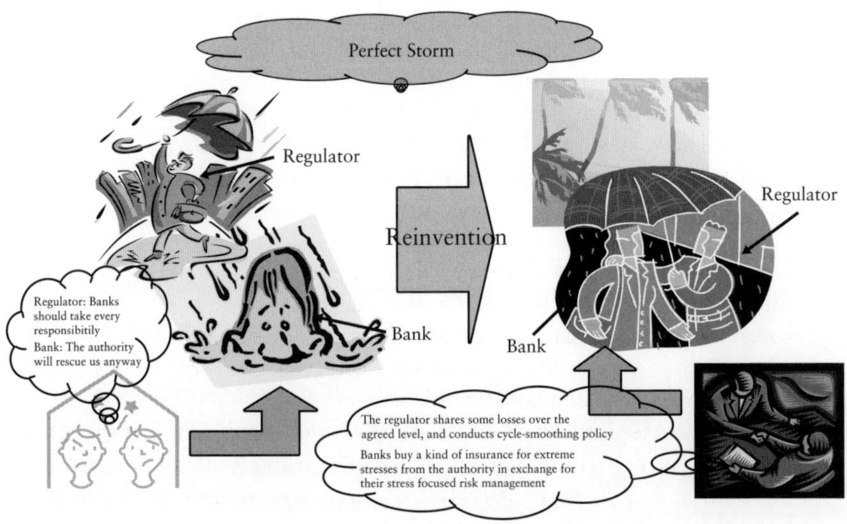

Figure 5.1 Reinvention of the incentive mechanism of financial system

2. Each bank and the supervisor discuss the bank's stress scenarios to ensure if they are in line with the degrees of stress indicated by regulators.
3. So long as the bank and the supervisor agree in point 2, the authorities provide the bank with public guarantees to absorb losses that exceed the agreed stress level.
4. Meanwhile, the authorities will not provide any guarantee to banks that cannot reach an agreement with them, although this will not be accompanied by the penalties because the preceding requires only voluntary add-ons to the required minimum capital.
5. This process motivates banks to agree with the supervisor on the stresses to be braced for.
6. Meanwhile, this process also motivates the supervisor not to allow easy stresses to be set by banks, which could bring in treasury criticism of the supervisory agency.

Introduction of a Credit-Cycle-Smoothing Macroprudential Policy

1. The authority sets indicators that represent developments of the credit cycle (or the cycle of financial bubble).
2. As a tool to conduct this macroprudential policy, the authority may use the scaling factor (currently set at 1.06) for the Basel II capital calculation.
3. The government selects (or newly establishes) a public entity to conduct this cycle-smoothing macroprudential policy, which should be politically independent and be equipped with a strong capability for macroeconomic research.

Introduction of Stress-Focused Risk Management at Financial Institutions

1. Banks measure the risk amount that corresponds to the stress scenarios agreed by the supervisor in the following process.
2. Banks first classify the risks based on root causes regardless of the current risk category, and measure the risk amount based on this classification.
3. Banks collate stress scenario data that covers the tail part of loss distribution in a comprehensive and objective manner.
4. Banks focus on the risk where their capital goes under the level of the minimum requirement, rather than zero.

Introduction of a Compensation Mechanism that Induces Management to Work for the Long Term

All senior managers are required to sell to the authorities put options structured to pay the bulk of their compensation received during the period preceding their financial troubles to compensate the authorities' financial support for them.

In the following sections, I will first discuss the micro issue that might be seen as most familiar by risk managers, that is, the introduction of stress-focused risk management by financial institutions. Then I will discuss the issue of clarification of stress sharing based on the micro-foundations established by the first discussion. These are followed by the issue of the introduction of a compensation mechanism that induces management to work for the long term, and by the issue of the introduction of credit-cycle-smoothing macroprudential policy and other policy issues.

Comparison with the Proposal of Kashyap, Rajan, and Stein (2008)

Before proceeding, I would like to briefly explain the policy proposal reported by Kashyap, Rajan, and Stein (2008) at the Symposium held by the Kansas Fed in August 2008, and then compare it with my proposal. The policy purpose of the proposal of Kashyap, Rajan, and Stein (2008) is more or less the same as mine: to prepare ourselves for the next perfect storm. And their anatomy of the causes behind the crisis also seems to be similar to the one this book gives: a structure of moral hazard embedded into the financial system, and an understanding that improved regulation alone cannot prevent a repeat of the creation and bursting of a financial bubble without dealing with this structure of moral hazard.

Kashyap, Rajan, and Stein (2008) proposed a kind of accident insurance, which is supposed to be bought by financial institutions. The main features of this insurance are 1) conditions for an insurance payout: an occurrence of systemic financial crisis, 2) insurance coverage: losses of the insured bank, 3) insurance provider: pension funds, wealth funds, and so on, 4) insurance managers: no clear indication, but this party is supposed to hold from the insurance provider funds to be paid for insurance payments, 5) the relation with the current regulation: mutually complementary.

This proposal has many aspects in common with mine. One of them is the idea of using insurance against the losses under a huge stress. This book also proposes that losses from stresses that are larger than what banks and authorities agree should be absorbed by banks, should be borne by the authorities, and this mechanism is the same with insurance.

There are, however, many differences between the two. The insurance provider is one of them. I propose that the authority plays this role, but Kashyap, Rajan, and Stein (2008) propose that private investors play this role. I am quite skeptical of private investors' capability of providing this type of insurance. As noted, the objective of this insurance is to protect many global financial institutions from a perfect storm. And if this is the case, we need insurance that can cover huge amounts of losses that occur simultaneously. Let's take the case of this global financial crisis. If the insurance is to cover the shortage of bank capital, which was estimated by IMF

(2008a) to be ¥67 trillion (US$742 billion), there seems to be no private institution that could cover such a huge amount. Otherwise, banks would have to pay huge premiums to buy such an insurance policy.

Indeed, some global banks have started to discuss the idea of transferring op risk held by banks as in the cases of market and credit risks, and discussion of op risk transfer actually has many features in common with the insurance idea of Kashyap, Rajan, and Stein (2008), including the potential size of losses and uncertainties concerning the insurance coverage. This op risk transfer transaction has not yet had significant success, particularly in the area of the tail part of loss distribution. This is partly because banks and product providers do not have enough data to estimate the frequency and severity of losses accurately. Besides, no mechanism has yet been established to avoid moral hazard. Also, to make these products tradable in the market, we need clear information on how much capital is required under the AMA of Basel II. This is because banks determine the price of risk transfer products based on the reduction of required capital owing to this risk mitigation effect. In other words, it is difficult to have tradable products in this area without knowing clearly the regulatory treatment of these products.

The insurance proposed by Kashyap, Rajan, and Stein (2008) might also face the same difficulties as the op risk transfer products. First of all, there is no sufficient data for measuring the risk to be insured against. Also, the moral hazard might be limited because its coverage is limited to impact from systemic factors (more specifically speaking, this size is associated with all the losses caused by systemic factors except the concerned bank's losses), but cannot be avoided if all the market participants head in the same direction of further stimulating the financial bubble (or underestimation of overall risks), as in the current financial crisis. An issue to be answered in this crisis is how banks could correctly analyze the macroeconomic situation, quickly stop dancing, and leave the party at its height. The insurance proposed rather encourages banks to continue dancing so long as others are still on the floor.

Finally, it should be noted that Basel II does not necessarily clarify its position on how much these systemic risks should be reflected in the calculation of required minimum capital. In this sense, the insurance proposed by Kashyap, Rajan, and Stein (2008) faces a similar situation to op risk transfer products. It will be necessary to clarify the risk mitigation effects owing to the insurance of systemic risks under Basel II to facilitate its pricing, and thereby make the insurance workable and tradable. Currently, in the area of AMA, total risks that can be mitigated by insurance are capped at 20 percent. Some argue, however, that this cap may be too low to encourage the market for op risk transfer products. This type of discussion in the op risk area should be considered in further discussions of insurance for systemic risk.

Table 5.1 A comparison of Kashyap, Rajan, and Stein's proposal and Oyama's proposal

Item	Kashyap, Rajan, and Stein	Oyama
Purpose	Mitigation of negative effects associated with moral hazard embedded into the financial system	Same
Policy tools	Developing insurance against systemic risks	Agreement between the authority and banks on loss sharing, and the introduction of stress-focused risk management by banks, which enables them to measure the agreed levels of stress to be absorbed by banks
Reactions to moral hazard	Trigger for insurance payment limited to the materialization of systemic risks (losses of other banks), which might rather stimulate the taking of moral hazard by banks in a financial crisis	Stress sharing between the authority and banks with conditions on their agreement. (In this process, whether each bank can accurately measure the risk corresponding to the agreed levels of stress becomes important.)
Insurance providers	Pension funds, sovereign wealth funds, and the like	The government
Relation with the current regulation	Mutually complementary	Same

In table 5.1, I compare the proposal of Kashyap, Rajan, and Stein (2008) with my own proposal on major important items.

IMPROVEMENT OF INDIVIDUAL INSTITUTIONS' RISK MANAGEMENT

In the following, I will discuss how we should improve the risk management of individual institutions, focusing on 1) identification of risk factors, 2) measurement of risk amounts, 3) ICAAP based on the measured risk amounts, and 4) the involvement of senior management, based on the lessons learned from the crisis.

Identification of Risk Factors: The Importance of Breaking Silos

Identification of risk is the starting point of risk management. Still, few experts argued seriously over whether the current way of identifying risk is right or wrong. This is partly because a comprehensive review of the methods for identifying risk factors could lead to a comprehensive review of risk management itself. No one (not only banks but also regulators) wants to scrap a familiar system to introduce a new one that costs a lot. However, as noted in chapter 4, it is this aspect that led financial institutions to be unprepared for the current financial crisis as far as risk management is concerned.

When identifying risk factors, it is important to remove the silos that have long been used for risk management, and to analyze and classify loss cases based on economic causes instead of transaction types or the sections that deal with them. This helps avoid the oversight of loss cases between risk categories, and enables banks to measure risk amounts corresponding to their predetermined risk appetite in a more precise way. To identify the risk factors beyond the conventional silos, we need further analysis based on the data. Past studies in the op risk management area, however, have shown some examples of categories of economic causes, including 1) human error, 2) crime, 3) system failures, 4) failures of internal management framework, 5) external factors—regulation changes, 6) external factors—the macroeconomy's various cycles, 7) external factors—structural changes in the domestic macroeconomy, 8) external factors—structural changes in the global macroeconomy, 9) external factors—natural disaster, and 10) market random walk.

This actually shows that even losses normally classified under the category of credit risk could have many different causes, that is, not only the typical (6) but also (1), (4), (5), and (7), for example. In this sense, the so-called Swiss cheese case (various contingent elements happen to occur simultaneously and then lead to loss cases) may sometimes be true of these loss cases. And the same is true of market risk loss cases.

After clearly identifying risk factors, we then need to classify loss cases under them. It should be noted that the introduction of this new management would not necessarily scrap the conventional risk management system. The risk management system that is helpful to business front lines and the one helpful in assessing the robustness of the financial institution as a whole against risks can be different. Even if banks introduce an analysis based on the new risk factor classification, it is not necessary to replace all the existing ones with the new classification. For the time being, for example, it may be enough to flag all the loss data collected by market, credit, and op risk management areas with information indicating new risk factor categories.

Anyway, the current financial crisis reminded us that risk measurement based on the conventional risk categories could not be effective in capturing real stress events in a serious way. Therefore, we need to introduce a new risk management framework based on the lessons we learned.

Treatment of Invisible Risks

As indicated by NIRA (2009), in general, the risks taken by financial institutions can be divided into two types. The first is "visible risks," or risks that can be statistically measured, and the other is "invisible risks," or risks that cannot be statistically measured (often called "Knight's uncertainty"). Some top tier European or US banks have long been believed to be good at managing visible risks, while this crisis actually showed us that they have easily dismissed invisible risks, in part due to confidence in their management of visible risks. Interestingly, some Japanese and Asian banks, which recently experienced their own crises, generally tend to have a very cautious stance toward invisible risks. They have usually restrained themselves when expanding into new businesses if they have been uncomfortable with "too good to be true" risk/return ratios, or if they could not determine the root causes of risks.

Regarding Japanese banks, this conservative stance also derives from their emphasis on the PDCA (Plan, Do, Check, Act) cycle (a feedback cycle), which is embedded in their corporate culture. In contrast, European or US financial institutions tend to emphasize a framework of effective challenges provided by outside third parties (in particular, shareholders) to senior managers of financial institutions, and also compliance with appropriate self-control procedures that were established to be infallible. This system cannot function effectively, however, if the quasi-infallible process itself is found to be flawed. Meanwhile, Japanese financial institutions put their emphasis on self-control "mechanisms." They assume that their procedure could be fallible and thus always ensure by themselves if there are any possible weaknesses to be corrected. This process looks very similar with Toyota's "Kaizen" which entails voluntary actions of front business lines to improve their management. This mechanism, once employed by financial institutions, would surely change the risk-taking behaviors of front business line, which previously might seek the chance to cheat the outside third party but now be forced to check them by themselves.

One caveat: the above mechanism would surely damage the possible dynamism of financial institutions. Given that excess risk taking behaviors by some financial institutions are severely criticized, however, I believe that all financial institutions in the world should follow the Japanese way in this area and thereby deal with invisible risk in a more conservative way.

Collection of Risk Factor Information

It may be possible to use the data collection framework that was already used for AMA purposes. As noted, loss data classified under op risk losses are then further classified into event types and business lines. In the case of op risk, however, because the event types are very close to economic causes, we may not need much effort to reclassify them into cause-based categories. Also, many elements of market risk might be classified into (10) and credit risk into (6). As the current financial crisis showed, however, even if market risk losses were caused by (10) and credit risk losses were caused by (6) at first glance, on further analysis we might find out that other risk factors also influenced these cases. This type of factor analysis should be done in detail for each loss case.

It should be noted that the factors behind market risk include positive impacts (factors for profit), and those behind credit risk include rating migration that has not yet reached the materialization of losses. The AMA framework does not necessarily capture this type of information. In this case, we do not have to stick to the AMA framework and may use this information, for example, to estimate the loss distributions of (6) and (10). Also, even in the case of op risk management, it is possible to include the data on "near misses" into its framework, and thus deal with all the data in a similar way.

Next to be considered is the use of scenarios for risk factors, of which actual samples can be very few (e.g., (5), (7), and (8)). For example, the factors highlighted by the current financial crisis could also belong to this category. In this process, we can again depend on the technique developed by the AMA. The measures to keep comprehensiveness and objectivity of scenarios, as explained in chapter 4, are good examples.

Also, in the process of scenario making, it is important for senior managers to be deeply involved. This process could raise the issues of risk management against the crisis to the level of business strategy issues. Moreover, the regulator should ask banks' senior managers whether they are really satisfied with the banks' robustness against stresses, which is required by the regulator, and gain satisfactory answers. The regulator should take a serious stance in this dialogue with banks' senior managers, implying that it might request a change in senior managers who cannot pass this process. At the same time, regulators that are satisfied with banks' explanations should take some responsibility once this bank suffers huge losses due to factors not mentioned in the preceding process. (Of course, this does not exempt financial institutions' senior managers from their own responsibilities.) In this financial crisis, we have not yet seen any penalty against regulators that allowed for the intensification of crisis.

If we reach a conclusion that these events are "force majeure" after various analyses, we might be able to dismiss the responsibility of the authorities to preempt the crisis. Unfortunately, this type of analysis has rarely been done before now. It goes without saying that the same is true of Japan's nonperforming loan problem. In this regard, a rare "self-criticism" was published by the UK FSA in March 2008. This type of clear sense of responsibility on both sides could entail serious dialogue between the two.

Risk Measurement Methods

Through the preceding process, data concerning movements of risk factors are collected and the lack of real data is supposed to be supplemented by scenario data. As highlighted by the current financial crisis, even market risk amounts measured with a high confidence level such as 99.9 percent (often expressed as an event that occurs once every 1,000 years) could be easily realized once the external environment changes. In this regard, even in the case of market and credit risks, information on the real risks faced by financial institutions can be gained only from scenario-type data. This is why scenario data is so important for risk measurement.

Meanwhile, the problem is, as noted in chapter 4, how to estimate the loss distribution that is followed by each risk factor based on a combination of real data and scenario data. Because of this problem, in the area of market and credit risk management, scenario analysis is mainly used only in the area of stress testing, and is separated from the area of VaR for the purpose of risk assessment and ICAAP. As a result, stress testing tends to lack clarity, robustness, and comprehensiveness if compared to the case where it is integrated into the risk measurement framework.

Another issue is how we should establish a framework to raise the standard of objectivity and comprehensiveness of scenario data to a level comparable to real data. As noted, AMA's experience is also helpful in this area. Even though AMA's approach is still in the developmental stage, its methodology to assign frequency and severity to each scenario data can be used to estimate the shape of the loss distribution followed by risk factors. Also, various methods to realize comprehensiveness and objectivity of scenario data were already proposed in the area of op risk management (please see chapter 4 for more details).

For example, to realize comprehensiveness and objectivity, we need to establish the process of making a stress scenario, which is clearly modularized to be sufficiently granular in each module from risk diversity point of view (comprehensiveness), and also sufficiently transparent from the third party's point of view (objectivity). I will discuss this issue in more detail in the next section. Also to realize comprehensiveness, we need to create a framework that could combine the macro and micro perspectives by setting up a workshop inviting economists who specialize in macroeconomics and financial stability analysis as well as experts in each business line.

Meanwhile, to gain objectivity, as noted in chapter 4, we should do rough back-testing using the benchmark provided by theoretical assumptions proposed by the industry and the academic world, while trying to remove biases using behavioral economics. In this regard, it would be interesting work to use the power law to estimate the tail part of the loss distribution. (Please see, e.g., Nagafuji (2008) and Fontnouvelle and Rosengre (2004) for more details.) Also, a simple application has been given in chapter 4. Once this type of method has been established, it can surely help increase precision in estimates of the tail part of loss distribution.

To validate the objectivity of scenarios, we need, for example, more cooperation with authorities that are engaged in macroeconomic analysis, such as central banks. One of the great lessons learned from the crisis is that there can be rapid contagion of stress events from one country to another, with the increasing trend of synchronization of world business cycles. So even regional banks in Japan are now required to include the perspective of a global economy into their stress scenarios. However, it is quite hard for individual financial institutions to make such a scenario. Therefore, it might be helpful to use a macroeconomic scenario presented in, for example, the financial stability review, which is periodically published by the central banks for the purpose of financial stability.

This way, a proactive use of the most recent developments observed in the area of AMA enables banks to integrate the risks that cannot be captured by conventional methods for market and credit risk into their enterprise-wide integrated risk management.

In addition to this method that uses scenario data as an input for risk quantification, stress scenarios can be used for risk quantification in a slightly different way. As indicated before, the current credit VaR and market VaR models are not supposed to assume any significant changes in external environments. If a model is used assuming possible changes in external environments, however, the outcome could be very different. For example, in the case of the credit VaR model, its estimated risk amounts and credit costs could vary depending on macroeconomic conditions in one year, two years, and three years, which surely affect the financial conditions of obligors at each future time. So even in the case that the VaR model structure itself does not capture significant changes in the external environment, it is possible to assess the impact of the changes in external environments (the impact of changes in macroeconomic environments on obligors' financial conditions) based on the current VaR model if the scenarios of different external environments can produce different VaR output.

Stress Testing Methodology

Generally speaking, we recognize that a desirable stress test should be accompanied by the following elements: 1) forward looking nature; 2) sufficiently severe degree of stresses; and 3) the structure that could capture risk contagion mechanism over the multiple years. Meanwhile, we also recognize the difficulties in having the above elements mainly due to the following reasons.

1. Forward looking scenarios, which are not necessarily based on the historical events could often be seen as subjective.
2. Reverse stress testing could be helpful to identify sufficiently severe degree of stresses but could not show financial institutions any hint of the probability of the scenarios, which is another important element to be considered to plan the possible reactions.
3. In order to incorporate the risk contagion mechanism over the multiple years into the stress scenarios in a precise way, we might need to have the world macroeconomic model that might be owned by major central banks. The natural question is, is it possible? The second question is, is it meaningful, given that even many central banks could not recognize well this contagion of effects in this crisis beforehand?

Against the above questions, I would argue for the following realistic answers. They emphasize the importance of senior managers' sense of crisis and their reactions, as well as the importance of modularization of risk elements to be scenarionized, which could facilitate the third party to verify comprehensiveness and objectivity of scenarios.

1. Regarding the plausibility of scenarios, financial institutions should consider all the risk scenarios which are surely not likely to happen but at the same time the one which we could not negate their occurrence in the coming 5 to 10 years. This time horizon matches well with the senior managers' ones. Also it could help financial institutions highlight many past crises that seem to have been conceivable beforehand but not be seen seriously by senior managers as clear and present danger. If we set clearly the time horizon of 5 to 10 years, however, most seeds of crises could be covered by the imagination of senior managers or risk managers. Thus, I believe the above could be a reasonable starting point to narrow down the range of scenarios to be considered seriously.
2. All the scenarios selected in the above process should be the ones used for reverse stress testing. However, this does not mean that financial institutions are expected to put aside enough capital to manage all the

stress scenario cases. Of course, they have to have enough capital to overcome the clear and present dangers. Otherwise, they should prepare for the crises in a different way based on their views on the plausibility of stress scenarios. One way is to classify all the scenarios into three categories, such as, the red zone—likely to occur in the coming two years, the orange zone—likely to occur in the coming five years, and the yellow zone—the others, and then attach them with the different reactions. For example, we might have such a rule that the red zone scenario outcome should be prepared by capital, the orange zone scenario outcome should be prepared partly by capital and partly by contingency planning, and the yellow zone scenario outcome should be prepared by contingency planning. For this process, we should pay special attention to monitoring and updating the above categorization based on the current situation. This should be done at least every quarter by senior managers. The precise updating rather than the initial classification of scenarios could be the key factor for success of this framework.

3. In order to enhance objectivity of the above process, financial institutions might make reference to the risk heat map made by the authorities, such IMF and major central banks. Also, we might expect the use of the early warning indicators which are now newly developed by the IMF. A caveat is that too much dependence on these type of indicators for judging crisis plausibility might cause another problem which is similar with the one caused by VaR.
4. The risk scenario making process should start with identifying various risk factors based on the category of root causes so that the focused risk factors could be granular enough. For this purpose, I suggest to use the category of root causes discussed in this chapter ("Collection of Risk Factor Information"). For each category, we need at least two to three serious scenarios to have granular level of scenarios.
5. As a next step, financial institutions should identify primary risk factors that would be influenced by the above root causes and directly pose impacts on their capital adequacy, such as loss or latent loss. For example, they are interest rate, stock price, foreign exchange rate, real estate price, debtors' financial indicators related with their credit ratings, and various prices in the financial market.
6. Then, financial institutions should make forward looking scenarios based on their captured contagion mechanisms. This contagion mechanism should be captured by multifaceted perspectives as much as possible and thereby obtaining the contagion mechanism triggered by root causes and leading up to primary risk factors. For example, it is desirable to set up the following categories and then see the feedback effects between them in the matrix structure.

A. Domestic macroeconomy/domestic regional economy (private consumption, capital expenditure, public spending, exports, etc.);
B. Various financial and asset markets (stock, real estate markets, etc.);
C. Overseas macroeconomies and overseas financial markets; and
D. International capital flows.

7. Articulation of the contagion mechanism in the above process is helpful to bring in more objectivity in the scenario-making process as they are now visible and thus able to be challenged by the third parties.
8. The above contagion mechanism should capture the dynamism for two to three years since the materialization of risk factors.
9. As already discussed in the above, in order to bring in objectivity in the scenario making process, financial institutions should benchmark their scenarios with the one by the authorities at home and abroad, such as the IMF and central banks. Also, as is the case of data pooling for op risk data, the benchmarking study of stress scenarios among financial institutions should also be helpful for financial institutions to find possible weaknesses of their scenarios. This type of activity should be initiated by the industry group such as IIF or Japanese Bankers Association. One caveat: excessive convergence to a few stress scenarios among financial institutions could enhance herding behaviors of the market and thereby increase systemic vulnerability of the financial system. Thus, we should stop at emphasizing the importance of sharing the methodology and risk elements information and should not go so far as to sharing the same risk scenarios.
10. Finally, as the above enables the scenario making process transparent, the third parties such as internal auditing department should challenge the appropriateness of the process and whereby improving the quality and objectivity of stress scenarios.

ICAAP Based on the Measured Risk Amounts and Senior Manager Involvement in Risk Management

ICAAP first becomes possible by comparing measured risk amounts after the abovementioned process with bank holding capital. The current financial crisis also showed that this process could be improved upon in some respects.

First is the way of expressing the degrees of stress. In the past, the representative indicator is the confidence level of VaR. As shown in chapter 4, however, this represents only horizontal frequency, and does not sufficiently reflect the idea of historical frequency, which is more important for capturing perfect storms. Such degrees of stress, in other words, should be equal to the degrees of risk allowance by each financial institution. Consequently, if financial institutions try to learn something from this financial crisis, it is necessary for them to express their own risk allowances by historical frequency as well as by the confidence level of VaR. On this issue, I introduced in the previous section a method to measure the risk amounts by VaR using scenario as well as real data. The degree of frequency to be attached to this scenario data actually depends on the degree of risk allowances set by senior managers.

The next issue is the type of capital to be compared with the measured risk amounts in this process. In conventional economic capital management, it is usually Tier I capital, and sometimes Tier I plus latent profits of holding securities, depending on banks. The question is whether this, too, should be kept in the future.

In the current financial crisis, we observed that the financial institutions were attacked by strong market pressures, and consequently not a few of them faced a liquidity crisis and then failed. This indicated that these financial institutions actually face challenges on whether they can keep the minimum required capital, rather than on whether they consume all the capital they have. In other words, their survivability is questioned long before their capital is consumed by losses, or when their capital adequacy ratio is still positive (often even higher than the minimum required level). If this is the case, the capital to be compared with the risk that concerns senior managers should be enough to satisfy the market. This means that if the current capital adequacy ratio is 14 percent, and the level at which the market would lose its confidence in the stability of this institution is lower than 12 percent, the difference between these two, that is, 2 percent, is the capital to be compared with the risk (or the capital above 12 percent).

This argument does not necessarily mean that financial institutions can totally dismiss the possibility that they will lose all their capital (or that the capital adequacy ratio of 14 percent will reduce to zero) as a result of risks materializing. Particularly, from the perspective of the authority that protects deposits, this probability is also very important. So as long as the regulatory authority remains one of the most important stakeholders of banks, banks are also required to answer to this request.

In principle, however, this objective should be aligned with the objective and concerns of senior management to use it as a tool in business decision making. And if the largest concerns of senior management are events that force the vulnerabilities of their institutions to be attacked by the market, these financial institutions are naturally required to manage this risk. And these should not only be the concern of senior managers of financial institutions, but also of the authorities. This is because the net value, or economic value, of capital could decrease significantly once the concerned banks are attacked in the market. And in this process, the difference between this net value and accounting capital amounts based on the fundamental values of assets widens. If the financial institutions can survive this crisis, market net value is likely to become closer to fundamental values, which would not entail big problems for the regulating authority.

However, if the financial institutions fail as a result of a market attack, as some did in the current crisis, fundamental values might become closer to market net value. In this case, the regulating authority suddenly finds that the credited capital adequacy ratio of 8 percent has already become negative once it tries to liquidate all the assets and liabilities of the banks.

Constantly keeping capital that is more than the minimum required level (say, 12 percent) indicates that banks need to keep more capital (say, 14 percent) in a normal period. This level depends on at what level a senior managers' view would get them fired by shareholders. Whether the frequency of this risk is once every 10 years or 20 years has to be determined by senior managers as their own risk to be managed. In this sense, as in the case of risk scenarios that are directly associated with business judgments, senior managers' interest in this type of ICAAP could be invariably raised.

This crisis, similar to Japan's banking crisis, reminded us of the importance of financial institutions' capability to raise capital. At the beginning of the financial crisis, there were surely some financial institutions that succeeded in raising capital from the market, and such amounts might be considered in the scenarios used for ICAAP. However, this scenario should not be over optimistic in emphasizing banks' capabilities to raise capital during the crisis. The current crisis actually indicated that even though capital could be raised in the first phase of crisis, this might possibly have declined rapidly as the crisis grew more serious. The scenario should be constructed so as to include the process of deterioration.

Liquidity Risk Management

In this financial crisis, liquidity risk from the viewpoint of fund raising and also of market liquidity was highlighted as shown in chapter 4. As was explained, however, it is quite hard to integrate this liquidity risk into economic capital management, on which ICAAP is based. Therefore, the framework of liquidity risk management, in particular fundraising liquidity risk management, has to be established in addition to the economic capital management framework.

The risk factors identified by ICAAP and the risk factors to be identified to prepare for this fundraising liquidity risk do not necessarily overlap. Of course, some of the latter might reflect the former, but there are also many unique features. Therefore, we need a separate framework from economic capital management.

First, I would like to discuss the overlap between the former (the risk of losing capital) and the latter (the risk of losing liquidity). One of them is the op risk element related to liquidity risk management, such as fund-raising operation failures and wrong estimates of one's liquidity condition. Also the former (which often materializes in a downgrade by rating agencies or the authorities' corrective actions) leads to a negative reaction from the market and then to liquidity troubles in the market. Meanwhile, a unique overlap is the market attack (a bank run in the money market) or malfunction of a payment system, which is not necessarily associated with bank fundamentals.

Another important aspect of liquidity risk management, which was highlighted by the current crisis and might be judged to be unique is its heavy dependence on the central bank regime of providing funds to the market. In particular, this regime could significantly influence the probability and the size of a market-wide liquidity crisis, against which financial institutions are now expected to deal with.

As discussed in chapter 4 and also indicated by NIRA (2009), the actual tools with which central banks conduct the liquidity management of financial institutions vary significantly among major countries. For example, significant differences are sometimes observed in the frequency of communication between the central bank staff in charge of money market operations and the staff of financial institutions in charge of liquidity management and the amounts of information gained from these communications, in the formation of trust relationships between the parties, and in the availability of tools for providing funds to individual financial institutions and their usability. In this environment, I would argue for the idea that financial institutions (in particular the internationally active ones) should consider explicitly the following "central bank regime" elements in their own liquidity risk management.

1. The capability of collecting information concerning the status of liquidity of individual financial institutions.
2. The scope of monitoring of status of liquidity.
3. The effectiveness in guiding the status of liquidity of individual financial institutions.
4. The effectiveness in tools for providing liquidity to individual financial institutions.
5. The degree of access to solvency information regarding individual financial institutions.

At any rate, banks need to develop various scenarios including these, and then ensure the adequacy of their current liquidity level by comparing it with the liquidity level required by the scenarios, or possible increases in liquidity in response to a rapid increase in liquidity requirements. This process is basically the same as ICAAP that we discussed in the previous section from the methodological point of view. There might be a nuanced difference because liquid assets could be easier to increase in comparison with sticky capital, so the differential approach (i.e. ensuring the capability to increase liquid assets against the increase in required liquidity in the stress) could become more important in liquidity management than in capital management. Another nuance is that liquidity risk management is more seriously lacking in data than other risks for capturing the movements of risk factors, so it has to depend excessively (even compared to op risk events) on scenarios in many respects. There might be ways, as I noted, however, to improve this area.

Last, I would like to emphasize again that the following process is very important in liquidity risk management: 1) making various scenarios related to fundraising liquidity risk as objective and comprehensive as possible; 2) determining clearly the degree of liquidity risk allowance by senior managers; 3) identifying the scenarios that correspond to the degree of risk allowance by senior managers; and 4) ensuring a framework that can secure required liquidity under stress and protect the entity. In addition, senior managers are required to be able to explain the above to the regulators and the market in a persuasive way.

FORMATION OF A NATIONAL CONSENSUS ON SHARING LOSSES

The Authorities' Reactions to the Crisis So Far

We have already discussed the lessons to be learned from the crisis concerning individual institutions' risk management. The lessons to be learned, however, cannot be limited to individual institutional issues. At the same time, we face a big challenge to the overall macroprudential framework, including the authorities as well as individual institutions' ability to stabilize the financial system. And this issue is very closely related to the former individual institutional issues, too. This is because, as explained in chapter 4, there are many risks faced by individual institutions that are associated with macro phenomena including the current financial crisis. Also, the authorities' macroprudential framework to deal with those macro events will be influenced by micro situations such as the status of individual institutions' risk management.

On this, as I have noted often, there is one important issue that remains to be seen: how the authorities and banks should share the losses under extreme stress. The phenomenon that we observed mainly in the US and UK up to the summer of 2008 was that the authorities requested banks to absorb all the losses by their own efforts regardless of the size of the total losses, and only at the stage at which the authority found banks' incapable of dealing with losses did they offer a public bailout for some and leave others to fail based on seemingly ad hoc criteria. This was not limited to the cases of the US and UK. If you look at financial stress events in the world in the past, you can easily find similar actions by the authorities despite some differences in the speed of reaction. My view is that these reactions themselves pose serious threats to the process of establishing an efficient and effective risk management framework, that is, the so-called happy marriage between the micro risk management of individual institutions and the macroprudential policy framework of the authorities.

In the following, I would like to discuss the rationality of the past authorities' reactions, focusing on the following issues: 1) whether we should admit the existence of macro-stress that is out of the control of individual financial institutions; 2) and if we admit that, what kind of stress is it; 3) and once we admit that, how should we share those losses between financial institutions and the authorities?

Recognition of the Limited Ability of Individual Institutions to Deal with Stresses

The first question, whether we should admit the existence of macro-stresses that are out of the control of individual financial institutions, does not ask whether it is possible. If it did, the answer is definitely "yes." The issue is rather the occurrence of moral hazard on the side of banks or their expectation of public bailout under such stresses, once we admit their existence. In other words, the authority will be concerned that the scope of what it is admitting is not only real systematic issues involving the whole macroeconomy, but also individual institutions' micro risk management issues. Consequently, the real issue is whether we can distinguish systemic impacts that are beyond the control of individual institutions from the idiosyncratic issues they should manage. Frankly speaking, this is surely not an easy task. Meanwhile, it is not efficient either to keep using the idea of a so-called "constructive ambiguity," or using ad hoc criteria to bail out those institutions considered too big to fail.

In this environment, it might be better for the authorities to consider the option that they share some extreme losses that are clearly defined as losses out of control of individual institutions beforehand for some banks that are too big to fail, at the cost of the introduction of more strict risk management than before. This could enable the authorities to deal with extreme stresses while containing the moral hazard of financial institutions (details will be explained later).

Stresses to be Shared by the Authorities (or Stresses Beyond Individual Institutions' Management)

Once we admit the existence of stresses to be shared by the authorities, then we have to answer the next difficult question, that is, what these stresses are. To be sure, risk that can be captured by VaR, or measured only by horizontal frequency, is very unlikely to be included in this category. This idea should not cause any surprise, because horizontal frequency is just a yardstick for idiosyncratic factors.

The events that are included in this category should be defined by historical frequency. However, even in the case of events defined by historical frequency, some could be idiosyncratic. Also, even in the case of systematic shocks, some such as the ordinary business cycle are expected to be dealt with by individual financial institutions' efforts. On this issue, I would like to emphasize again the importance of the authorities to clearly show their expectations of the degree of stresses to be absorbed by banks, as discussed in chapter 4. If it is an event that could occur once in every 25 years, this definition removes the losses that could occur from events with a lesser frequency than once in every 25 years. In other words, they are the losses that the banks must stand.

Moreover, because they are huge systemic phenomena (on the quarter-of-a-century level), it is very likely to develop into a macro-level crisis if the authorities just stand by only expecting private initiatives. It still might be too abstract, but these risks are hard to be dealt with by individual institutions, and would not cause any serious moral hazard because most banks have no intention of managing this sizable risk by themselves. Consequently, the authorities should share some part of such losses. Even if we look at history, we find that at first the authorities refused to share such losses, but later did, and the losses were much bigger than expected.

How to Share the Losses Between the Authorities and Financial Institutions

The next question to be answered is, once admitted, how losses should be shared between financial institutions and authorities. This question might be put into other words, such as what level of historical frequency should the authorities require financial institutions to prepare for. For example, if it is on a level of once every 10 years, as is the current case for many countries, the size of losses to be shared by the authorities could be huge. Meanwhile, if it is like the case of the UK, that is, on a level of once every 25 years, the size of losses to be shared by financial institutions might be too big. From the authorities' point of view, they naturally prefer the lower level of losses, so they have an incentive to set the frequency higher (e.g., once every 25 years, rather than once every 10 years). Meanwhile, from the macroeconomic point of view, as indicated in chapter 4, requesting financial institutions to put aside huge capital to manage events on an every-quarter-century level might significantly impair the efficiency of financial intermediation in the macroeconomy. At any rate, it is important to start a discussion to form a national consensus on this issue.

If the authorities can catch early warning signs of credit shock or inflating credit bubbles set to burst, it might be better for them to warn financial institutions against the shocks only when they are approaching them instead of warning them permanently. I will discuss this method of changing the reactions of the authorities over different phases of the credit cycle later.

As discussed, two major stakeholders of financial institutions, that is, shareholders and regulators, basically have a different degree of risk allowance. Therefore, there are arguments that setting the risk allowance or risk appetite of financial institutions should not be left to the institutions or their economic capital management. It is argued that the authorities, instead, should force them to set a tougher risk allowance. This might be right, but, at the same time, I wonder whether financial institutions' risk allowance measured by historical frequency might be much closer to that of the authorities than we usually expect. Here are my main reasons.

As indicated in chapter 2, the risks that are appealing to senior managers of banks would be risks of their own banks facing a critical situation. This situation should come much earlier and more frequently than the case where their net values are reduced to zero or even become negative. Let's suppose that this crisis corresponds to the situation in which the capital adequacy ratio goes under the minimum required level, say, 10 percent of the capital adequacy ratio. And this institution's senior managers would like to limit their risk taking to a level at which they would face this situation no more than once every 10 years (to keep their own reputation, they would like to keep management stable at least while they are in office). In this case, it is not necessarily clear whether the amount of capital required to ensure that the capital adequacy ratio goes under 10 percent no more than once every 10 years is higher or lower than the amount of capital required to make the ratio go under 0 percent with the confidence level of 99.9 percent (and with a historical frequency of, say, once every 25 years).

We need further study on this issue, but if we find there is no big difference between them or that the former is, rather, bigger than the latter, the issue is much easier to solve. In this case, even in the area of regulation such as SREP against ICAAP, it may be better to introduce the idea of the former so that the regulation requirements could be more easily aligned with the incentives of senior managers.

Judgments of Specific Risks to be Shared by the Authorities

Now I would like to discuss how we should strictly judge the risk amounts that are over the certain level of historical frequency to be shared by the authorities. For example, if the losses rose from systemic stress events that had not been identified as risk management weaknesses by inspectors in on-site examinations, or much beyond inspectors' expectations, they should at least be candidates for those losses to be shared by the authorities. The reasons are as follows.

Suppose a case where the extreme stress event that goes beyond the stress level agreed upon by financial institutions and the regulators occurs. There are four different reasons behind this event: 1) the size of shock to the fundamentals of the macroeconomy was larger than previously expected by the authorities; 2) the authorities have dismissed for some reason shocks to the fundamentals of the macroeconomy, which should had been captured by the authorities much earlier; 3) the fundamentals of the macroeconomy projected by the authorities departed from the market's assessment; and 4) individual financial institutions failed to react to the shocks despite proper early warning from the authorities.

In case (1), the size of shocks was too large to be expected in a pre-emptive way, so this might be easy to agree upon as a case for public rescue. Case (2) might also justify public rescue, but also exposes the authorities to criticism from the public or treasurer. So the authorities would have strong motivation to improve the quality of their monitoring. This also suggests that if individual financial institutions do not follow the degrees of stress suggested by the authorities (case (4), or the case of the UK in 2005, as noted), the authorities would not opt to rescue them (they might rescue those too big to fail, but only in very uncertain circumstances). This mechanism could motivate financial institutions to try to agree on the degrees of stress to be considered unless they have very strong confidence in their capability to manage extreme stresses.

Finally, case (3) is the case in which financial institutions have higher capital than required by the authorities and have not been shown any weaknesses in risk management by the authorities before facing serious challenges from the market, such as difficulty in obtaining funding, a drop in stock prices, and downgrading by rating agencies. If the market judgment is likely to be more adequate than that of the authorities, this could be case (2). Meanwhile, if we have enough information to justify the authorities' judgment, the authority

Table 5.2 Injection of public funds during the Japanese banking crisis

Purpose of funds	Amount (trillion ¥)	Breakdown, recoveries (trillion ¥)	P/L (trillion ¥)
Depositors' protection	18.6	Banks: 8.1 Nation: 10.4	All losses
Buying assets from defaulted institutions	9.7	Recoveries: 7.1	Profits from selling recovered assets: 1.5
Increase of capital of banks	12.4	Recoveries: 9.2	Profits from selling recovered assets: 1.3

Source: Nihon Keizai Shinbun, October 15, 2008

should act as in case (1). In this context, it should be noted that the public funds injected into the Japanese banking industry during the banking crisis actually resulted in profits, except for the funds for bank liquidation, in other words, the funds to cover the losses (see table 5.2).

Generally speaking, the mass media tends to focus only on the size of funds in the midst of crisis, and then very easily forgets the situation after the recovery. (To be fair, a part of this responsibility is attributed to the authority side, which has not reviewed the crisis and past reactions.) Looking back in time, the authority has often done a pretty good job of assessing the fundamentals compared to the market in the crisis.

These arguments indicate that reasons (1) to (3) should be good enough to justify the rescue of financial institutions in a perfect storm. However, these type of arguments are useful only in a sober atmosphere. The history of the crisis actually demonstrated to us that they are very hard to accept for politicians and the public in the midst of crisis in general regardless of their rationality.

PREPARATION BY THE AUTHORITIES AND INDIVIDUAL FINANCIAL INSTITUTIONS FOR STRESSES

The Type of the Current Financial Crisis

It is often heard that the US authorities' reaction to the current crisis looks similar to that of the Japanese banking crisis in the 1990s, particularly their manner of allowing the market to prompt them to act. As shown in chapter 1, there may be many commonalities between the current US crisis and Japan during the 1990s in that both countries faced a shock that rocked the core engine of economic growth. Indeed, if you look at the fundamentals of the macroeconomy, you can easily find that both countries' high economic growth up to the bubble bursting heavily depended upon the innovation factor, or total factor productivity (TFP) (see figure 5.2). This TFP can often be seen as a reflection of the financial bubble and might be lost after a bubble burst, as in Japan. If this is the case for the US, the US could also expect a significant drop in potential growth rate from now on.

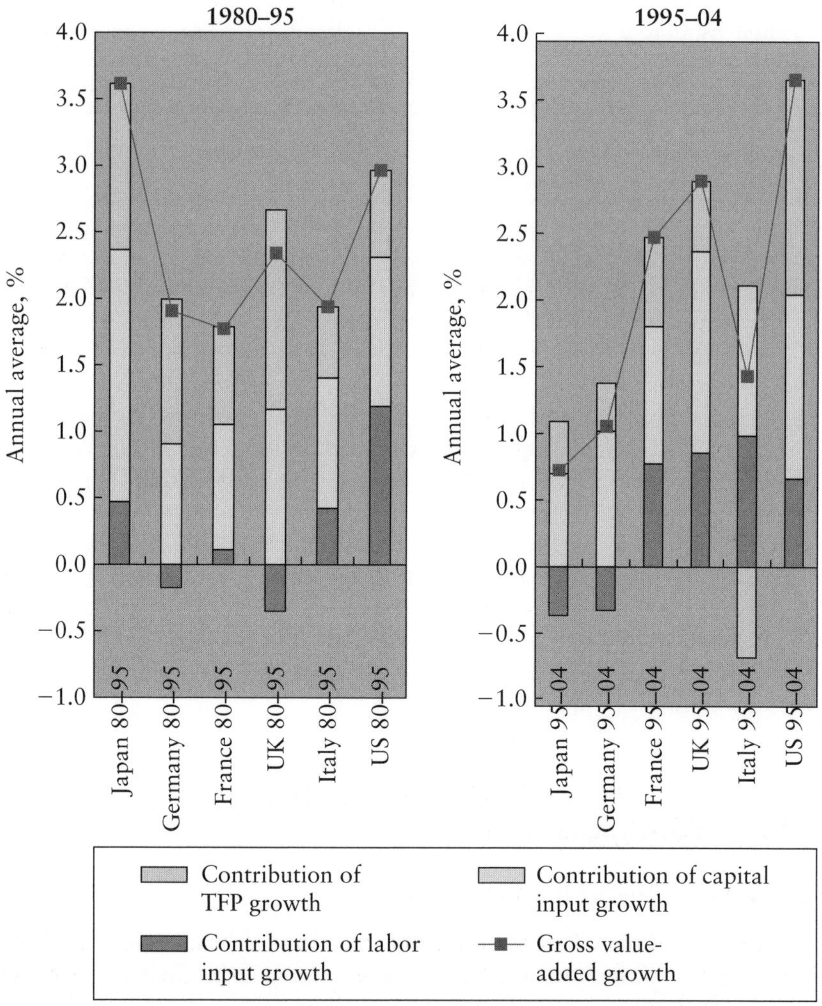

Figure 5.2 Development of contributing factors to major countries' potential growth rate

Source: Fukao and Miyagawa (2007)

Also, there are some similarities between the two cases in that they did not well prepare the institutional setting against systemic risk that could cause disastrous damage to the macroeconomy because of benign conditions that continued for too long before the bubble burst. Besides, the US is now feeling deflationary pressure, as did Japan during the 1990s (and also now), indicating an occurrence of a vicious circle, in which a hovering high real interest rate pushes asset prices further down, another sign of further deflation.

However, there are some differences between the US and Japan. For example, the drop in the potential growth rate could be much smaller for the US compared to Japan, where the contribution of labor factors to potential growth rates went down from positive to negative over the period of the bubble bursting. Also, up to the bubble's burst in Japan, real estate asset prices and stock prices were very hard to explain, for example, by the discounted cash flow (DCF) method. If compared to Japan at that time, real estate prices in the US (in particular, commercial mortgage) can be more easily explained from the DCF perspective, so they have less the flavor of a financial bubble, despite some regional variations.

For example, if you look at the development of price/earnings ratio of real estate in Japanese major cities (the inverse of the cap rate (risk-free interest rate + risk premium – expected rate of increase in rent)), it was more than 40 times in 1991 or only less than 2 percent cap rate. This then went down to 15 times up through the middle of the 2000s (6–7 percent cap rate) and hovered around this level later (see figure 5.3). Meanwhile, in the US, the average cap rate was a little more than 7 percent in New York in 2005, a level that was actually higher than the level of other countries' major cities (see figure 5.4). The cap rate then slightly went down in the US but still hovered around 6 percent in 2007.

If you look at the residential mortgage situation, which is often said to be more serious in the US now than in Japan at that time, many indicators actually support this argument. For example, the ratio of household debt to GDP is much higher for the US now than for Japan at that time (see figure 5.5). However, if you look at the ratio of debt service to household disposable income, this ratio increased very rapidly from the beginning of the 1990s but still stopped at a little less than 15 percent (see figure 5.6). This seems to be a similar level to that of Japan in 2004 (see figure 5.7). So there are surely a lot of financial bubble elements in the prices of residential mortgages in the US, but, at the same time, as Dynan and Kohen (2007) showed, demographic factors might also have worked in a positive way on their prices. These factors may need to be discounted from the degree of the bubble if compared to the Japanese case.

This implies that the quality of the macro-shock to the financial system in the US might be different from that of Japan during the 1990s. According

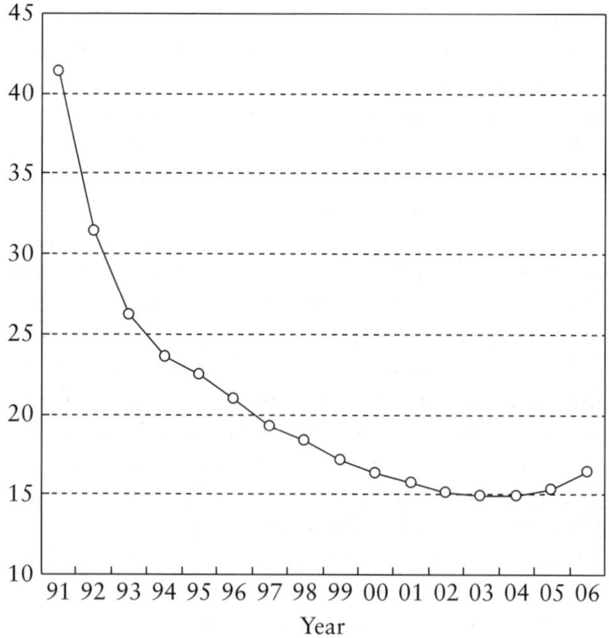

Figure 5.3 Development of price/earnings ratio in major cities of Japan

Source: Mizuho Research Institute (2006)

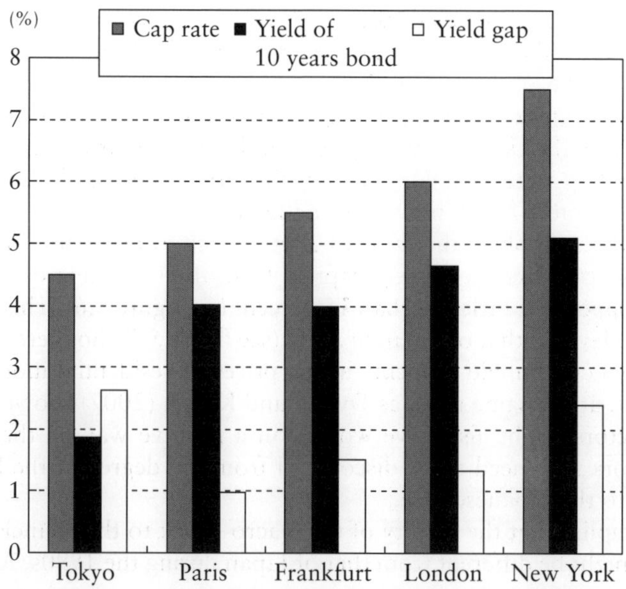

Figure 5.4 Yield gap of major cities of Western countries

Source: Mizuho Research Institute (2006)

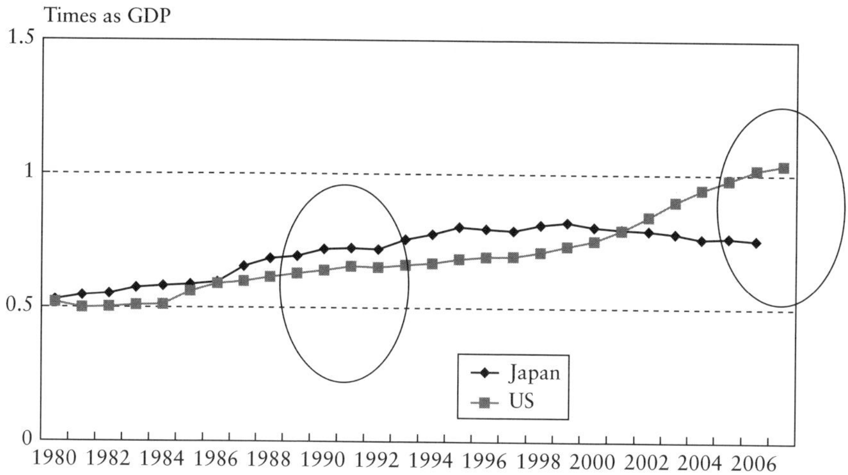

Figure 5.5 Comparison of household debt between Japan and the US
Source: Haji and Shinohara (2008) based on material from the Cabinet Office, the US Commerce Department, FRB

to the types of shocks discussed in this chapter, the strongest feature of the shock in Japan during the 1990s was 1) a shock that was much larger than expected by the authorities, and this was followed by; 2) the authorities' failure to capture it; and 3) a difference of recognition between the authorities and the market. Meanwhile, in the case of the US, points 1 and 3 are very substantial, and they are followed by point 2. (Of course, point 2 could not be dismissed even in the US because some financial institutions such as investment banks, insurance, and non-banks that were weakly monitored by the regulatory agencies suffered huge damages.)

In other words, while late recognition of the rapid deterioration of economic fundamentals aggravated the problem in Japan during the 1990s, market overreaction, as well as more rapid deterioration of fundamentals than expected, seemed to play an important role in the US. This is partly because the losses of Japanese banks at that time were mainly recorded on an accrual basis (and neither were sufficient impaired losses recorded either), while a large part of losses of the US financial institutions occurred because fair value accounting was applied to trading book transactions and AFS transactions. And the divergence between market values and fundamental values were actually pointed out by the OECD (2008) and BOE (2008a).

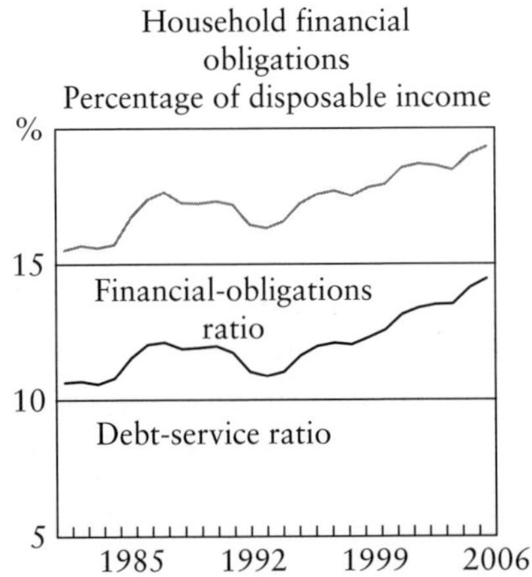

Figure 5.6 Ratio of debt service against disposal income of the US household

Source: Dynan and Kohn (2007) based on material from the Board of Governors of the Federal Reserve System, FOF, SCF

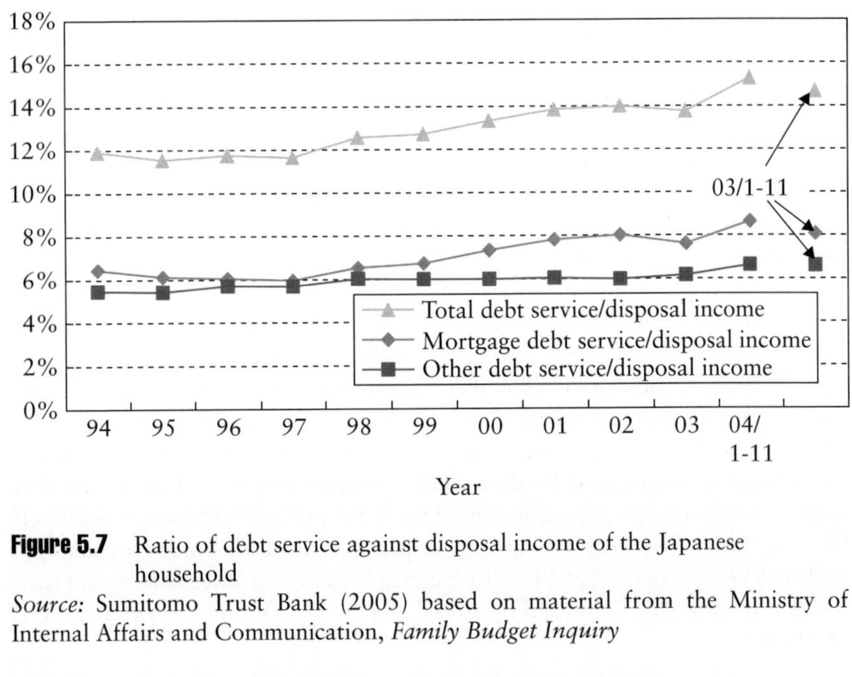

Figure 5.7 Ratio of debt service against disposal income of the Japanese household

Source: Sumitomo Trust Bank (2005) based on material from the Ministry of Internal Affairs and Communication, *Family Budget Inquiry*

This way, the events that are occurring in the US now can be said to contain elements of the Asian crisis in 1997 (or pound sterling crisis in the UK in 1992) as well as the Japanese banking crisis. In other words, they were commonly intensified by market attacks capitalizing on the disequilibrium of fundamentals in certain countries. And these investors expanded their attacks from one to another country that seemed to be implied by the original one, capitalizing on uncertainties in the market. In the case of the Asian crisis, the first attacked country was Indonesia, followed by Thailand, and even by Korea at the end. This picture looks very similar to the current financial crisis, in which a crisis for non-banks that were deeply involved in subprime loans was followed by a crisis for monoline insurers and GSEs that were once seen to be implicitly protected by the government, and then by the top investment banks, including Goldman Sachs and Morgan Stanley, and finally by the largest insurance company in the world and some large US and European banks.

As we saw in the Asian crisis, in an environment in which market evaluations were formed independently of fundamental values, the quality of balance sheets of financial institutions from the short-term point of view could change in any direction. Once we lose the implicit anchor of the market (for example, the ratings assigned by rating agencies, DCF values of loans based on risk parameters including probability of default), it is quite difficult to find any market participants brave enough to provide prices without introducing other new anchors.

So it is inevitable that a new anchor must be established to bring stability to the market from the long-term point of view. However, if it takes too long, the market may collapse first. From the short-term point of view, we have no option but to expect parties that have strong confidence in the fundamental values of the market (i.e. large financial institutions and the authorities) to protect themselves by using more funds to influence market prices than speculators do, or to regulate market prices directly to contain investor speculation. Whether these actions would end in success depends on the rationality of these parties' confidence in fundamental values, and also the amount of funds for market intervention and the power of regulation.

In the case of the Japanese banking crisis, the rationality of the judgments of authorities (i.e. rationality of the so-called "convoy system") was questioned. Meanwhile, in the case of Asian crisis, many economies saw rapid recovery once the crisis ended from 1999–2000, testifying to the lack of funds and regulation to protect them, not a lack of rationality. And now the US, which has already entered the process of dealing with the O&D model and establishing a new reasonable anchor, can be seen to lack the funds and regulation (or a flexible manner for using them) to protect itself from market attacks at least up to the end of 2008.

The Authorities' Preparation for the Crisis

So when a financial crisis like the current one occurs, how should the authorities and financial institutions react in the short term? So long as the financial instability leads to huge *accounting* capital losses or a huge increase in risk amounts, the authority might be required to finance some of the financial institutions' accounting losses and consequent loss of capital or transfer the risks by budget. This phenomenon has been repeated in history. I emphasize the term "accounting" because the market value from the short-term perspective (or fair value) could depart from fundamental values based on estimated risk/return variables.

In this case, if financial institutions suffered huge losses because of "force majeure" causes or those that the authorities completely overlooked, the authorities should help the concerned banks (which had permanently prepared a kind of buffer for systemic risk, as discussed later) by injecting public funds into them. In this case, the capital (or losses) to be financed should be based on the losses caused by the difference between fundamental values and market values. This idea is consistent with the principle that the authority should protect the anchor (or fundamental values) for the financial system. Also, this would be returned to the authorities as profits once the authority succeeded in stabilizing the financial system. As shown before, in Japan this part was actually returned later to the authorities as profits.

Indeed, very similar reactions on the part of the authorities had been seen in many financial crises in the past (IMF 2008b). However, many of them were passive (pushed by the crises) rather than active reactions. The problem is that the framework for these reactions tended to be ad hoc, and were often twisted by political battles. They often began effective policies only after the crises had intensified. The best example for this is the Japanese banking crisis, but the current US case has also shown that the Japanese case is not the only exception.

The big question is why the authorities would not prepare any budget buffers for crises while they ask banks to prepare capital buffers themselves. Do they have to pretend that all the losses, including ones caused by systemic risks, should be absorbed only by financial institutions to avoid moral hazard, or believe that they could introduce some budgetary measures very quickly once the crisis occurs? Unfortunately, history shows that the former only intensifies the uncertainties and consequent losses, and the latter is simply not the case. So the authorities should prepare a sufficient budget to mitigate stress events in the financial system, and thereby stabilize the macroeconomy permanently. As the history of financial crises showed, the size of this budget treatment could be about 10–20 percent of GDP. To contain the uncertainties of the financial system, the authorities should secure a budget sizable enough to reassure the public, regardless whether they will actually ever use it.

Indeed, this is a lesson that we had already learned from the Asian crisis. In other words, Asian countries not only improved their financial system as a result of this crisis, but also significantly increased their foreign currency reserves (see figure 5.8). Even if they improve their financial system, they understand that they cannot manage investor herding behavior in a very uncertain market environment. To prepare for this case, the Asian crisis showed us the need for keeping a certain buffer.

It should be noted that there were no serious concerns of a recurrence of an Asian crisis in the midst of volatile currency movements triggered by the current financial crisis, even though some tensions were observed in Korea. This reminded us of the importance of a buffer to stabilize the financial system.

The other measure that could be taken by the authorities in a financial crisis is to buy specified assets from banks. This is the measure that was actually taken in many cases, including the US in the S&L crisis and Japan

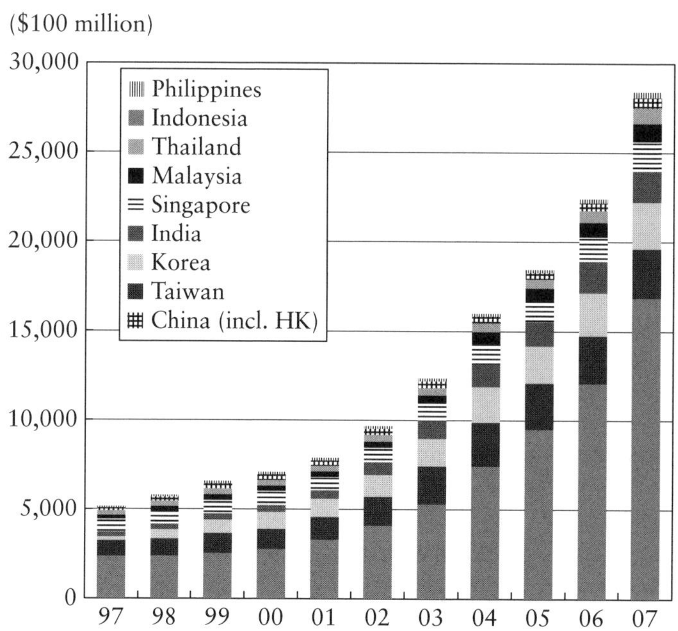

Figure 5.8 Development of Asian countries' foreign currency reserves

Source: Fidelity (2008) based on material from the ADB

in its banking crisis. Also in the current crisis, US authorities were supposed to buy nonperforming assets such as mortgage lending and securitized products from banks when the Emergency Economic Stabilization Act was enacted. (Later, however, because the authorities decided to make injecting public capital into financial institutions a priority, the US authorities instead started to secure future losses arising from the nonperforming assets that were separated from other assets). Also in Japan during the banking crisis, the organization that was established by the banks and government bought nonperforming loan assets from banks, and the BoJ bought bank holding stocks.

These measures could have a different feature from the injection of public funds into banks. From the banks' point of view, the injection of public funds is to finance the shortage of capital (or the losses that have already occurred), increasing banks' robustness to manage risk. Meanwhile, buying specified assets is done to transfer the risk from financial institutions to the authorities. Both measures are helpful for improving the bank capital adequacy ratios, but the former is a contribution to the numerator while the latter is a contribution to the denominator of the ratio. Also, if the size of the budget is the same, the contribution to the numerator (injection of public funds) could improve the capital adequacy ratio significantly more than the case of contributing to the denominator (buying specified assets from the banks).

Meanwhile, from the authorities' point of view, a capital injection takes on the risk of the firm as a whole, while buying assets takes on the risk of the specified assets. The difficulty in the former is the process of deciding which firms are qualified for capital injection. Also, the former requires involvement in financial institutions' management, which is a big burden on the authorities. On the other hand, the latter could have less problem of impartiality because the deals are supposed to be done by public offer. Besides, buying specified assets could transfer their risks from banks to the authorities without causing a fire sale of these assets in the market, contributing to the stabilization of the financial system through the stabilization of the specified market. The authorities can also benefit from their limited involvement in market activities compared to the capital injection.

As mentioned, however, the possible biases arising from the purchase of assets could be bigger depending on the purchase prices that are expected to protect the anchor of the financial system. Above all, so long as major market players including large financial institutions are robust enough, they should be responsible for managing the market. This logic indicates that this option (asset purchase) itself might implicitly assume that another option (capital injection) has already been taken for major banks that could not perform as major players in the market.

History indicates that it is very hard to get the arguments for using taxpayer money for securing the financial system accepted politically, regardless how logical they may be. The typical question posed by the general public and politicians is, "Why do we have to use our taxpayer money to cover losses caused by greedy bankers?" And the typical authorities' answer is "If we do not use it now, we will see further losses to be covered down the road." The answer might be right, but it is also understandable that the public could not put a lot confidence in such authorities' statements, so long as they view the authorities as a kind of accomplice to the banks. To be ready for this situation, we have to establish a contingency framework in ordinary times, not in extraordinary times.

Finally, I would like to make a comment on the Japanese authorities' reactions to the current crisis, including the framework for injecting public funds into banks (mainly targeted at regional banks), and the measures announced by the FSA on November 7, 2008, "Partial Relaxation of the Regulation of Banks' Capital Adequacy Ratio" and "Measure for Relaxing the Conditions for Loans to SMEs."

First, on the framework of capital injection, it should be highly valued that Japanese authorities introduced this framework with sizable budgets in a pre-emptive way before actually seeing the banking crisis. Meanwhile, there remain some questions on this framework. The first concern is that this framework is supposed to deal mainly with regional banks, which are less important from a systemic risk point of view. The second concern is that the minimum capital adequacy ratio is set at only 4 percent for regional banks in Japan, against 8 percent for other banks in the world. If the main purpose of capital injection is to prevent the materialization of systemic risk, we should not resort to this so long as this concern is not so big. Easy use of this last resort could cause not only a moral hazard, but also the loss of budget discipline.

In this sense, we should set a higher capital adequacy ratio and more advanced risk management for financial institutions that are qualified for capital injection by the systemic risk criteria. The idea is that these banks that are too big to fail should pay the corresponding costs for their qualification. This suggests that these banks might be required to have a capital adequacy ratio of higher than 8 percent, and implement IRB and AMA under Basel II. If the authorities inject capital into banks that do not reach this stage at all, this could cause a serious moral hazard. Similar problems seem to exist concerning "Partial Relaxation of the Regulation of Banks' Capital Adequacy Ratio" (see table 5.3) and "Measure for Relaxing the Conditions for Loans to SMEs" (see table 5.4).

This change in the definition of loan reorganization led to a change in definition of the "need special attention" grade of loans, consequently changing

Table 5.3 Overview of "Partial Relaxation of the Regulation of Banks' Capital Adequacy Ratios"

		Before	**After the revision**
Domestic criteria	Governmental bonds	Latent profits: not reflected in capital	Latent profits: no change
	Equity, corporate bonds	Latent losses: 60% is excluded from Tier 1 capital	Latent losses: not reflected in capital
International criteria	Governmental bonds	Latent profits: 45% is added to Tier 2 capital Latent losses: 60% is excluded from Tier 1 capital	Latent profits: not reflected in capital Latent losses: not reflected in capital
	Equity, corporate bonds		No change

Source: Japanese FSA (2008a)

Table 5.4 Overview of "Measure for Relaxing the Conditions for Loans to SMEs"

	Revision of supervision guideline/financial inspection manual
Before	Some loan reorganizations with certain conditions can be seen as highly likely to be serviced and consequently not classified under "need special attention" (the default status under Basel II). One of the conditions is that business turnaround will be completed, so the concerned loans will be upgraded to "normal" grade within about three years.
After the revision	The three years can be lengthened depending on the size of firms. More concretely speaking, the financial inspection manual relaxed this thee-year condition to five years as far as SMEs are concerned.

Source: Japanese FSA (2008b)

the default definition for the banks that implemented Basel II. Besides, the problem is that this proposal was not a temporary measure, but was permanent. If the authorities introduce this measure permanently, they should show some evidence to demonstrate that the criteria used so far were wrong.

Unfortunately, there is a political movement to capitalize on this crisis, jeopardizing the robust framework that was established in the process of managing the Japanese banking system. The phenomena that occurred since the summer of 2008 were indeed extraordinary, and it is surely the case that special measures have to be taken against the special environments. Also, capital injections into regional banks can be seen as a part of business stimulus policy as well as of prudential policy. Even in this case, however, the introduction of those measures to treat some institutions favorably permanently, instead of temporarily, without having enough discussion in the name of a crisis could surely damage competitiveness and the credibility of the Japanese financial system. Moreover, to avoid the introduction of ad hoc measures biased by political influences, we need a credit-cycle smoothing, macroprudential policy, which will be discussed later in this chapter.

The Individual Institutions' Crisis Preparation

I have already argued that financial institutions should manage their risk based on agreed upon degrees of stress with the authorities. The implementation of this measure is expected to increase the stability of financial system significantly.

In addition to this measure, if the authorities judge that some losses even beyond the agreed stress level should be shared by financial institutions because of budget constraints, large financial institutions could set up a collective loss-sharing system. For example, the Cooperative Credit Purchasing Co. was established by banks in Japan in the midst of the so-called Jusen crisis (1993), and participating banks collectively shared the losses of purchased assets on an ex-post basis. (This scheme in Japan, however, did not necessarily succeed in promoting the disposal of nonperforming loans because of banks' reluctance to materialize losses by transferring the assets to this organization and also because of some strong resistance from the obligors to which the assets were being transferred.)

The scheme proposed here is to make financial institutions prepare a certain level of capital (e.g. one percentage point of capital adequacy ratio) even against the materialization of systemic risk, which is beyond the control of individual institutions, and then use this amount alongside public funds. Taking these measures could motivate financial institutions to bring more discipline into their behavior. This is because if a few financial institutions relaxed lending conditions too much, then all participants could also be damaged by having to pay capital for the organization. In other words, these policies try to internalize external diseconomies or macro-shocks that are beyond the control of financial institutions. (There are some commonalities between Kashap, Rajan, and Stein (2008), as explained earlier in this chapter, and this policy.)

According to the IIF report published in August 2008, a new organization called the Market Monitoring Group (MMG) is expected to be established, which will play a role in confirming whether excessive relaxation of lending conditions of the industry as a whole is occurring, and whether banks have dismissed macro-type risks too easily. If we can establish the abovementioned collective loss-sharing scheme against stress events, the MMG should have a monitoring function to ensure that the scheme is effectively functioning. Otherwise, it may be difficult to suppose that this scheme would work as expected without having a penalty for free riders. No financial institutions will pay voluntarily for a free lunch (external economies).

Finally, the compensation system for senior managers of financial institutions should also be changed on their own initiative. In the case of financial businesses, it often takes quite a long time to see the deficiencies of services or products after they are offered. This was the case of Japanese banks' nonperforming loan problem, and also the case for the current problems of subprime loans and securitization products in the US (although the speed in the US seemed to be much faster than in Japan). This feature increased the size of the crisis, and at once caused a cycle of credit risk. In the current crisis, public criticism concentrated on the senior managers of Wall Street's top financial institutions in the US because they pushed the sale of defective products during the bubble period, earning excessive salaries. In the crisis, they might have been fired, but paid no penalties, even though they caused huge losses to their respective organizations. According to the media, it was actually this type of negative public feeling against them that delayed the political agreement on the Emergency Economic Stabilization Act in the US. As shown by the IIF report, this problem was well recognized by financial institutions themselves. The current big question is how we can change the compensation system from the current type that stimulates bubbles to one that contains bubbles.

An idea is to request senior managers to repay a part of their received compensation to partly pay for the public capital that is injected to cover capital shortages. In the following, I will show my concrete idea, which requests all the board members of financial institutions to sell the following put option to the authorities.

Overview of the put option:

- *Underlying asset:* The difference between the banks' actual holding capital and the minimum required capital under the regulations (its negative value equals the size of public capital injection) multiplied by the ratio of the concerned board member's compensation during the past five years to those of all board members.
- *Execution price:* The value of underlying assets = zero (specifically, the timing of needed public capital injections to keep the certain level of capital adequacy ratio). If the capital is not injected, however, this option is, of course, not executed.

- *Cap:* All the compensation received by the certain board members during the past five years minus certain minimum living expense amounts.
- *Term:* Five years.

This scheme requires all board members during the past five years of financial institutions in trouble to pay back some of their received compensation (capped by living costs) during this period to cover their financial institution's losses. The price of this put option should be calculated based on the expected default rate of the concerned financial institution, which is consistent with its economic capital assumptions. This condition makes the premium of put option minimal under normal conditions because it is very unlikely that financial institutions will claim a high probability of their own default to the authorities (even if some did, then the authorities would take corrective measures to improve their capital).

There may be various questions about this proposal, for example, whether the period of five years is long enough, or how we should decide living costs. At any rate, forcing every financial institution to sell this type of put option to the authorities could, from the viewpoint of the incentive mechanism, contain elements of bubble creation. Another important aspect of this policy is to soothe public nerves when discussing a public capital injection.

There may also be the view that the payment of a large part of compensation for senior managers in the form of stock options without allowing its execution for a certain period, which will be terminated once the banks receive public funds, could have similar effects to this proposal in a more feasible way. So long as the compensation is associated with stock prices, however, this mechanism could also stimulate bubble creation and therefore, unless the option execution period is set very long, it might be a little difficult to discourage senior managers from a bubble-favoring mentality.

THE SCOPE OF INDUSTRIES TO BE COVERED BY PRUDENTIAL REGULATION

We have already discussed the issue of the consensus to be formed between the authorities and financial institutions on loss sharing under a stress situation. We also need another agreement on sharing responsibility between the public and private sectors. This is the issue concerning the scope of the industries to be covered by prudential regulation, or whether non-banks should come under current bank regulation.

In the current financial crisis in the US, we observed intensified criticism over the authorities' loose supervision of various non-banks, ranging from non-banks originating mortgage loans to insurance companies and investment banks. Previously, we acknowledged that banks have externalities or that there can be materialization of systemic risks, and do not have enough incentive to deal with them by themselves. Consequently, the authorities share some risks through the deposit insurance scheme, which then requires measures to contain the moral hazard of insurance buyers, that is, authority supervision and monitoring of risk held by financial institutions.

In the case of the US, the industries that have mainly been supervised by agencies with enough capability, such as the FRB and OCC, are limited to the banking industry. Of course, insurance companies are supervised by state regulators, and investment banks are mainly supervised by the SEC. Still, state regulators do not have enough capability to assess the risks associated with complex financial products in the global markets. Similarly, the SEC does not have enough capability, and focuses only on compliance checking, rather than SREP-type exercises.

Now the question is how broadly we should expand the scope of bank-level prudential regulation. The fact is that integrated supervision by one agency covering a wide variety of financial industries has long been the global trend. Also, in Japan, the Japanese FSA has the power to supervise securities houses and insurance companies in addition to banks. Meanwhile, the US was far behind this global trend. Therefore, this issue can be seen as an issue of the global risk monitoring system, which has long allowed the US to keep a very special archaic system.

Even if one supervisory agency covers every financial industry, however, the level of supervision could be very different depending on the type of industry. For example, in Japan, the Basel II-type regulatory framework has been applied only to the banking industry, and not yet to securities houses or insurance firms. The arguments in this book so far have tended to be limited to the banking industry, but that does not necessarily mean that we do not have to consider how to deal with systemic risks caused by investment banks (securities houses) and insurance companies.

In Japan, we already experienced the failures of large securities houses and life insurance companies during the 1990s, as well as large banks. They were sensational enough to be compared with Lehman Brothers or AIG, but the Japanese authorities never crossed the Rubicon at that time. In other words, while many securities houses (e.g. Yamaichi Securities and Sanyo Securities) and insurance companies (e.g. Chiyoda Life Insurance and Toho Life Insurance) failed during the Japanese banking crisis, in no case did the authorities bail them out. This indicates that the authorities at that time maintained the notion that the impacts of failures were fundamentally different between banks and others. Meanwhile in the US, in addition to AIG, the wave of bailouts also reached investment banks. The authorities might judge that 1) from the global point of view, the impact of their failure could be too big, and 2) their difficulties are mainly caused by liquidity problems with keeping high positive net values, and consequently not solvency problems. This criterion itself, however, is not applied in a uniform way to every institution. For example, Bear Stearns and AIG were rescued, and Lehman Brothers and Merrill Lynch (being merged with BOA) were not.

So the authorities' judgments might vary, but the current crisis shows that we might need a new set of criteria regarding the "degree of business globalization" and the "degree of involvement in derivative transactions," in addition to the traditional one of a "run on the bank," when considering the size of systemic risk impact. In addition, the US authorities might also consider the increase of concerns about moral hazard or market sentiment.

It should be noted that a positive step was already taken by the US authorities to change the supervisory agencies for investment banks such as Goldman Sachs and Morgan Stanley from the loose SEC to the strict FRB. In the future, supervision for insurance companies might also be transferred from loose state regulators to a strict federal regulator.

Now, we will discuss the case of other countries. In Europe, there has been no strict boundary between commercial banks, investment banks and insurance companies, so there should be no serious problems arising from the separation of supervisory agencies. Meanwhile, in Japan, commercial banks and securities houses are still regulated to be separated. There are also a few cases where the same financial groups have banking and insurance entities.

In this financial crisis, even though the size of losses was significantly smaller than those of European and US peers, some Japanese securities houses suffered relatively big losses. For example, total subprime loan-related realized losses of Japanese banks at the end of FY2007 were ¥1,453 billion (¥2,433 billion including latent losses), and ¥1,762 billion (¥2,433 billion including latent losses) at the end of the first half of FY2008. This number includes the losses of securities houses belonging to mega bank groups, and Mizuho Securities alone in the Mizuho group accounts for ¥413 billion at the end of FY2007, or a third of total losses. Also, the losses of the Nomura group, which was not included in these numbers, reached ¥258 billion, so the sum of losses of only two securities houses (¥671 billion) reached about 70 percent of total losses for banks (excluding the Mizuho Securities number).

Also, in this financial crisis, the only financial institution to collapse in Japan was a life insurance company. This might imply that the Japanese authorities would also need to introduce systemic risk criteria of a "degree of business globalization" and a "degree of involvement in derivative transactions," and consequently bail out even securities houses or insurance companies in the future. If this is the case, the authorities should better encourage these institutions to advance their risk management further.

ESTABLISHING THE INFRASTRUCTURE FOR FINANCIAL TRANSACTIONS (ACCOUNTING AND DISCLOSURE)

Securitization is often cited as one of the factors behind the current financial crisis. The importance of securitization transactions for financial institutions is closely related to how broadly banks should expand the range of counterparties for trading risks in the market. The basic function of securitization is to convert bilateral trading of risks in the form of lending to trading with parties that are not directly involved in the risk origination process. In this process, the associated risks are converted to various different types of risks that are easily assumed by other market participants.

One complicated issue in this process is that this risk conversion process may often be too complicated to be understood by outside third parties, so the risk sellers could have an incentive to cheat buyers (or have loose discipline to comply with the conditions). Besides, if the risks are widely traded in the market, the prices formed in the market would become the basis for valuation of these risks. Even if these prices widely deviate from the prices used in the bilateral trades, they become the basis of accounting, and might sometimes entail bankruptcy of the entities that hold the assets.

Regarding this information asymmetry, a similar problem can also be found in manufacturing industry. A big difference between the manufacturing and financial industries, however, is that consumers tend to find out much earlier about the defects of products in the case of manufacturing than the case of finance. This is because the products (or services) dealt with by the financial industry usually have a longer lifespan, which means it requires longer to reveal their defects. This feature of the financial industry actually caused the financial bubble and the credit cycle of the macroeconomy.

Indeed, the current crisis poses the question what is the right degree of loan securitization to balance its merits and demerits, which were significantly changed as a result of the crisis. We are now required to consider the measures to be taken to change again the right degree of securitization in its favor. This is currently quite hard to estimate in an environment in which the resecuritization market has simply evaporated and trade volume, even in the ordinary securitization market, is very thin. However, we have already seen, for example, that rating agencies have clarified the basis for ratings, increasing their quality. Also, a trend of increasing disclosure information on securitization transactions was gradually established. So the environment surrounding securitization transactions has now started to move in the right direction, although it will take a long time for market participants to regain confidence.

Are there any other measures that can push securitization further in this direction? For example, can any measures expand the scope of securitization in financial transactions, that is, expand the tradability of risk, improving the efficiency of the macroeconomy? An answer could be the establishment of a market infrastructure that increases information quality, thereby expanding risk tradability. More specifically, the following three measures can be taken for this purpose: 1) the establishment of a framework to motivate third parties (mainly rating agencies) to increase the quality of their risk assessment continually; 2) clarification of the definition of fair value in the accounting system and the expansion of the level 3 (model price) concept; and 3) increased disclosure of risk information.

Concerning the first measure, the issue is how we should establish such an incentive mechanism to motivate the rating agencies to provide accurate ratings. For example, we might be able to make an index that evaluates the medium-term relative performance of rating agencies, which could influence fee levels for the rating agencies. Also, as in the case of SWIFT, a global settlement organization, over which several countries' authorities conduct joint supervision, it may be possible for several concerned major regulatory authorities to supervise the globally influential rating agencies jointly in some specified areas. In particular, because the risk weight of securitization transactions depends heavily on the judgments of external rating agencies in Basel II, the authorities may have a good reason to justify supervision of them.

The second issue is currently being discussed, but the expansion of the area in which fair value accounting is applied looks to be an inevitable trend from the viewpoint of objectivity of financial conditions of firms, and also of accounting rule-setting bodies that put emphasis on information values for major stakeholders. This trend itself may be moving in the right direction despite events in the current financial crisis. In other words, while there is a tendency in the market to overreact to events from a macroeconomic point of view (a con for fair value accounting), there could also be fraud from a micro-transaction point of view if price setting is left to a few concerned parties (a pro for fair value accounting). There is no need to sacrifice the micro perspective for the macro perspective. The bottom line is that the so-called frequently observed "violence" of the market can be seen as a side-effect of accounting measures to ensure impartiality or fairness of trades under ordinary conditions. This indicates that we should now think of measures to "contain" this side-effect.

There are some overlapping areas between containing violent market movements and maintaining the fairness of market transactions, where we do not have to worry about a possible trade-off between macro and micro issues. This is the issue involved in defining the concept of the level 1, 2, and 3 hierarchy of fair value, which is used in the US. This issue relates to the question of how we should recognize the timing when transformation of market information from the highest common factor of all market participants moves to a biased one by a few market participants with extreme positions (or how whether we can really recognize this timing). Another question is how we should revise the biased information based on the answer to the first question.

These questions actually reveal a fundamental problem of the current accounting system. This is its principle of not considering "forward-looking" information in the judgment of the appropriateness of price. The market naturally forms prices considering the impact of business cycle factors on prices in a forward-looking way. Under the current accounting system, however, it is difficult to keep continuity of prices if normal prices suddenly evaporate in the market. Indeed, it seems to be inevitable to consider forward-looking elements in price formation explicitly, even in the world of accounting.

We have already discussed the third and final issue in chapter 4. The important point is the increase in disclosed information to match the demand of market.

On this issue, for example, it may be an interesting idea to establish a system that clarifies the traceability of risk, as recommended by the report made by a financial market strategy team set up by the financial services minister of the Japanese government in 2007. This could surely increase the trading costs, which then could be reduced by innovations. Establishment of risk traceability can be interpreted as the increase in transparency of risk assessment at each step of securitization. For example, if we can label all the derivative transactions made in the market with a standardized code number that is accompanied with the basic risk profile information, and can access easily all this information on the internet, risk traceability could be significantly improved.

Also, in this case, we do not have to wait for the reactions of the accounting rule-setting bodies regarding derecognition criteria as the regulatory authorities could easily request all financial institutions to perform a strict "look-through" for all transactions under the Basel II Accord based on the traceable data. It becomes clear that, if financial institutions adopt Basel II and are required to look through their assets backing up their securitized papers as a regulatory restriction for them, the off-balance standards would not yield any significant problem, regardless of their accounting standards. Based on this lesson, all the regulatory authorities should request all financial institutions to strictly look through their off-balance standards.

Meanwhile, it is necessary to declare that this type of disclosure would not be required for one-off bilateral transactions between financial business professionals (while the authorities should not allow these transactions to be securitized in the market). This is because these transactions would not be assumed to be tradable. Therefore, accounting value should also be based on fundamental value calculated by the models. The idea is that we should request financial institutions to recognize model and accounting risk associated with liquidity risk in return for the merits of tradability or the increase in liquidity owing to securitization. Conversely, we should not request them to recognize these risks for the transactions that do not enjoy merits of liquidity.

To improve the reliability of the risk profile information discussed, the authorities might be required to check some samples periodically. Also, to facilitate the authorities' conduct of a credit-cycle-smoothing macroprudential policy, it is important to establish a system that enables the authorities to analyze risk scenarios based on information with various angles such as product features, originators, arrangers, geographies, and rating agencies.

At any rate, it is next to impossible that we will see the renaissance of the near-dead securitization market in the near future if we cannot establish a new market infrastructure with the joint efforts of market participants and the authorities, as shown.

INTRODUCTION OF FLEXIBLE AND PROACTIVE MACROPRUDENTIAL POLICY

Concerns about Procyclicality

This financial crisis highlighted the issue of procyclicality caused by Basel II. In other words, financial institutions and some authorities feared that Basel II would further increase the swing of credit cycle. This mechanism is as follows. First, in a crisis, an increase in losses and in estimated risk amounts decreases financial institutions' capital adequacy ratio. Then this decline pressures financial institutions to recover the ratio by raising capital in the market or reducing the size of risk assets. Third, if financial institutions heavily depend on the latter, this would reduce their lending and thus deepen the recession. Risk-sensitive Basel II surely has these types of characteristics. However, it has also already introduced various measures that contain this side-effect (see table 5.5).

There are, however, some limits to the effects of the above measures. For example, if we set the degree of stresses at the level of once every 25 years for assessing the required capital, then required capital might be too high to help the macroeconomy grow in a smooth way through lending. Besides, if we require financial institutions to use very prescriptive scenarios for the stress testing purpose, this would surely discourage them from thinking of measures that would be really helpful to their risk management. Meanwhile, if the authorities react to the crisis only after it comes, they tend to be too late and fall off the cliff without doing anything under political pressure.

Table 5.5 Various measures of Basel II to contain its procyclicality

Pillar 1	Pillar 2
IRB requires financial institutions not to stop at point in time (PIT, or assigning ratings based on the different phase of business cycle of the time) but also to assume the element of through-the-cycle (TTC, or assigning ratings based on the bottom conditions over the business cycle). Loss given default (LGD) estimates should be at the bottom of the cycle (so-called, downturn LGD). Weighted average by probability of default may satisfy the above. Op risk amounts in BIA and TSA are associated with gross profits, so are expected to be anticyclical (although this is not explicitly mentioned in Basel II.) Risk parameters used for IRB (such as probability of default) should be long-term average. Stress testing assuming two consecutive quarters with zero growth rates should be done.	Outcome of stress testing including Pillar 1 should be considered in financial institutions' assessment of capital adequacy. Stress testing assuming some structural changes in macroeconomy is expected to be done by financial institutions.

The Need for a Credit-Cycle-Smoothing Macroprudential Policy

To overcome these problems, there is an idea of introducing the policy measures that would impose uniform regulation on all financial institutions, and that is flexible and proactive enough to react to changes in the credit cycle in a proactive and pre-emptive way while leaving room for financial institutions to improve their own risk management. This is a policy measure that assumes a feature of Pillar 2 (leaving more room for individual institutions' discretion) in terms of horizontal frequency but also assumes a feature of Pillar 1 (imposing uniform restrictions on all institutions) in terms of historical frequency.

More specifically speaking, this should be a policy measure that would affect all institutions evenly to contain bubble factors in a pre-emptive way based on some targeting indicators that represent bubble factors. This should look quite similar to the conduct of monetary policy. Some might wonder whether the purpose of monetary policy already includes containing financial bubbles, and whether this should be enough. However, the current financial crisis was not necessarily judged as a result of the failure of monetary policy alone. In the US, there seems to be quite a few who argue that this is the case. Of course, many experts actually argue that the long-continued easy monetary policy in the era of Chairman Greenspan surely laid the ground for creating the financial bubble. Still, generally speaking, it is well understood that the central bank, which is expected to stabilize the general price level, cannot easily manage asset prices. For example, it is hard for the central bank to tighten monetary policy only because of an increase in asset prices or a decline in risk premiums.

This is exactly the same dilemma that was faced by the BoJ during the bubble era. In other words, the central bank usually has only one policy tool, money-market operations, and even if we provide more policy objectives than policy tools, it is quite hard to attain them.

Policy Targets

We have recently heard many arguments for a so-called credit-cycle-smoothing, macroprudential policy from the authorities' side. However, it is not necessarily clear what kind of cycle the discussed policy is trying to manage. In this context, some authorities have argued for the introduction of "dynamic provisioning," which has already been introduced in Spain as a prototype of a credit-cycle-smoothing, macroprudential policy. In this provisioning system, the level of provision against loans is decided considering the situation at the bottom of the cycle. So when we approach the peak of the cycle, the system requires financial institutions to put aside more provisions for the coming bottom.

This dynamic provisioning, however, has a similar feature to the monetary policy because both polices try to manage the same ordinal business cycle. And the current financial crisis, for example, seems to follow a quite different cycle from the ordinal business cycle represented by, say, real GDP growth rate. Besides, if you look at the macroeconomic situation of Spain, which introduced this system a few years ago, you will soon find that its economy among the major European countries, was the most badly plagued by residential mortgage bubbles after the UK. So looking at the case of Spain, dynamic provisioning does not necessarily seem to be effective in containing bubble factors leading to the current crisis in a pre-emptive way.

This indicates that we should first discuss clearly the type of cycle to be smoothed by the new macroprudential policy. As already discussed in chapter 4, the basic purpose of macroprudential policy is to prevent shocks that menace the stability of the financial system. History indicates that these shocks will not occur as frequently as an ordinal recession. Experts in financial crises often mention a frequency of roughly once every 10 years. In other words, previous crises to the current one are the events from the middle to the end of the 1990s, the Japanese banking crisis, the Asian and

Russian crises, and the turmoil caused by the failure of LTCM. Before these crises was Black Monday during the end of 1980s, and before that was the Latin American debt problem during the end of 1970s and the US S&L crisis at the beginning of 1980s.

Strictly speaking, there were many other shocks, and also the degrees of shocks varied significantly. So they do not necessarily indicate the length of the credit cycle precisely. They, however, surely provided some images (or a kind of common factor) of shocks to be managed by credit-cycle-smoothing, macroprudential policies. They are the creation of a financial bubble and an excessive decline in risk premiums in the asset market, which were often followed by long-continued high profitability of financial institutions and benign macroeconomic conditions. Based on the experiences of the Asian crisis, for example, some Southeast Asian countries and the IMF have been developing early warning indicators that could indicate the signs of a currency crisis. We might adopt a similar approach to shocks that menace the stability of the financial system.

If we seek simplicity, as in the case of the Taylor rule for monetary policy, we have to select a small number of representative indicators. The simpler rule is often expected to lead to a surer attainment of the policy, thanks to the transparency of the policy-deciding process that it entails. For these indicators, for example, we might use the following indicators of risk appetite and credit, market, or liquidity risks, which have long been shown in the GFSR published by the IMF (see figures 5.9, 5.10, and 5.11). It should be noted that these indicators have actually been used by international organizations and the authorities as major indicators of vulnerability of the financial system.

Policy Tools

Because the central bank uses mainly money market operations to set market interest rates at the targeted level, the macroprudential authority needs policy tools to smooth the credit cycle. For this purpose, we might use the scaling factor that is currently used for the calculation of capital adequacy ratio by financial institutions.

Basel II does not use the direct output from the IRB formula for capital calculation. It actually uses the output of the IRB formula multiplied by "1.06." This 1.06 is called a "scaling factor," and was not necessarily set to calculate the risk amounts more precisely. The reason for this scaling factor lies in the authorities' wish to keep continuity of financial institutions' capital amounts between Basel I and II. In other words, when the authorities tentatively calculated the Basel II number for financial institutions, they found that the required capital under Basel II could decrease by

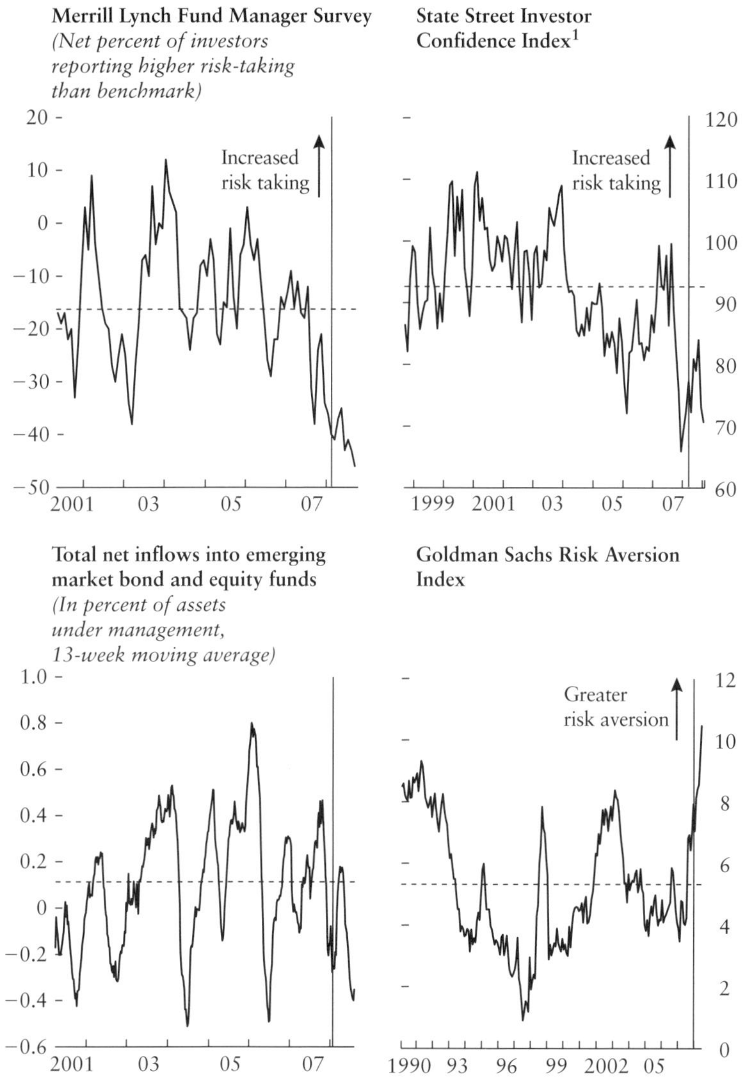

Note: Dashed lines are period averages. Vertical lines represent data as of the April 2008 GFSR.

[1]The estimated changes in relative risk tolerance of institutional investors from Froot and O'Connell (2003) are integrated to a level, scaled, and rebased so that 100 corresponds to the average level of the index in the year 2000.

Figure 5.9 Developments of risk allowance

Source: IMF (2008a) based on source material from Emerging Portfolio Fund Research, Inc. Goldman Sachs, Merrill Lynch, State Street

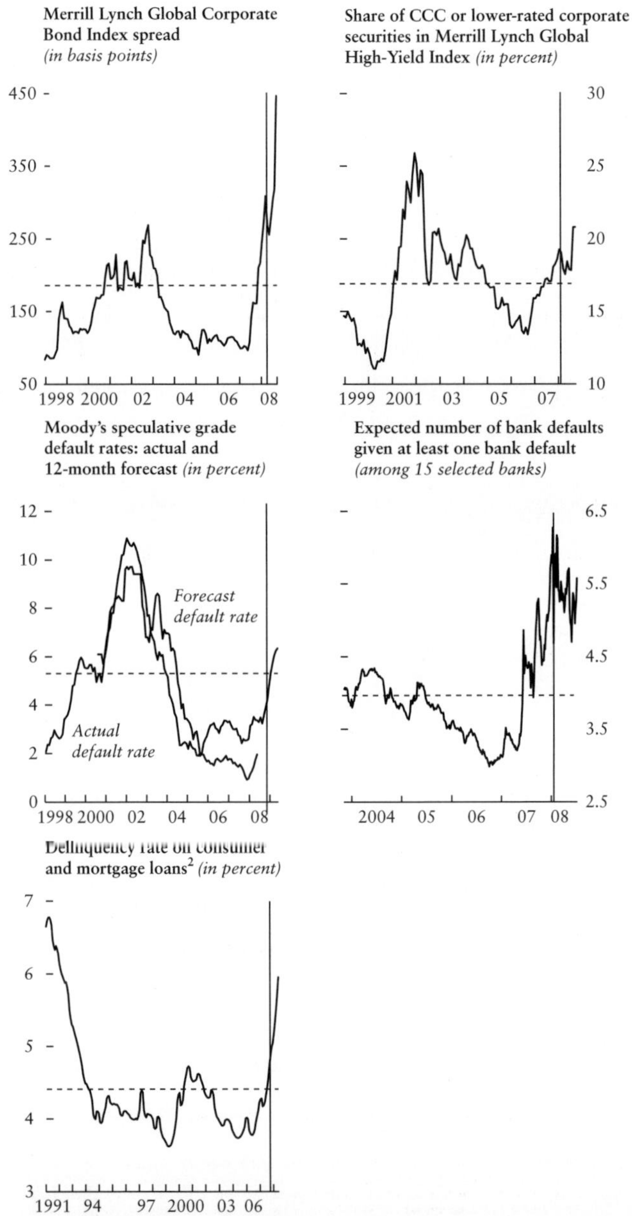

Note: Dashed lines are period averages. Vertical lines represent data as of April 2008 GFSR.

[1]Measuring the largest probability of default among the sampled 15 banks each day.

[2]30-, 60-, and 90-day delinquencies for residential and commercial mortgages, and credit card loans in the United States.

Figure 5.10 Developments of credit risk indicators
Source: IMF(2008a) based on source material from Merrill Lynch, Moodys, Bloomberg, L.P., MBA, Federal Reserve

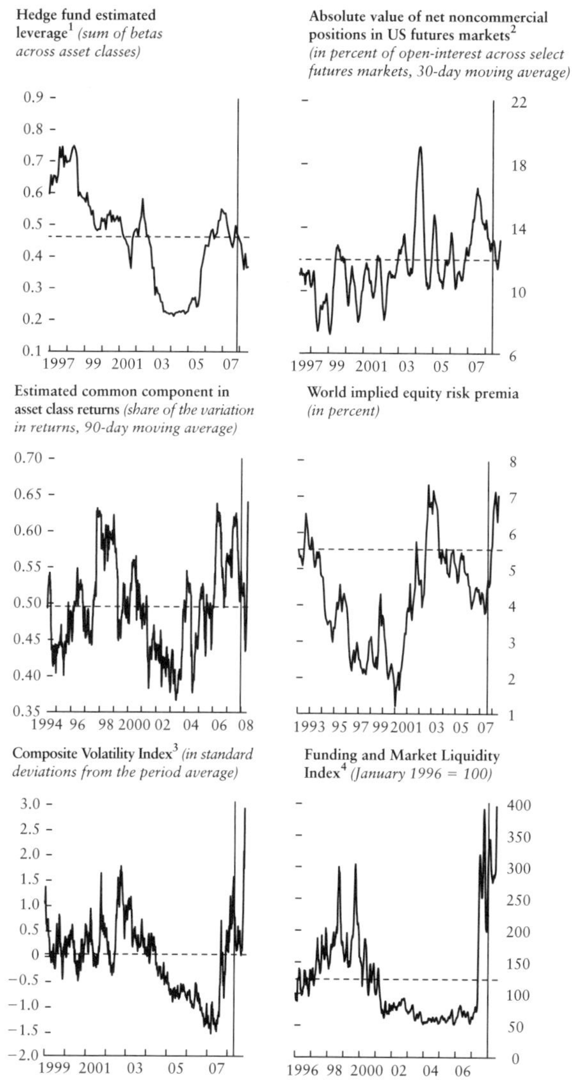

Note: Dashed lines are period averages. Vertical lines represent data as of the April 2008 GFSR.
[1]36-month rolling regressions of hedge fund performance versus real asset returns.
[2]Data represent the absolute value of the net position taken by noncommercial traders in 17 selected U.S. futures markets. High values are indicative of heavy speculative positioning across markets, either net-long or net-short.
[3]Represents an average z-score of the implied volatility derived from options from stock market indices, interest, and exchange rates. A value of 0 indicates the average implied volatility across asset classes is in line with the period average (from 12/31/98 where data are available). Values of +/−1 indicate average implied volatility is one standard deviation above or below the period average.
[4]Based on the spread between yields on government securities and interbank rates, spread between term and overnight interbank rates, currency bid-ask spreads, and daily return-to-volume ratios of equity markets. A higher value indicates tighter market liquidity conditions.

Figure 5.11 Developments of market and liquidity risk indicators

Source: IMF (2008a) based on source material from Credit Swiss, Tremont Index LLC, Bloomberg, L.P., JP Chase Morgan, IBES, Morgan Stanley Capital International

6 percent compared to that under Basel I, on average. Therefore, authorities that feared a sudden decline in capital argued for this measure to be taken. If the authorities were to have strong confidence in the outcome of the Basel II formula, they might not care about the drop. Otherwise, however, authorities' fears of a significant drop in required capital as a result of the change in regulation was understandable. And this concern was more than sufficiently borne out by the current crisis.

So the scaling factor was invented to fill the gap between the numbers calculated by the IRB formula and the expectation of authorities, which have not yet been confident enough in the new formula. And I think we should use this factor as a candidate for the tool of a credit-cycle-smoothing, macroprudential policy (see figure 5.12). The most appealing merit of this tool is its simplicity. What we have to do is increase or decrease this scaling factor from the current 1.06 according to the level of selected reference indicators. Meanwhile, the most serious demerit is that this tool looks too simple for one to be sure whether it is really effective in smoothing the credit cycle.

For example, a large part of the financial losses that occurred in the current crisis were not necessarily well covered by Pillar 1 of Basel II. Given the

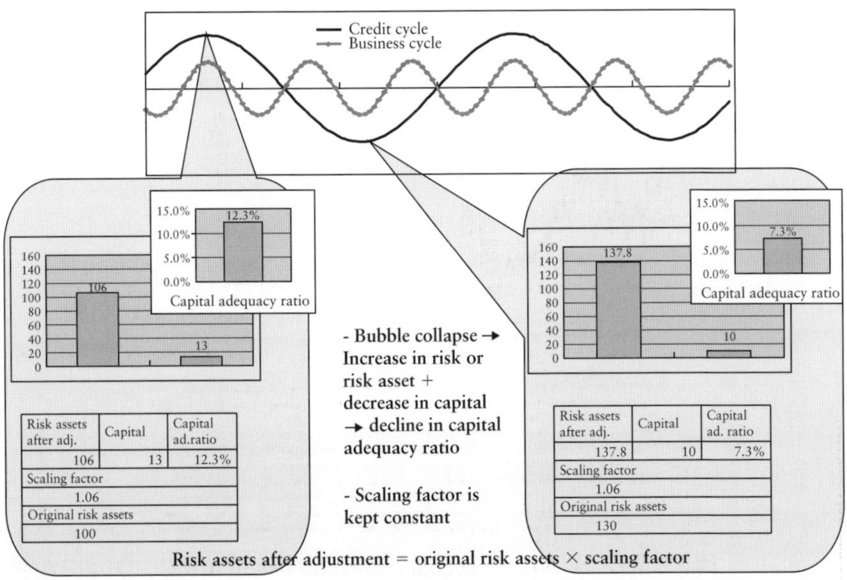

Figure 5.12(a) Macro impacts of capital adequacy ratio—the current situation

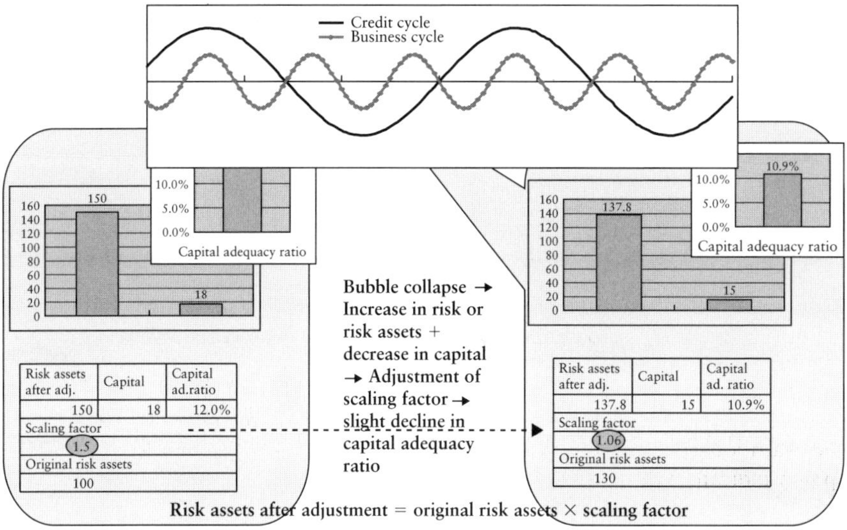

Figure 5.12(b) Macro impacts of capital adequacy ratio—after the introduction of credit-cycle-smoothing, macroprudential policy

financial institutions' diverse positions that are not covered well by Basel II, requesting them to put aside larger capital based on a uniform formula might cause some inefficiency in attaining the policy target. Besides, we might hear the complaints of globally active financial institutions that "the use of different scaling factors among different countries could impede this global-base business," or "business in one country could be better than in another." This type of complaint, however, could be flatly dismissed, because even now in the area of monetary policy, we see different levels of interest rates, about which no one has complained.

The Agency to Conduct the Policy

Finally, I would like to discuss the issue of the agency that would conduct this credit-cycle-smoothing macroprudential policy. This should naturally be the bank regulatory agency, and in Japan, for example, it is the Japanese FSA. In this case, however, these agencies would need to be equipped with more macroeconomic research capability. Because central banks are in general very good at doing this type of research, it may be better that the regulatory agencies seek more cooperation with the central banks in deciding macroprudential policy. Moreover, the regulatory agency that decides macroprudential policy should be politically independent as the central banks are required to be. To implement this policy framework successfully, we need to establish a framework that can facilitate the effective conduct of prudential policy. Table 5.6 compares a credit-cycle-smoothing macroprudential policy with monetary policy in some important aspects.

Table 5.6 Comparison of credit-cycle-smoothing macroprudential policy and monetary policy

	Macroprudential policy	Monetary policy
Policy target	Prevention of a financial system crisis	Price stability (smoothing the business cycle)
Forward-looking policy indicators	Risk premium information as variously observed in markets	Various leading indicators of business conditions (e.g. money supply, yield curve, and industrial production)
Policy tools	Adjustments of the scaling factor that is currently used for the capital adequacy ratio	Money-market operations to set money-market rates at the targeted level
The agency to conduct the policy	Bank regulatory agency with political independence	Central bank

CHAPTER 6

Strategic Reaction to the Financial Crisis: The Japanese and Asian Perspective

FRUSTRATION OF ASIAN COUNTRIES

The Differences Between the Japanese Banking Crisis, the Asian Crises, and the Current Financial Crisis

If you compare the Japanese banking and Asian crises during the 1990s on the one hand and the current financial crisis on the other, you might find another important difference besides the ones already discussed in this book. In the case of former crises, the countries or the region that caused the crises were forced to follow various advice and pressures on stabilization measures coming from other countries, in particular the US, which showed strong concerns about their development into global financial crises. Consequently, these countries could expand their hegemony through expanding their countries' business models.

Meanwhile, we have not seen any such developments in the current crisis. If you look at the accumulated loss amounts of financial institutions by region, you can easily find that most losses were taken by the US and European financial institutions, and only a small portion is accounted for by Japanese and Asian financial institutions (see figure 1.3 in chapter 1). Strangely enough, what we have observed in this crisis is, however, that the country that caused the crisis still tries to advise other countries that have maintained a sound banking system. The logic behind this is that the problem that occurred in the US could occur some time in the future in any other country. But is this really true?

Certainly, the O&D financial model has been developed in the US and some European countries, and recognized as the most advanced not only in these countries but also in others. In this sense, as discussed in this book so far, there are many lessons to be learned from this crisis even for Japanese and Asian banks. At the same time, however, there are also many different aspects of authorities' reactions to financial system stability between Asia and the US and Europe. As also discussed before, Japan and Asian countries have already experienced their own financial crises in recent history, and this made the authorities and banks' attitudes toward risk assessment more conservative than those of their counterparts in the US and Europe.

For example, concerning the risk assets of investment funds under the Basel II, the Japanese authority requests financial institutions in principle to look through all the underlying assets regardless of IRB and standardized approaches, and only if it is impossible to look through them will the Japanese FSA allow financial institutions to use investment guidelines as a base to calculate the required capital. Meanwhile, in Europe, it is possible to choose between risk weights based on external ratings or the look-through method for the standardized approach, and between the look-through method and the simplified method for equity for the IRB approach, indicating that financial institutions do not have to select the look-through method even if it is possible. This treatment is definitely looser than Japan's. Similarly in the US, the hierarchy at the top of the look-through method is not as clear as the case of Japan.

So US and European regulatory reactions to the problem that occurred in the US and European countries could not always be applied to Japan and Asian countries. Also, the macroprudential framework (deposit insurance system) was better prepared in Japan and Asian countries than in the US and Europe thanks to their crisis experience. From these points of view, the US proposal to other countries, published in the middle of September 2008, to follow its initiative of a financial system stabilization policy looked quite arrogant (although it might substantially be proposed on the other side of the Atlantic Ocean).

Reasons Japan and Asian Countries Cannot Place Policy Demands on the US and European Countries

Then why were Japan and Asian countries forced to put up with this situation? Just as the US and European countries requested prudential policies on the part of Asian countries during the 1990s, why didn't Asian countries try to do the same this time? One of the reasons is that Asian countries, particularly Japan, do not have enough information and studies to explain clearly the strengths and features of their own financial system. In most cases, they were only stored in the heads of concerned bureaucrats.

For example, we had various discussions and experimental measures taken in the Japanese banking crisis during the 1990s, but most of the internal information concerning the process of these discussions have simply gone without being summarized or reviewed from the policy assessment point of view. It is a little surprising, but we have not yet seen any formal reviews of Japanese authorities' policy reactions to the banking crisis by the authorities themselves. Indeed, in the midst of the current crisis, there were many inquiries from the US and European countries for Japanese authority reaction to the crisis at that time, but there were only a few official documents that summarized them in Japanese, much less in English. In this environment, it is quite hard to explain the strengths of a Japanese financial system persuasively to outside parties.

Another reason is that we do not prepare well in sending these types of policy messages from Asian countries to the US and Europe. First, Japan faces a serious shortage of staff involved in global policy or the rule-making process. In this area, the Japanese FSA and BoJ cooperated to deal with the increasing number of working groups, say, under the BCBS for Basel II implementation and crisis management, but the number of the staff has not increased in correspondence with the increase in working groups. Even if high-quality staff members were to work 24 hours a day to contribute to the discussions, it would be next to impossible to compete in argument with their US and European peers who wield large staffs. In addition, Japanese staff in general are seriously handicapped by language and a lack of expertise (there are very few Japanese bureaucrats who have stayed in the same working area for more than 10 years, as is common in the US and Europe). So if Japan would like to compete with the US and European countries evenly in this area, Japan actually has to invest more resources in them. Unfortunately, this understanding is not necessarily well shared beyond the international section in each bureaucracy. In this environment, even if the Japanese authorities make the right arguments, it is a little difficult to be heard in international forums.

Also, Japan and Asian countries have not yet availed themselves sufficiently of the potentiality of working with countries in the region nor of the experience of making a consensus of divergent views of different countries in international forums. This might be why Asian countries' views are given only little weight in the process of global rule setting. In this respect, we should learn more from the experiences of European countries.

On the discussion of prudential issues, the European situation was similar to that of Asian countries during the 1980s, and they did not try to coordinate their variant views on this front. Consequently, I remember that the international arguments at that time in this area tended to be strongly influenced by the US, the UK, and sometimes by Japan. Since the 1990s, however, European countries have made progress in market integration and also accordingly have coordinated regulations and implementation, giving them more and more weight in global discussions.

This heavier weight can be attributed to the number of countries (and also the number of staff) that one agency represents, and also their strong arguments and skillful negotiation techniques (including having discussions in English, which was not necessarily easy for some European countries before), gained from their experience in earning a consensus among many different countries. Many European countries do not use English as a mother tongue, so they are not necessarily good at using it for technical discussions. Still, based on the discussion among European countries, they now argue their views strongly in international forums regardless of how well they speak English.

Meanwhile, Japan and East Asian countries (including Southeast Asian countries) have long believed that it is next to impossible to ride tandem in this area because of the significant differences in levels of economic development and also in the forms of social systems. Recently, however, in addition to Asian financial centers such as Hong Kong, Singapore, and Korea, which have already attained a high level of economic development, many ASEAN countries have also succeeded in advancing their industrial and financial infrastructures after the bitter experience of the Asian crisis. Moreover, China is rapidly catching up, and its economy will soon be the biggest in Asia. This region also has Australia and New Zealand, countries that have already established a US- or European-style financial system.

This all shows that current conditions are much better than before for authorities in the region to start discussions in the direction of more regional coordination in the area of financial system stability. Indeed, countries in the region have already discussed bank regulatory issues quite actively in meetings such as the Working Group of Bank Supervision under the Executive Meeting of East Asian and Pacific Central Banks (EMEAP). This meeting could become the mirror image of the BCBS in the Asia–Pacific region. These discussions, however, have not yet reached the stage of standardization of the regional financial system, or the formation of "Asian views" against, say, US or European views.

Lastly, another reason for a relatively poor Japanese and Asian showing in this area lies in the small number of mighty global financial institutions in the region. Authorities' views gain heavier weight once they have their own experiences of supervising such financial institutions. It goes without saying that notable work on the part of the authorities alone would not be enough to increase the region's influence in the process of global rule making; it would have to be accompanied by the global presence of local financial institutions in the region.

SECLUSION OF THE JAPANESE FINANCIAL INDUSTRY FROM THE GLOBAL PICTURE

Japan: A Rare Country that has Few Home–Host Issues

Japanese and Asian frustrations might also originate from the fact that their voices in the global policy decision-making process do not correspond to their economic power, which has rapidly developed. It is particularly true of the financial world because there the frustration is derived not only from their small presence in the global policy making process but also from the small presence of the financial industry itself. Its most representative case is Japan. For example, the share of the financial industry in its economy is smaller than 7 percent, compared to 9.4 percent of the UK and 8 percent of the US. Besides, another remarkable feature of Japan is the seclusion of its financial industry from other parts of the world. Indeed, there are very few Japanese banks that have large subsidiaries in other countries, and also very few foreign banks that have large subsidiaries in Japan.

In the discussion of Basel II, one of the most serious issues is the so-called "home–host" issue. This issue originated from the fact that the regulators' powers cannot easily go beyond their own borders when financial institutions increase their global business. In other words, there is a question of which country's regulator should approve the Basel II advanced approaches for a bank that does extensive businesses in country B but of which the parent bank is located in country A. So long as it is the subsidiary that was established in country B, it is, in principle, the regulator of country B that has the prime responsibility for supervising this entity. However, globally active banks in general have a globally integrated risk management system, which tends to be developed and managed by the parent bank. In this case, this bank might have trouble in explaining the same things to the regulators of country A and B to apply for the approval of AIRB of Basel II. Only two countries might not present major problems, but if this number reaches 100, things could get very difficult.

Besides, there might be the case in which the subsidiary side does not capture well the details of the management system that was developed by the parent side. In this case, the regulator of country B faces the question of whether or not, and to what extent, it could outsource the assessment of the model to the regulator of country A. In Basel II, it is expected that the home country's regulator would play a major role in this approval process to lessen the burdens of financial institutions, but also that some host country regulators are supposed to share some responsibilities if concerned subsidiaries are seen as important from a material point of view (e.g. the size of subsidiary). Some countries, such as eastern European countries, are very sensitive to this issue because their own financial markets are often dominated by subsidiaries of US and western European banks.

Fortunately or unfortunately, there are few serious home–host cases in Japan. It is indeed a rare case in the world. Not only in the US and major European countries, but also in East Asian countries, there are at least one or two very serious home–host issues to be discussed. Regulators in East Asian countries usually have the issue of host countries to supervise subsidiaries of the US and European global financial institutions, but also often have home–host issues among East Asian countries. Meanwhile in Japan, except for new merger cases that occurred in this financial crisis, Japanese banks owning huge subsidiaries in foreign countries is limited to the case of MUFG, which owns UBOC in the US, foreign banks owning huge subsidiaries in Japan is limited to Citibank Japan, which has only recently been established.

Reasons for Seclusion

Why doesn't Japan have serious home–host issues? This is mainly because of its very special financial structure. Up to now, Japan has kept an overbanking situation, in which many banks do cutthroat competition in limited business areas, entailing very low profitability of the banking industry (Shiratori and Oyama 2001). Meanwhile, we have not seen any remarkable shareholder movements to restructure the industry to improve its profitability. Moreover, in an environment where there are still many regulations that strictly limit and at the same time protect the areas of business for banks, the Japanese banking industry tends to be seen by shareholders as another utility industry that has a solid and stable business base protected by regulations. In this environment, there is not a lot of room for foreign banks that would like to create dynamic businesses with high profitability. Some exceptions are a part of investment banking and private banking businesses, a kind of niche business that Japanese banks do not do.

In addition, the very special Japanese macroeconomic conditions over the past 15 years have surely influenced the situation. A continued deflationary situation during this period put the Japanese banking industry under significantly severe profit conditions. Deflation naturally leads the policy interest rate to an extremely low level. In the case of Japan, we had experienced a very long period of a zero interest rate policy. On the other hand, we could not reduce the costs of deposits to zero. Even if banks set the deposit interest rate at zero, there must be the fixed capital to collect deposits and associated costs. So the net profit margin of deposits (market rate minus total costs of deposit) would usually be negative in a deflationary situation.

Commercial banks normally enjoy a relatively stable and wide margin on deposits as a core part of their profits. In Japan, however, this had long been kept negative, providing a good reason for foreign banks not to have a strong interest in establishing an extensive retail network in Japan. The same is true of the lending side, which has long seen a continuous decline in Japan under deflation.

The next natural question may be why major Japanese banks did not depart from such an unprofitable market and expand their business into foreign countries. This is partly because of the after-effects of their failure to expand their businesses actively in foreign countries during the bubble period. Another reason is the shortage of capital that followed the banking crisis. Moreover, the Japanese banks' business model is not unique enough to cultivate new markets in foreign countries. Finally, there might be a sense of security so long as they stuck to the Japanese market, which is still the world's number two, despite the hard deflationary conditions. At any rate, the Japanese financial industry has long been virtually secluded from the other parts of the world, despite no regulation forcing it to be.

FUTURE STRATEGIES OF THE JAPANESE AND ASIAN FINANCIAL INDUSTRIES

The Importance of Risk Management of the Financial Industry from the Strategic Point of View

There might be some arguments that Japan and Asian countries should not necessarily try to take the initiative in the world of finance given that they have already established a respectable presence in the manufacturing industry. I would like to say "no" to this argument. The reason is that the financial industry is often positioned to design the structure of whole industries and household consumption through the services it provides, and in this regard, is close to macro-level policy. If we dominate finance and influence the business practices in this area, we can also influence industry structure and consumer behavior. Besides, there should be no national boundaries that restrict leading business models.

Also, as noted, the presence of globally active financial institutions could facilitate the authorities of their home countries to participate or lead the discussion of global rule making and its actual implementation. In the 1980s, when Japanese financial institutions rapidly expanded their businesses in the world, the world always demanded Japanese involvement in the global rule-making process, although the Japanese side was modest enough to be silent. It was still true even during the 1990s when Japan faced serious banking problems owing to its massive size. And now the time has come to remind the Japanese that this is all in the distant past.

When Japanese and Asian banks are seeking chances to expand their businesses globally, most important is to digest the lessons learned from the current crisis by their own judgment, and consequently establish more advantageous new business models than those of the US and European banks, which are now so busy reacting to short-term crisis management. And in this area, we need close cooperation between financial institutions and the authorities, which are expected to introduce new macroprudential policies and new institutional frameworks.

ASIAN STRATEGY

An effective way to increase the involvement of Japanese and Asian authorities in the global rule-making process is to form a collective Asian view and convey it to international forums. It is no doubt not so easy to extract common views from the various countries in the region, among which the differences are surely much smaller than before, but still much bigger than those among European countries. Moreover, these differences arise not only from the level of development but also from the social and economic structure.

There are, however, also many common features among them. As mentioned, Japan and many East Asian countries have already established financial systems that are fairly robust against the crisis based on their own experiences of the 1990s. Moreover, there are common interests in the region from the strategic point of view. It is a fact that all these countries do not belong to the European or American blocs that have strongly influential powers over the global rule-making process, and unless they build another new regional bloc, they cannot easily send their messages to global rule-making bodies. Japan is the only country that is a member of BCBS, but, as noted, this membership itself does not assure the chance of getting global agreement on its message.

Unfortunately, Asian countries including Japan have a kind of biased preference to discuss with or learn from the US and European countries, instead of countries in their own region. It is important for the region first to remove these biases and then, like European countries, seek common views on various issues of prudential institutional setting and regulations in the region. The deeper this process is, the better the ideas and the better the logic for negotiation can be gained before facing the discussions in Basel. For this purpose, it may be better to start with, for example, discussing the introduction of the aforementioned macroprudential policies, and the establishment of the framework for mutual surveillance. In this context, the movement toward the improvement of the Chiang Mai initiative (the agreement to mutually provide foreign exchange among East Asian countries), and also the increase of assistance for emerging countries through the increase in fund provisions to the IMF in the latter half of 2008 were very encouraging signs of regional cooperation and coordination, which would contribute to the stability of the global system.

Given the close linkage of financial systems across the region, we should also not forget the need to oversee countries in other regions to maintain the global financial stability. For example, the US, the country that caused this financial crisis, happened to be the only major country that has long rejected the IMF's FSAP mission (periodical reviews focusing on member countries' financial system stability). In other words, a country that has long escaped the international surveillance of financial system stability caused this crisis. I would never argue that the FSAP mission for the US could have pre-empted this crisis. However, if Asian countries raised their concerns about the one country that has long not accepted the FSAP mission that has caused this crisis, and then proposed a new scheme (possibly with some capable staff) that focuses more on the multilateral surveillance of countries in trouble at this moment, the global organization might find it difficult to ignore.

Also, once the region established a robust macroprudential framework, it could ask other regions to follow their standards because the weaker standards of other regions would pose a risk to the region. For example, if a region decides to secure a permanent budget of a certain percentage of GDP to deal smoothly with failed institutions, then the region might request other regions to follow this initiative. And if other regions did not follow it, then the region should consider imposing some penalties on financial institutions from other regions, motivating them to improve the stability of their own financial systems. This may be a similar strategy to that taken by European countries, or the IASB in the process of converging accounting systems.

In this environment, the only remaining option for Japan is to take some policy initiative to lead discussions in the region. For this, we need to significantly increase staff and organization for these regional and global discussions. Without these efforts, even neighboring countries would simply ignore this secluded country.

CHAPTER 7

Conclusion: Post-Crisis Risk Management to be Established

In the following, as a summary of all discussions in this book, I will discuss the post-crisis risk management to be established by financial institutions and authorities, and also specific strategies to be developed and the roles to be played by Japanese and Asian financial institutions and authorities to promote this new system in the world in the coming years.

RISK MANAGEMENT OF INDIVIDUAL INSTITUTIONS

To show the advantages of one's own business models capitalizing on the current financial crisis outside, we need to show clearly how financial institutions in the region can react to the weaknesses of risk management that were highlighted by the crisis. Particularly when the US and European financial institutions are busy dealing with one regulatory requirement after another to fix the ongoing crisis, establishing a robust risk management framework focusing on the stress events from a long-term point of view could contribute to the global expansion of the businesses of the region's financial institutions. And for this purpose, in addition to each individual institution's efforts to improve its risk management and establish a new business model based on the new risk management, we also need the assistance of the authorities, which are expected to introduce a financial stability framework based on the lessons learned from the crisis.

We already discussed in detail how individual financial institutions should improve their risk management in chapter 5. The following is a brief summary of this discussion.

- Regardless of conventional risk categories, financial institutions should reclassify loss events and movements of risk factors based on "causes" of risks, and analyze the risk profile based on this classification. This framework also includes liquidity risk, model risk, accounting risk, and reputational risk, which are not explicitly covered by conventional economic capital modeling.

- Financial institutions should pay enough attention to "invisible risks" and have the PDCA cycle embedded in their corporate culture to manage them.
- Regardless of risk category, financial institutions should apply the same basic idea to their risk assessment. And they should pay more attention to the idea of historical frequency as well as horizontal frequency when expressing their own risk appetites and quantifying risks.
- Financial institutions should establish a framework to maintain the objectivity and comprehensiveness of scenarios for quantifying risks based on the historical frequency, and also should clarify that the owners of stress scenarios are senior managers themselves.
- Financial institutions should reset capital to be compared with risk and the degree of stresses (or historical frequency) that are used for risk quantification to be aligned more with a level that could be appealing to senior managers. In the case of the former, for example, this capital could be set at additional capital over the level of the minimum requirements. Also, liquidity risk should be compared with the liquidity buffer and not capital.

This requires financial institutions to change the framework of risk management radically, so it might face tough resistance. It is feasible to introduce the new system gradually, starting from the part related to the ICAAP, jointly using a legacy one for the time being. Also, to increase the incentives of financial institutions to move in this direction, we need a strong push from the side of regulators, an important stakeholder of financial institutions. Having the new risk management framework made jointly by financial institutions and the regulators in advance of the US and European countries could further ensure the active global development of financial institutions in the region.

FINANCIAL INFRASTRUCTURE

Increased risk management surely ensures that financial institutions' businesses strategy can develop into various areas. It is not only individual institution's risk management that controls the risks associated with various businesses. There may also be the risks that could be reduced significantly by improving the infrastructure of the whole financial market. This new infrastructure could also often develop new transactions and new markets. As a good example, in the following I will discuss the case of securitization.

When considering the financial industry in the region in the future, how we should incorporate securitization and the O&D model, which have long promoted the rapid expansion of financial businesses in the world, into our own business model is quite important. If we can control the risks associated with the increase in tradability brought by securitization and the O&D model well, it is no doubt that they can improve the efficiency of financial intermediation significantly. On the other hand, the aforementioned risk management may contribute to capturing the risks precisely but not to reducing them. Consequently, only introducing new risk management could only lead to larger required capital and its associated cost, and subsequently narrow the scope of financial institutions' businesses.

Therefore, if we want to reinvigorate the securitization business, we need to improve the market infrastructure so that it can reduce the inherent risk. For this purpose, as discussed in chapter 5, we need the following additional measures to enhance this market infrastructure:

- Establishing the mechanism to bring in more discipline in the management of rating agencies, including the direct supervision by the regulatory authorities;
- Considering forward-looking elements in price formation explicitly even in the world of accounting; and
- Establishing the system that clarifies the traceability of risk associated with securitized products.

MACROPRUDENTIAL POLICY

Finally, I would like to briefly discuss the expected initiatives of the authorities in Japan and Asian countries to design and implement the new macroprudential framework. The following is the summary of the policies and regulations introduced in chapter 5:

- *Clarifying loss sharing between the authorities and financial institutions under extreme stresses.*
  We need this clarification for 1) smoothly overcoming the extreme stress cases such as the current financial crisis and also for 2) curbing the moral hazards of regulating authorities as well as of financial institutions. I would like to remind you that this is a kind of insurance scheme where financial insurances buy the guarantee of the authorities over the extreme losses under the crisis at the cost of their preparation against the agreed stress cases. This policy is expected to motivate financial institutions to establish their stress-focused risk management in line with regulatory expectations.

- *Encouraging individual financial institutions to enhance their risk management based on agreed upon stress levels.*
  We definitely need this micro-foundation to make feasible the loss or stress sharing between the authorities and financial institutions.
- *Preparing a framework for dealing with failed institutions and injecting public capital into institutions in trouble based on the agreed stress levels.*
  We need this framework to stop the escalation of a financial crisis. The level of stresses to be absorbed by financial institutions, which is indicated by the authorities, should be a benchmark of this backstop. In other words, the stresses going beyond this level should be expected by the market as well as financial institutions as the ones to be dealt with primarily by the authorities.
- *Restricting compensation for senior managers of financial institutions using the idea of put options to facilitate dealings with failed institutions under extreme stress.*
  We need these restrictions to motivate senior managers' risk taking behavior to be more aligned with regulatory expectations. This is also a mechanism that penalizes senior managers who allow the gap between the regulatory reporting risk numbers and actual risks taken by them, and thereby motivates them to narrow this gap.
- *Conducting a credit-cycle-smoothing macroprudential policy.*
  We need this prudential policy as only the efforts of micro-level (e.g. enhancement of risk management of individual institutions or supervisions of the authorities) could not pre-empt the creation and bursting of financial bubbles. As was the case where a series of serious recessions and depressions encouraged the authorities to establish the politically independent central bank, we should now clearly recognize the need for establishing another public entity that should directly be involved in the battle with the credit cycle.

Some might express concerns that the above lining-up of measures might expect too much from the role of authorities, which should not be desirable nor even possible. The essential idea of these measures, however. does not lie in the heavy dependence on the authorities' judgment. It rather lies in the balanced sharing of responsibilities between the public and private sector in proportion to their capabilities. The current financial crisis actually demonstrated that there have been many systematic factors working behind this crisis rather than idiosyncratic factors. Another note is the difference in time horizon of utility function between the private sector and the one owned by the nation. The public sector is not necessarily good at reflecting the utility over the long-time horizon, e.g. the one including the next generation. Management of the extreme stresses could belong to this category. In order to deal with possible economic disutility over the multiple generations, we definitely need the public judgments.

Even the public sector, however, cannot be superman. It also needs the cooperation of the private sector. So what is the best way to cooperate with each other? My answer to this question is that the authorities should provide the price for this economic disutility and thus enable the private sector to function based on this price. All the ideas demonstrated in this book actually lead to the pricing of extreme stresses under the financial crisis. The authorities' request against the private sector to have enough capital so as to withstand the certain level of stresses is equal to the provision of the price for this stress, which is determined by the additionally required capital multiplied by capital cost.

Some readers might have already recognized that the above idea is quite similar with the idea of pricing carbon dioxide. In order to save the earth, the global community has already taken a first important step in the direction of containing carbon dioxide. Following this step, I believe that it is our turn to take a brave step in the direction of containing the financial crisis.

Epilogue

Seven months have already passed since I finished drafting the Japanese version of this book at the end of 2008, and the world looks like it has finally gotten over the worst of the crisis. Thanks to massive liquidity provision and ultra-easy monetary policy by central banks of all the major countries, and also thanks to governments' moves to bail out major financial institutions and sometimes even major manufacturing industries, we have seen some stress moderation in interbank money markets and others including CDS and stockmarkets. The economies of major countries recorded their worst ever minus growth rate up to the first quarter of 2009, but then saw some recovery (although not a V-shaped recovery), again thanks to their massive fiscal stimulus packages.

Once some market stability had been regained by quick-fix measures, the world then swiftly stepped into the next phase. This is the phase of reforming the global financial system from the long-term point of view, thereby establishing a crisis-free sustainable global financial system. This movement can be compared to a search for the twenty-first-century version of the Bretton Woods regime, interestingly keeping the same main cast over more than 60 years apart, that is, the US and UK, which endeavored to take leadership in drafting the rules for the global system. For example, the UK FSA published "the Turner Review" in March 2009, just before hosting the G20 summit in London. This review officially declared a departure from the long-pursued light-touch regulation and actually initiated the global chorus calling for re-regulation and also for a significant increase in required capital for financial institutions. The revision to the Basel II market risk framework published by the BCBS (draft version in March and final version in July) followed exactly the same proposals (such as the controversial requirements of capital being equal to VaR + stress VaR for market risk of trading book transactions) made by the UK FSA. The EU also published its own report (called the "de Larosiere Report") covering almost all major issues highlighted by the crisis but uniquely emphasizing the importance of establishing the framework of Europewide supervision and macroprudential monitoring.

Meanwhile, the US showed its intention, for example, through the Supervisory Capital Assessment Program (SCAP) in April and the proposal of financial regulatory reform in June, of advocating its new prudential regime, such as a core Tier 1 ratio-based capital requirement and leverage ratio as the essential elements to be introduced in the global rules as well as improving the regulatory framework by establishing a "Financial Services Oversight Council." Actually, some international bodies, such as the Financial Stability Board (FSB: the former FSF was renamed the FSB in April 2009) and BCBS, have already committed to this US direction, promising a review of the definition of capital and the introduction of the leverage ratio in the future improvement of global prudential rules.

Besides, in a similar vein to the arguments made in chapter 5, almost all recent reports pointed out the need for introducing some measures to contain the procyclicality of Basel II (e.g. "Report of the Financial Stability Forum on Addressing Procyclicality in the Financial System" by the FSF in April) and the compensation mechanism to discourage financial institutions' senior managers from taking excessive risks (such as the "FSF Principle for Sound Compensation Practices" by the FSF in April). They, however, often seem to face the hard realities. For example, as pointed out in chapter 5, the world regulators are now agonizing over the questions of how they should define the cycle to be smoothed and how they should smooth it, or of which institution should implement the smoothing, or whether there is any overlapping or conflict of interest with the conduct of monetary policy by the central bank. In this connection, the Financial Crisis Advisory Group, set up by the IABS and FASB, also published a report in July, advocating the need for reasonable reactions on the accounting side to tackle the weaknesses highlighted by the crisis, despite its recognition that fair value accounting itself was not a cause of the current crisis.

Finally, in May, the BCBS published a paper titled "Principles for Sound Stress Testing Practices and Supervision," which articulated the regulators' expectation of stress testing to be conducted by financial institutions. Although many post-crisis reports made by various international organizations strongly recommended the use of stress testing to supplement the limits of VaR, so far only the UK FSA had disclosed its idea of what constitute sound practices of stress testing in 2008. The BCBS basically endorsed the ideas of the UK FSA, but widened their scope and increased to some extent the level of abstraction in the form of principles.

In sum, we have actually seen something similar to the Keynes–White-type initiative that was observed during 1940s to lay the ground the Bretton-Woods regime. And the current Keynes and White again represent the same countries as 60 years ago, although, unlike in the 1940s, there seem to be very few disagreements between these two (US and UK) camps. Their arguments can basically be summarized in the following points:

Enhancement of Regulations for Financial Institutions

- A significant increase in required capital (particularly for securitization and general market risk)—FSA 2009, BCBS 2009c, d, EU 2009b:

  - The UK FSA (2009), BCBS (2009a, b), and EU (2009b) require a significant increase in required capital for investment in securitization products and also for trading activities, using the unusual idea of "sum of VaR + stress VaR multiplied by a multiplier."
- Introduction of a simpler capital requirement such as a leverage ratio—UK FSA 2009, BCBS 2009a, FSF 2009a, US Department of Treasury 2009:
  - An agency of the US (FDIC) has long argued for the importance of simple leverage ratios rather than the very complex risk-sensitive Basel II, and this argument gained momentum in the midst of the crisis, being endorsed by the UK FSA (2009) and BCBS (2009a), as well as the FSF (2009a).
  - The US Department of Treasury (2009) also emphasized the importance of introducing the leverage ratio as a part of the global rules.
- Purification of capital to be counted for capital adequacy ratio—UK FSA 2009, FRB 2009, BCBS 2009a:
  - The UK FSA (2009) introduced the idea of core Tier 1 capital, which excludes any hybrid capital products being counted as a part of Tier 1 under Basel II, and requested banks to keep it to more than 4 percent. The FRB introduced a similar idea called "tangible common equity" in the SCAP and also requested financial institutions to keep it to more than 4 percent.
  - BCBS (2009a) declared that "strengthening the quality of bank capital" is one of three new standards to be introduced by the program to strengthen the regulatory capital framework.
- More prescriptive regulation, rather than principle-based or process-focused oversight—UK FSA 2009, BCBS 2009b, US Department of Treasury 2009:
  - The UK FSA (2009) declared a significant shift in emphasis of its supervisory approach from the previous "light touch," or an approach based on its strong belief in self-correction capabilities of markets and individual institutions to lead them to take appropriate risk, to "intensive supervision," or more direct intervention in financial institutions' risk management and business strategies, focusing more on key business outcomes, rather than on systems and processes. The new approach includes the assessment of approved persons, with a focus on technical skills as well as probity, implying frequent UK FSA examinations to be passed by senior managers of financial institutions.
  - BCBS (2009b) demonstrated supplemental Pillar 2 guidance and some parts (e.g. "Specific risk management topics") went beyond the principles to indicate specific ways of managing specific risks.
  - US Department of Treasury (2009) proposed that 5 percent of credit risk of securitized exposures should be retained by the originators or sponsors of securitization.

Improvement of the Risk Management of Individual Financial Institutions

- Improvement of stress-testing methodologies—BCBS 2009e, UK FSA 2008b, FRB 2009:
  - The BCBS (2009e), partly following the UK FSA (2008b), emphasized the importance of establishing the right governance structure over the use of stress testing and its integration into firmwide risk management, and also of capturing the impacts of interactions/feedback effects of stresses or the hidden risks through a reverse stress-testing method.
  - The FRB (2009), for the first time among major regulators, requested major financial institutions to conduct stress testing based on the common macro-stress scenarios indicated by the authority to assess their capital adequacy. The BCBS (2009e) also suggested that regulators might better consider common macro-stress scenarios to be applied to the stress testing of financial institutions.
- Introduction of a compensation mechanism that discourages senior managers of financial institutions from taking excessive risks—FSF 2009c, UK FSA 2009, EU 2009b, US Department of Treasury 2009:
  - The FSF (2009c) and others emphasized the importance of establishing sound governance over the compensation system, of aligning the system with modest risk-taking incentives, and of increasing effective supervision by major stakeholders, including regulators and shareholders.

Enhancement of the Means of the Authorities to Stabilize the Financial System

- Establishing a framework to deal smoothly with failed financial institutions that have systemic importance or are internationally active—FSF 2009b, EU 2009a, UK FSA 2009, US Department of Treasury (2009):
  - The US Department of Treasury (2009) proposed an increase in required capital for systemically important financial institutions and also a more transparent process of resolving failed financial institutions under the initiative of the Department of Treasury.
  - The FSF (2009b) identified some important principles to be maintained in managing the financial crisis and subsequent failures of globally active financial institutions by multiple supervisory agencies to deal smoothly with cross-border supervisory issues.
  - The EU (2009a) indicated the need for establishing the European System of Financial Supervisors (ESFS), which is expected to coordinate the application of supervisory criteria among EU members and also be in charge of supervising globally active financial institutions.

- Introduction of some measures to contain the impacts of procyclicality of Basel II and the current accounting system—FSF 2009a, EU 2009a, UKFSA 2009, FCAG 2009:
  - The FSF (2009a) and others proposed some measures including adjustable capital requirements corresponding to the phases of the business cycle, and also regulation less dependent on VaR and more dependent on stress-testing outcomes.
  - The FSF (2009a, d) and others strongly argued for the revision of the current incurred loss model to determine loan loss provisioning so as to reflect forward-looking information and thereby reduce the procyclicality effects of provisioning. The FCAG (2009) also recommended that the IASB and FASB should explore alternatives to the current incurred loss model that use more forward-looking information.
- Improvement of the macroprudential monitoring framework—EU 2009a, UK FSA 2009, US Department of Treasury 2009:
  - The EU (2009a) pointed out the need for establishing the European Systemic Risk Council (ESRC), headed by the ECB chairman, which is expected to report early warning signs of macro-prudential risk to the European regulatory agencies.
  - The UK FSA (2009) urged more cooperation between it and the BOE to improve their macroprudential analyses, which should be the basis for the conduct of appropriate prudential policy.
  - The US Department of Treasury (2009) proposed setting up the Financial Services Oversight Council, headed by the Treasury Secretary and composed of the heads of major regulatory agencies including the FRB chairman. This organization is expected to 1) fill in the regulatory gaps between different financial markets, 2) promote policy coordination among different agencies, and 3) find and report the early warning signs of macroprudential instability to the government. It also proposed that the FRB should have responsibility for supervising all major financial institutions categorized into Tier 1 FHCs.

Some of these measures or proposals were surely in line with the proposals that I made in the previous chapters. For example, the introduction of various measures to contain the procyclicality impacts of Basel II and the accounting system more or less overlaps the idea explained in chapter 5, though we have not yet seen any discussions of difficult issues to be tackled before its introduction, which were highlighted in the same place. Besides, the nationwide framework to deal with the financial crisis became more transparent, and the stress testing required for banks was also articulated. These actions were surely a step toward the proposal made in chapter 5 on the formation of a consensus on loss sharing of extreme stresses between the authorities and financial institutions. Finally, many organizations proposed various measures to tackle the weaknesses of financial institutions' compensation mechanisms, although they stopped at a kind of moral suasion and short of concrete measures.

Despite these advancements, however, many other policy initiatives actually just reinforced my concerns mentioned in chapter 4, rather than mitigating them. The following are some more detailed explanations why I cannot but feel strong concern about the current regulatory trend.

LACK OF ANALYSIS OF ROOT CAUSES OF LOSSES UNDER THE FINANCIAL CRISIS

As was the case for many reports published in 2008, those recently published emphasized many weaknesses of risk management highlighted by the crisis, such as excessive dependence on VaR and credit rating agency ratings for risk assessment and inadequate use of stress testing, lack of firm (or group)-wide perspectives on risk management, weak liquidity risk management that does not consider evaporation of market liquidity, and so on. Very few pointed out, however, why banks did not conduct appropriate risk management. Almost all reports indicated that financial institutions "should" have conducted it, implying that financial institutions already knew how to do it, but just did not. If this is the case, we need to identify why they were not motivated enough to conduct it, and then tackle this incentive mechanism to motivate financial institutions. Otherwise, just emphasizing the problems that appear without identifying their root causes would just cause the following negative consequences over the stability of the financial system.

Alienation of Regulation-Aligned Risk Management Practices

One of the unfortunate consequences of this is that the regulators request financial institutions to put aside higher capital requirements with illogical reasoning. Good examples were shown in BCBS (2009d). According to Section IV: "Changes to the internal models approach to market risk" of the document, banks using the internal model approach are required to use the sum of "VaR xmultiplier" and "Stressed VaR xmultiplier" for the capital calculation instead of "VaR xmultiplier" in the current treatment. This new treatment would significantly increase the amounts of capital requirement (at least doubling it). As I indicated in PricewaterhouseCoopers Aarata (2009), since the outcome of VaR and stressed VaR are not defined exclusively of each other, it must be very hard for many financial institutions to align this result with their measurement of "real risk amounts." Unfortunately, the BCBS has not offered us any economically reasonable explanation for this treatment.

The proposal of introducing the leverage ratio as a global rule is another example. This proposal might be near declaring that the regulators gave up identifying specific risks behind the losses of the crisis and consequently uniformly request financial institutions to put aside significantly higher capital regardless of their real risk profiles.

The third example is the move to limit the range of Tier 1 capital to be considered for capital adequacy ratio. General moves to purify Tier 1 capital so that it is considered in terms of capability to absorb losses should be welcome, but the abrupt changes in the rule only because of country- or bank-specific situations in a certain phase of crisis could again jeopardize the economic reasoning for quality of capital. Indeed, certain types of hybrid capital were rather highly evaluated by the regulators up to the first phase of crisis because they enabled some financial institutions to increase their capital base smoothly. This was also true of some Japanese banks that successfully increased their capital bases with hybrid capital and thereby survived its banking crisis. It was only in the second phase of this crisis, when some US and European banks faced difficulties in raising further capital through using hybrids or were attacked because of their excessive dependence on hybrid types by the market, that it was understood that certain conditions could reduce the workability of this capital.

These three examples surely discourage financial institutions from aligning their own risk management with regulations and motivating them to improve their own risk management. It is very understandable that the regulators at epicenter countries, partly owing to strong political pressures, were obsessed by the idea that they had to do something immediately to tackle financial institutions' capital insufficiency, even before precisely identifying its causes. However, what's very hard to understand is the request of all other countries to introduce the same rules regardless of the size of losses actually occurred in them. Many Asian countries naturally wonder why they have to request financial institutions to have more capital at the cost of alienating institutions' efforts to align their own risk management with regulatory ones even though the causes of losses in epicenter countries might be epicenter specific. I will discuss this issue again later.

Greater Incentive for Financial Institutions to Work Around Regulations and Take Higher Risks

Another unfortunate consequence of the lack of analysis of root causes is the introduction of more regulation without changing incentive mechanisms. Indeed, the UK FSA (2009) showed that it put too much confidence in financial institutions' voluntary efforts to deal with their weaknesses of risk management, which were motivated by market pressure. The only alternative to this idea for the UK FSA is to introduce more prescriptive regulations to force the risk appetite of financial institutions to be aligned with its own. This, in turn, could give financial institutions more incentive to work around the regulations. This is exactly the vicious circle already observed in the past history of regulation and pointed out in chapter 4.

More regulation and higher capital requirements without being aligned with the incentive mechanism of financial institutions could rather motivate these institutions to take more risks that are not captured by the regulations, satisfying shareholders by offering higher returns. This is unfortunately a very reasonable reaction on the part of financial institutions that need to maximize the utility of all major stakeholders, and indeed this type of phenomenon has actually occurred in the current crisis (i.e. the materialization of the risks associated with securitization, which were not well captured by the Basel II). This point was correctly emphasized by the Japanese FSA (Sato 2009) and NIRA (2009), which should be well considered.

Wrong Incentive for Financial Institutions in Non-Epicenter Countries

Facing the arguments for the new global rule that requires higher capital and more regulations regardless of actual losses, the most perplexed seem to be regulators and financial institutions in the non-epicenter countries, in particular in Asian countries. As indicated by figure 1.3, the size of losses of Asian financial institutions was significantly lower than that of the losses of US and European financial institutions. Still, they are required to be subject to the same new rule that was revised according to the fiascos of epicenter countries. The consequence is that even though many regulators and financial institutions in the region have not necessarily recorded huge losses or recognized serious weaknesses of risk management, these financial institutions suddenly face a significant increase in required capital.

If, as advocated by the regulators in the epicenter countries, all other countries could face a similar situation in the near future, they may be right to argue for the new rule based on their experiences in the crisis to be adopted globally. As indicated in chapter 6, however, we can find many possible regional variant factors that could explain the difference in inherent risks of financial institutions. The first factor is the different composition of business lines. As indicated by table E.1, we have seen some big differences between US/European and Japanese banks, for example. The former shows high shares of gross profits of retail banking business, trading and sales, and corporate finance, while the latter shows high shares of commercial banking and payment and settlement, indicating that this difference in business lines could largely explain a big difference in losses during the crisis. This difference can only partly be reflected in the capital increase for trading book transactions.

Also, if this different share of businesses just reflects the degree of incentives of financial institutions to work around the regulations, we should

Table E.1 Banks' business line gross income

Business line gross income as a percent of consolidated gross income (results reported as medians)	All participants	Australia	Europe	Japan	North America	Brazil/India
Corporate Finance	2.1%	1.1%	3.0%	0.9%	4.2%	0.5%
Trading & Sales	7.7%	11.1%	11.4%	3.2%	4.8%	8.8%
Retail Banking	44.2%	51.3%	42.3%	20.3%	49.5%	38.4%
Commercial Banking	24.6%	17.2%	24.9%	54.0%	17.5%	21.0%
Payment & Settlement	2.1%	4.9%	0.7%	4.9%	1.1%	3.4%
Agency Services	1.1%	.	0.7%	2.5%	2.2%	1.3%
Asset Management	4.0%	.	3.4%	0.6%	4.0%	6.7%
Retail Brokerage	2.8%	na	2.3%	3.0%	4.7%	0.2%

Source: BCBS 2009f, "Results from the 2008 Loss Data Collection Exercise for operational risk"
Note 1. Cases where there are results from fewer than four banks are denoted by "." in the tables.

better focus on the causes of financial institutions being motivated to abuse the system. This may be related to the compensation mechanism. On this front, for example, the ratios of salaries of CEO/average employees of major US/European banks even after the current crisis are still significantly higher than those of Japanese banks. Or this may be related to a general loose governance system or loose supervision by the authorities. For example, table E.2, which was shown in BCBS (2009f), indicated that the size of op risk losses could be completely different between US/European and Japanese banks (the losses of the former tend to be about 10 times higher than those of the latter), implying possible large differences in corporate ethics and governance structure.

Ignoring all these differences and simply applying the same regulations revised by the epicenter countries could discourage financial institutions in other regions to improve their risk management in tandem with the regulators' efforts to improve their regulations. In most of the regions in the world, the implementation of Basel II contributed significantly to improving general risk management of financial institutions and increasing the credibility of regulators rather than to intensifying the abuse of the system by financial institutions. The abrupt introduction of leverage ratio and significant increase in capital requirements owing to the failures of some specific regions could surely damage the sound relationship being established between regulators and financial institutions in other regions, thereby discouraging the latter from further advancing their risk management.

Undue Damage to the Macroeconomy

As the Japanese banking crisis showed, a drastic increase in disposal of non-performing loans and an increase in capital are often sufficient to regain the stability of the financial system. These drastic measures are usually supposed to help mitigate the loss of confidence of the market, which felt betrayed by the misjudgments of the prudential authorities. So these measures are supposed to be temporary and country specific. In this sense, many might naturally wonder if the US SCAP assumes a severe enough scenario to assess financial institutions' capital adequacy because the unemployment rate of even the worst scenario will easily be topped by the real number. A big surprise is that no other countries publicly criticized this seemingly low severity of stress, which could not even match the degree of stress required under Pillar 2 of Basel II.

Meanwhile, if these conservative prudential measures were introduced as permanent measures, they could in turn surely impede the efficiency of the macroeconomy and, at any rate, are very unlikely to be sustainable. In this sense, the distinction between the short-term crisis management and the

Table E.2 Annualised loss amounts

Table ILD11
Annualised loss amount normalised per €billion of assets, Tier 1 capital, gross income and operational risk capital (Results reported as medians)

		Annualised sum of losses ⩾ €20,000					
		All	**Australia**	**Europe**	**Japan**	**North America**	**Brazil / India**
Consolidated assets	All	155,555	170,747	129,811	13,750	387,437	394,482
	AMA	196,655	230,369	186,528	25,242	504,497	
	Non-AMA	116,838	94,121	108,300	8,820	224,287	394,482
Consolidated Tier 1 capital	All	2,932,878	3,882,245	3,375,191	291,174	5,498,439	5,422,736
	AMA	5,640,662	5,760,028	6,376,932	551,558	12,128,746	
	Non-AMA	1,968,878	2,016,744	1,968,878	141,086	4,704,457	5,422,736
Consolidated gross income	All	4,860,322	5,550,147	5,125,736	726,431	8,076,643	7,711,110
	AMA	7,584,901	7,291,251	8,139,055	1,584,286	12,235,052	
	Non-AMA	4,162,786	3,211,629	3,527,860	486,563	7,024,900	7,711,110
Reported regulatory operational risk capital	All	43,268,410	29,093,167	56,283,482	5,708,683	67,153 605	
	AMA	63,408,911	84,100,786	84,049,051	18,896,063	73,898,537	177,956,321
	Non-AMA	29,093,167	21,440,604	39,381,024	3,245,737	54,602,027	177,956,321

Source: BCBS (2009f) "Results from the 2008 Loss Data Collection Exercise for operational risk"
Note 1. All participants in Brazil/India are non-AMA.
Note 2. All losses in the stable dataset.

long-term sustainable prudential framework should be very important. This may be particularly the case for the countries where the authorities have not necessarily lost market confidence over their conduct of prudential policy.

Lack of Governance of International Rule-Making Process

The issue of the uniform application of punitive measures against all financial institutions in the world regardless of the size of losses in the crisis might be unavoidable if the epicenter countries still would not like to see the loss of a level playing field with the non-epicenter countries. From the non-epicenter's point of view, however, this definition of "level" could be seen to be very biased. The source of the problem seems to lie in the current framework for making the global rules. If the countries that caused the global crisis could redesign the global system by themselves, it is very natural for them to emphasize the haphazardness of the crisis, as well as the commonalities rather than uniqueness of the factors behind the crisis.

As discussed, this type of policy making finds it hard to touch upon the heart of the problems (root causes) behind the crisis, and consequently finds it difficult to deal with them fundamentally. Fortunately, this was not the case for Japan, whose banking crisis during the 1990s and the 2000s was dealt with fundamentally by global standards that could not be biased by Japanese stakeholders' views. Strangely enough, while some reports such as the EU 2009a emphasized the importance of discussions of the IASB to be accountable and also to be politically independent, no reports mentioned the same thing about the discussions of the BCBS or FSB. From my point of view, the policy-making process of the IASB, which has long disclosed the minutes of many important meetings on its homepage, seems to be significantly transparent compared to the BCBS or FSB, which have not provided any answers to the questions posed about their consultation papers.

So to identify the fundamental causes to be resolved behind the current crisis, we might need another framework, such as a type of Financial Crisis Advisory Group of the IASB/FASB, which could be transparent and politically independent enough to provide all countries with unbiased views of the new global prudential rules.

References

Allen, Franklin and Elena Carletti. 2008. "Financial system: shock absorber or amplifier?" BIS working papers 257.

Algorithmics. 2007. "Operational risk at the core of "subprime meltdown" in the US." Algorithmics release.

Alvarez, Gene. 2001. *Operational risk quantification*, http://www.gloriamundi.org/detailpopup.asp?ID=453057460.

ASBJ. 2008. Saiken no hoyuu mokuteki kubun no henkou ni kansuru toumen no atsukai. *Jitsumu taiou houkoku dai 26 gou.*

Basel Committee on Banking Supervision (BCBS). 1999. *Capital Requirements and Bank Behavior: The Impact of the Basel Accord.*

—— 2004. *International Convergence of Capital Measurement and Capital Standards.*

—— 2006a. *QIS5: Fifth Quantitative Impact Study.*

—— 2006b. *Observed Range of Practice in Key Elements of Advanced Measurement Approaches (AMA).*

—— 2008a. *Basel Committee on Banking Supervision Announces Steps to Strengthen the Resilience of the Banking System.*

—— 2008b. *Principles for Sound Liquidity Risk Management and Supervision.*

Bank of England (BOE). 2006. *Financial Stability Report* 20.

—— 2007. *Financial Stability Report* 21.

—— 2008a. *Financial Stability Report* 23.

—— 2008b. *Financial Stability Report* 24.

Bank of Japan (BOJ). 2007. *Financial System Report*, September.

—— 2008a. *Financial System Report*, March.

—— 2008b. *Financial System Report*, September.

—— 2008c. *Monthly Report of Recent Economic and Financial Developments*, October.

Bank of Scotland (BOS). 2000. *Reform of the System of Insolvency Provisions.*

BCBS. 2009a. "Basel II capital framework enhancements announced by the Basel Committee."

—— 2009b. "Enhancement to the Basel II framework."

—— 2009c. "Guidelines for computing capital for incremental risk in the trading book."

—— 2009d. "Revisions to the Basel II market risk framework.

—— 2009e. "Principles for sound stress testing practices and supervision."

—— 2009f. "Results from the 2008 Loss Data Collection Exercise for operational risk."

Blundell-Wignell, Adrian. 2008. "The subprime crisis: size, deleveraging and some policy options." *Financial Market Trends*, OECD.

Blundell-Wignall, Adrian and Paul Atkinson. 2008. "The subprime crisis: causal distortions and regulatory reform." *Lessons from the Financial Turmoil of 2007 and 2008*. Reserve Bank of Australia conference, July.

BoJ. 2009. "Financial System Report," March, 2009.

Bookstraber, Richard. 2007. *A Demon of Our Own Design*. New York: John Wiley & Sons.

Center for Audit Quality (CAQ). 2007. *Measurements of Fair Value in Illiquid (or Less Liquid) Markets*, October 3.

Committee of European Banking Supervisors (CEBS). 2008a. *Report on Issues Regarding the Valuation of Complex and Illiquid Financial Instruments*.

—— 2008b. *Second part of CEBS's Technical Advice to the European Commission on Liquidity Risk Management*.

—— 2008c. *CEBS Report on Banks' Transparency on Activities and Products Affected by the Recent Market Turmoil*.

Committee on the Global Financial System (CGFS). 2005. "Stress testing at major financial institutions: survey results and practice." Prepared for the NBER Project on the Risks of Financial Institutions.

—— 2008. "Ratings in structured finance: what went wrong and what can be done to address shortcomings?" CGFS papers 32.

de Fontnouvelle, Jordan and Eric Rosengren. 2004. *Implications of Alternative Operational Risk Modeling Techniques*.

Cohen, Ben and Eli Remolona. 2008. "The unfolding turmoil: lessons and responses of 2007–2008." *Lessons from the Financial Turmoil of 2007 and 2008*. Reserve Bank of Australia conference, July.

Davis, Philip. 2003. *Towards a typology for systemic financial instability*. http://www.gloriamundi.org/detailpopup.asp?ID=453057460.

—— 2008. "Liquidity, financial crises and the lender of last resort—how much of a departure is the sub-prime crisis." *Lessons from the Financial Turmoil of 2007 and 2008*. Reserve Bank of Australia conference, July.

Dynan, Karen and Donald Kohn. 2007. "The rise in US household indebtedness: cause and consequences." In *The Structure and Resilience of the Financial System*, edited by Reserve Bank of Australia.

Duncan, Doug and Orawin Verz. 2007. *A Return to Normal Mortgage Banking*. January.

Economic and Social Research Institute. 2008. SNA (Flow) for FY 2007. Point Cabinet Office.

Egawa, Yukio. 2007. "Sub-prime mondai no kyokun." *Shouji houmu*.

EU. 2009a. "The High-level Group on Financial Supervision in the EU."

—— 2009b. "Commission proposes further revision of banking regulation to strengthen rules on bank capital and on remuneration in the banking sector."

Financial Crisis Advisory Group. 2009. "Report of the Financial Crisis Advisory Group," IASB.

Financial Market Department, Bank of Japan. 2008a. *Financial Market Report*. January.

Financial Market Department. 2008b. "Konjikinnyuukiki ni tanwohosshita tankikinyuushijouno douyou to chuuouginkou no taiou Bank of Japan."

—— 2008c. *Financial Market Report*. July.

Financial Stability Forum (FSF). 2008. *Final Report of the Financial Stability Forum on Enhancing Market and Institutional Resilience.*

Financial Service Authority (FSA). 2006. *Stress Testing Thematic Review.*

—— 2008. *FSA Moves to Enhance Supervision in Wake of Northern Rock.*

Financial Services Authority. 2008b. "Stress and scenario testing."

—— 2009. "The Turner Review: A regulatory response to the global banking crisis."

Fidelity. 2008. "Asia tsuukayasu to gaika junbi." *Fidelity Insights*, September 30.

Fischer, Stanley. 2008. Concluding panel comments. Financial System and Macroeconomic Resilience. BIS papers 41. BIS.

Freixas, Xavier and Jean-Charles Rochet. 1998. *Microeconomics of Banking.*

FSF. 2009a. "Report of the Financial Stability Forum on Addressing Procyclicality in the Financial System."

—— 2009b. "FSF Principles for Cross-border Cooperation on Crisis Management."

—— 2009c. "FSF Principles for Sound Compensation Practices."

—— 2009d. "Report of the FSF Working Group on Provisioning."

FRB. 2009. "The Supervisory Capital Assessment Program: Design and Implementation."

Fukao, Kyoji and Tsutomu Miyagawa. 2007. "Productivity in Japan, the US, and the major EU economies: Is Japan falling behind?" RIETI discussion paper, series 07-E-046.

Gieve, John. 2008. "Remarks on coping with financial distress in a more markets-oriented environment." *Financial System and Macroeconomic Resilience.* BIS papers. BIS.

Global Public Policy Committee (GPPC). 2007. *Determining Fair Value of Financial Instruments under IFRS in Current Market Conditions.* December 13.

Hamilton, Rob, Nigel Jenkinson, Adrian Penalver. 2007. "Innovation and integration in financial markets and the implications." In *The Structure and Resilience of the Financial System*, edited by Reserve Bank of Australia.

Himino, Ryozo. 2005. *Kenshou/Basel II to Nihon Kinyuuzaiseijijou kenkyukai.*

House of Commons Treasury Committee. 2008. *The Run on the Rock*, vol. 1.

Ikeo, Kazuhito. 1990. *Ginko-risk to kisei no keizaigaku Toyo keizai shinpou sha.*

—— 2008. "Saiteigata-gyoumu no genkai wo koeyo." *Nihon keizai shinbun*, September 18.

International Financial Risk Institute (IFRI). 2007. *Insights from the Joint IFRI/CRO Forum Survey on Economic Capital Practice and Applications.*

Institute of International Finance (IIF). 2008. *Final Report of the IIF Committee on Market Best Practices: Principles of Conduct and Best Practice Recommendations.*

IIF. 2009. "Restoring Confidence, Creating Resilience: An Industry Perspective on the Future of International Financial Regulation and the Search for Stability."

International Monetary Fund (IMF). 2006. *Global Financial Stability Report.* October.

—— 2008a. *Global Financial Stability Report*. October.

—— 2008b. *World Economic Outlook*. October.

Ishikawa, Tatsuya. 2004. "Juutaku kakaku hendou to kakei no shouhi oyobi shisan/fusai." *Nissay kisoken report*, 2.

Japanese Financial Services Authority (FSA). 2008a. *FSF houkokusho niokeru senshinteki kaijijirei wo fumaeta wagakunino yokintoriatukai kinyuukikan no shoukekashouhintou no hoyuugaku tounitsuite.*

—— 2008b. *Chuushoukigyou no tokusei ya keieijittai wo fumaeta kensa/kantoku no tetteini tsuite.*

—— 2008c. *Ginkoutouno jikoshihonhiritukiseino ichibu danryokukani tsuite.*

Japanese Bankers Association. 2009. "Comments on the UKFSA "The Tuner Review" and its Discussion Paper 09/2 (DP09/2)," this paper is available at the following site; http://www.zenginkyo.or.jp/news/entryitems/news210618_2.pdf

Jenkinson, Nigel, Adrian Penalver and Nicholas Vause. 2008. "Financial innovation: what have we learnt?," *Lessons from the Financial Turmoil of 2007 and 2008*. Reserve Bank of Australia conference, July.

Joint Forum. 2008. Cross-sectoral review of group-wide identification and management of risk concentration.

Kaminsky, Graciela and Carmen Reinhart. 1999. "The twin crises: the causes of banking and balance of payments problems." *American Economic Review* 89: 473–500.

Kashyap, Anil, Raghuram Rajan, and Jeremy Stein. 2008. "Rethinking capital regulation." Prepared for Federal Reserve Bank of Kansas City Symposium on "Maintaining Stability in a Changing Financial System", Jackson Hole, Wyoming, August 21–23, 2008.

Kearns, Jonathan and Philip Lowe. 2008. "Promoting liquidity: why and how?" *Lessons from the Financial Turmoil of 2007 and 2008*. Reserve Bank of Australia conference, July.

Kiff, John and Paul Mills. 2007. "Money for nothing and checks for free: recent developments in US subprime mortgage markets." IMF working paper, WP/07/188.

Kinyuu shijou senryaku team. 2007. *First report*. Japanese FSA.

—— 2008. *Second report*. Japanese FSA.

Kouzu, Takashi. 2008. "Konkai no kokusaitekina kinnyuukonrannwo fumaeta BCBS no torikumi." *Shouken Analyst Journal*, November 12.

McNeil, Alexander, Rudiger Frey and Paul Embrechts. 2005. *Quantitative Risk Management: Concepts, Techniques & Tools*. Princeton: Princeton University Press.

Mizuho Research Institute. 2006. *Ashimoto no fudousanshijou wo kenshosuru.*

Muermann, Alexander and Ulku Oktem. 2002. The *Near-miss Management of Operational Risk.*

OCC. 2007. "Subprime mortgage lending." *OCC Bulletin*, 2007–11.

OICU-IOSCO. 2008. *The Role of Credit Rating Agencies in Structured Finance Markets.*

Nagafuji, Tsuyoshi. 2008. "An analysis of Japanese banks' loss data: Possible use of external loss data." Presentation paper for the workshop "Use of external data for op risk management held by the center for advanced financial technology", Bank of Japan.

NIRA. 2009. "Preparing for the Next Financial Crisis—Proposal for a new financial system beyond present stopgap measures," National Institute of Research Advanced Report, October 2009, this paper is available at the following site; http://www.nira.or.jp/english/papers/papers2.html

Nihon keizai shinbun. 2008. Nichibeiou, 23chouen shikin kyouyuu. September 17.

—— 2008. "Naze koutekishikinha hituyounanoka—furyousaiken no shorikasoku." October 15.

—— 2008. "Oushuu, shihon chuunyuuwaku 37chouen." October 15.

Norinchukin Research Institute. 2002. "Beikoku ni okeru juutaku loan kashidashi shijou no henka to shouraizou." *Kinyuu shijou*, November.

Oyama, Tsuyoshi. 2007. "Plausibility of stress scenarios." Paper prepared for Second Expert Forum on Advanced Techniques on Stress Testing Applications for Supervisors, hosted by the IMF and DNB.

—— 2008a. "Learning from Subprime." *AsiaRisk*, October.

—— 2008b. "Constructive ambiguity." *The Asian Banker Journal*, 83.

Oyama, Tsuyoshi and Naguji, Tsusyoshi. 2007. "Loss data highlights characteristics of operational risks faced by Japanese banks." *Kinyuuzaisei jijou*, September 24. (English version on BOJ site, www.boj.or.jp/en/.)

Oyama, Tsuyoshi and Fukumoto, Tomoyuki. 2007. "Keizai shihon unei niyoru senryakuteki risk kanri no jissen" (Strategic risk management based on economic capital management). *Kinyuu zaisei jijou*, October 8.

PricewaterhouseCoopers Aarata. 2009. "Comments on BCBS's two consultative documents: 'Revisions to the Basel II market risk framework' and 'Guidelines for computing capital for incremental risk in the trading book,'" this paper is available at the following site; http://www.bis.org/publ/bcbs14849/ca/pwcaarata.pdf

Reinhart, Carmen and Kenneth Rogoff. 2008. "Is the 2007 US sub-prime financial crisis so different? An international historical comparison." Draft, February 5.

Reuters report. 2008. Nihon no kinnyuukikan ga hoyuusuru bei GSE kanrensaiken, 3megabank de 4.7chouen, July 16.

Rosenblum, Harvey, Danielle DiMartino, Jessica Renier, and Richard Alm. 2008. "Fed intervention: managing moral hazard in financial crisis." Economic Letter—Insights from the Federal Reserve Bank of Dallas, 3, no. 10, October.

Rosengren, Eric. 2008. *Risk-management Lessons from Recent Financial Turmoil*. May.

Saito, Makoto. 2000. "Kinyuu-gijutsu no kangaekata/tsukaikata." *Yuuhikaku*.

Sato, Takafumi. 2008. *Basel II to ginkou-kantoku—atarashii jikoshihonhiritsukisei*.

Sato, Takafumi. 2009. "Tightening capital rules could increase risk taking," *Financial Times*, June 30.

Securities and Exchange Commission (SEC). 2008. *SEC Office of the Chief Accountant and FASB Staff Clarifications on Fair Value Accounting*.

Senior Supervisors Group. 2008. *Observation on Risk Management Practices during the Recent Market Turbulence*.

Shiratori, Tetsuya and Oyama, Tsuyoshi. 2001. "Insights into the low profitability of Japanese banks: Some lessons from the analysis of the trends in banks' margins." Bank of Japan working paper series, 01-J-1.

Sumitomo Trust Bank. 2005. "Takamaru kakei no saimu futan." Sumitomo Trust Bank research report, February.

Tachibana, Tomohiro. 2008. *Shijou risk no keisoku shuhou—genzai kachi approach.* The Center for Advanced Financial Technology, Bank of Japan.

Takemori, Shunpei. 2008. "Shihonshugi ha kirai desuka." *Nihonkeizai shinbunsya.*

Tokyo Mitsubishi Bank. 2000. "RTGS dounyuugoto shijouheno eikyouni tsuite." *Focus on the Markets*, 3, June 30.

UBS. 2008. *Shareholder Report on UBS' Write-downs.*

US Department of Treasury. 2009. "Financial Regulatory Reform: A New Foundation."

Warsh, Kevin. 2008. "The promise and peril of the new financial architecture." Speech at the Money Marketeers of New York University, FRB.

Weiner, Susan. 2008. "Will the US subprime crisis be as bad as history suggests?" *Advisor Perspective*, February 26.

White, William. 2008. "Financial system and macroeconomic resilience." *Financial System and Macroeconomic Resilience.* BIS papers 41. BIS.

Yoshii, Kazuhiro. 2007. *Beikoku no SFAS157 kousei kachi no sokutei no gairyaku.* Daiwa Institute of Research.

Index